one world now

Praise for *One World: The Ethics of Globalization* and Peter Singer

Selected as an outstanding book by University Press Books for Public and Secondary School Libraries

"Many people have written about the economic meaning of globalization; in *One World* Peter Singer explains its moral meaning. His position is carefully developed, his tone is moderate, but his conclusions are radical and profound. No political theorist or moral philosopher, no public official or political activist, can afford to ignore his arguments."—Michael Walzer

"Peter Singer writes, as always, lucidly and with relentless logic. Getting states to behave ethically is a heroic aspiration, but this book will give even the most obdurate realist much to think about."—Gareth Evans, President, International Crisis Group, former Australian Foreign Minister

"Few issues are more critically in need of ethical assessment than globalization. When a leading ethicist like Singer addresses globalization, we all should listen very carefully."—Paul R. Ehrlich, author of *Human Natures: Genes, Cultures, and the Human Prospect*

"Timely and thoughtful. . . . A refreshing intellectual integrity in Singer's efforts to assess the facts on the ground."—Andrés Martinez, *New York Times Book Review*

"For readers in search of a different approach to globalization's typical themes, *One World* makes an interesting, thought-provoking read."—Meg Kinnard, *National Journal*

"Famed bioethicist Singer argues that the dangers and inequalities generated by globalization demand that we rethink the privileged rights of state sovereignty and devise new ethical principles of international conduct. In his view, the search for widely acceptable principles of global fairness is not simply an intellectual exercise but an imperative that even rich and powerful countries ignore at their peril."—G. John Ikenberry, *Foreign Affairs*

"*One World* is valuable reading for anyone interested in seeing whether globalization can be made to work for the benefit of many."—Philip Seib, *Milwaukee Journal Sentinel*

peter singer

one world now

the ethics of globalization

Yale UNIVERSITY PRESS   *new haven & london*

contents

preface

In 2000, in the wake of the protests against the World Trade Organization that disrupted the ministerial meeting held in Seattle the previous December, I began work on a book that would become *One World*. My goal was to examine ethical aspects of the way in which the world was, and was not, becoming a global community. I had not got far before George W. Bush became president of the United States, bringing with him an administration overtly hostile to global institutions, from the United Nations to the International Criminal Court, and to the Kyoto Protocol, which was the first attempt to stop or mitigate climate change by a binding international agreement to reduce greenhouse gas emissions.

Then, on September 11, 2001, while I was putting the final touches to my draft, I watched, together with shocked students and faculty at Princeton University, while the World Trade Center towers burned and collapsed. The notion of One World suddenly sounded a discord against the resonating talk of a clash of civilizations. Nevertheless, the terrorist attack on that day and

America's response to it confirmed the idea of a world that was increasingly becoming one, for it showed that no country, however mighty, is invulnerable to deadly force from the far corners of the earth. An American administration that had previously shown little concern for the opinion of the rest of the world found itself in need of the cooperation of other nations in a global campaign against terrorism, even if later it spurned global institutions in unleashing, without the approval of the United Nations Security Council, the misguided and ultimately disastrous invasion of Iraq. So I retained the original title, leaving it to stand both as a description of the increasing interconnectedness of life on this planet and as a prescription of what the basic unit for our ethical thinking should be.

One World reached a wide audience, both inside and outside colleges and universities. But the world has changed again since 2002. It is time to take a fresh look at globalization, including climate change, the global economy, international law, and global poverty. Hence *One World Now,* a book that retains the basic structure and, in revised and updated form, some of the contents of *One World* but takes account of major new developments, including

- The failure to reach an internationally binding post-Kyoto agreement on reducing greenhouse gas emissions, and the new approach taken by the nonbinding agreement achieved in Paris in 2015;
- The declining influence of the World Trade Organization as a result of the failure of its Doha Round of trade negotiations;
- The emergence and acceptance of the view that the world community has a responsibility to protect citizens of states when their government either cannot or will not protect them from crimes against humanity or genocide;

- The progress made in reducing extreme poverty, which, although substantial, leaves much still to be done; and
- The sharp rise in the number of refugees and internally displaced people desperate to find a safer place to live.

An invitation to give the Terry Lectures at Yale University in 2000 was the stimulus to begin work on *One World*. I thank the Dwight H. Terry Lecture Committee (Robert Adams, Robert Apfel, Radley Daly, Carlos Eire, Leo Hickey, John Ryden, Dianne Witte, and Richard Wood) for selecting me for this honor. The audience at Yale provided me with my first sounding board, and I then benefited from more detailed scrutiny and assistance from many wonderfully knowledgeable and helpful friends and colleagues. Paula Casal and Brent Howard read and commented on the entire draft of *One World*, and Matt Ball, John Broome, Michael Doyle, Gareth Evans, Nir Eyal, Peter Godfrey-Smith, Alex Gosseries, Lori Gruen, Dale Jamieson, Andy Kuper, Vivian Leven, Stephen Macedo, Jonathan Marks, Darryl McLeod, Branko Milanovic, Nick Owen, Thomas Pogge, Leif Wenar, and Melissa Williams all gave me comments on specific chapters within their various areas of expertise. Aaron Jackson and Diego von Vacano provided excellent research assistance while Kim Girman, my assistant, cheerfully and efficiently completed the many tasks I gave her. At Yale University Press, Jean Thomson Black was a consistently helpful and supportive editor.

In writing *One World Now*, I was assisted by all those who over the years gave me constructive comments on *One World*—too many to list, even if I could remember them all. I will, however, mention John Huss, who has for many years been using *One World* in the honors section of his Introduction to Ethics course at the University of Akron. He tried out the draft chapters of the present book on his class and gave me feedback, with additional comments coming from his teaching assistant Nevin Johnson and the students Zarek Bell, Joe Klein, and Nathan Nicholas.

Gareth Evans kindly read the section in chapter 4 relating to the responsibility to protect, and his comments enabled me to improve this section. Yale University Press's anonymous reviewers made helpful suggestions that saved me from several errors.

Princeton University and more specifically the University Center for Human Values have, over many years, given me ideal conditions for research and writing. Amy Gutmann, George Kateb, Stephen Macedo, Alan Patten, and Chuck Beitz all served as Director of the Center during the writing of *One World* or *One World Now*, and I thank them for their support. Students in my Practical Ethics course have been a critical audience for some of the material in this book. *One World Now* was completed in Australia, and I thank the School of Historical and Philosophical Studies at the University of Melbourne for providing me with an office and a congenial atmosphere for work. Finally, I thank Renata, my wife. Her love and companionship have added immeasurably to my life and work, and her readiness for adventure made it possible for us to try a new life in the United States. This book is one outcome of that decision.

Peter Singer
University Center for Human Values, Princeton University
&
School of Historical and Philosophical Studies, University of Melbourne

1 a changing world

Do Our Fellow Citizens Always Come First?

Consider two aspects of globalization: first, the ability of people living in Afghanistan, Iraq, or Yemen to bring sudden death and terror to New York, London, Madrid, Paris, and Sydney; and second, the emission of greenhouse gases from power stations, vehicles, and even cattle. The former leaves unforgettable images that are watched on television screens all over the world; the other causes changes to the climate of our planet in ways that can be detected only by scientific instruments. Yet both are indications of the way in which we are now one world, and the more subtle changes to which our vehicle exhausts contribute are already killing far more people than the highly visible deeds of terrorists.

Over the decades since the 1980s, as scientists piled up the evidence that continuing greenhouse gas emissions will imperil hundreds of millions, perhaps billions, of lives, state leaders struggled to agree on a plan for making sufficient cuts in those

emissions to prevent a serious risk of climate becoming catastrophic, although such a plan would clearly be in the interests
of the world as a whole. As we shall see later in this book, even
the agreement reached in Paris in 2015 does not do enough.

The lack of the necessary global perspective was never better
illustrated than by George W. Bush. As president of the United
States, the country that has, by its emissions over the past century, done more than any other to make climate change a problem, he said, "We will not do anything that harms our economy,
because first things first are the people who live in America."[1]
That remark was not an aberration but an expression of an ethical view that too many political leaders take for granted. His
father, the first President George Bush, had said much the same
thing at the 1992 Earth Summit in Rio de Janeiro. When representatives of developing countries asked the president to put on
the agenda the overconsumption of resources by the developed
countries, especially the United States, George H. W. Bush said,
"The American lifestyle is not up for negotiation." It was not
negotiable, apparently, even if maintaining this lifestyle will lead
to the deaths of millions of people subject to increasingly un-
predictable weather and the loss of land used by tens of millions
more people because of rising ocean levels and local flooding.[2]

But it is not only the two Bush administrations that put the
interests of Americans first. In the early 1990s, in the context
of the debate over whether to intervene in Bosnia to stop Serb
"ethnic cleansing" operations directed against Bosnian Muslims,
Colin Powell, then chairman of the Joint Chiefs of Staff under President Bill Clinton, quoted with approval Otto von Bismarck's remark that all the Balkans were not worth the bones of
a single one of his soldiers.[3] Bismarck, however, was not thinking
of intervening in the Balkans to stop crimes against humanity.
As chancellor of Imperial Germany, he assumed that his country

followed its national interest. To use his remark as an argument against humanitarian intervention was to return to nineteenth-century power politics, ignoring both the bloody wars that style of politics brought about in the first half of the twentieth century and the efforts in the second half of the twentieth century to find a better foundation for peace and the prevention of crimes against humanity.

In Kosovo, though the Clinton administration's policy of giving absolute priority to American lives did not prevent intervention to defend the Kosovars, it led to the restriction of intervention to aerial bombardment. This strategy was a total success: NATO forces suffered not a single casualty in combat. Approximately 300 Kosovar, 209 Serb, and three Chinese civilians were killed. President Barack Obama used a similar "air power only" strategy against the Islamic State, or ISIS, after 2014, when it was threatening to overrun Iraq. Again, this strategy avoids American casualties, but, as Ivan Eland pointed out, "If the U.S. uses only air power, ISIS will eventually hide in the cities and the U.S. will be faced with causing a lot of civilian casualties to get the group out or kill its fighters."[4]

Observing the American reliance on airpower to protect the people of Kosovo, Timothy Garton Ash wrote, "It is a perverted moral code that will allow a million innocent civilians of another race to be made destitute because you are not prepared to risk the life of a single professional soldier of your own." This does not mean that putting "boots on the ground" is always a good thing to do: the American invasion of Iraq in 2003 brought about the regional chaos in which ISIS has thrived. It also, according to an estimate by researchers at Johns Hopkins University, caused 654,000 more Iraqi deaths than would have been expected under prewar conditions.[5] Nevertheless, Ash's comment raises a fundamental ethical issue: to what extent should political leaders see their role as limited to promoting the interests of their citizens, and to what extent should they be concerned with the welfare of people everywhere?

As Ash suggests, there is a strong ethical case for saying that it is wrong for leaders to give absolute priority to the interests of their own citizens. The value of the life of an innocent human being does not vary according to nationality. But, it might be said, the abstract ethical idea that all humans are entitled to equal consideration cannot govern the duties of a political leader. Just as parents are expected to provide for the interests of their children rather than for the interests of strangers, so too anyone accepting the office of president of the United States takes on a specific role that makes it his or her duty to protect and further the interests of Americans. Other countries have their leaders, with similar roles in respect of the interests of their fellow citizens. There is no world government, and as long as that situation prevails, we must have sovereign states, and the leaders of those states must give preference to the interests of their citizens. Otherwise, unless electors were suddenly to turn into altruists of a kind never before seen on a large scale, democracy could not function. American voters would not elect a president who gave no more weight to their interests than he or she gave to the interests of Iraqis or Afghans. Our leaders feel they must give some degree of priority to the interests of their own citizens, and they are, so this argument runs, right to do so.

Beyond a World of Sovereign States

Is the division of the world into sovereign states a dominant and unalterable fact of life? Here our thinking has been affected by the horrors of Bosnia, Rwanda, and Kosovo. In Rwanda, a United Nations inquiry took the view that 2,500 military personnel, given the proper training and mandate, might have saved 800,000 lives.[6] Kofi Annan, who, as UN under-secretary-general for peacekeeping operations at the time, must bear some responsibility for what the inquiry termed a "terrible and humiliating" paralysis, learned from this situation, and when he became secretary-general, urged that "the world cannot stand aside when gross and systematic violations of human rights are taking place." What we need, he said, are "legitimate and universal principles" on which we can base intervention.[7] Subsequently, as we shall see in more detail in chapter 4, the United Nations World Summit unanimously accepted that the world community has a responsibility to protect the citizens of any state from genocide, ethnic cleansing, war crimes, and crimes against humanity, even if this means military intervention against a government that is carrying out such crimes within its own territory. The British historian Martin Gilbert called the acceptance of this responsibility "the most significant adjustment to sovereignty in 360 years"—in other words, since the Treaty of Westphalia ended the Thirty Years' War in Europe and established the principle of state sovereignty and nonintervention in the affairs of other states in 1648.[8]

How Terrorism Has Weakened State Sovereignty

In a very different manner, the aftermath of the terrorist attacks on the World Trade Center and the Pentagon in 2001 underlined the extent to which our thinking about state sovereignty has changed over the past century. More than a century ago, in the summer of 1914, another act of terrorism shocked the world: the assassination by a Bosnian Serb nationalist of Crown Prince Franz Ferdinand of Austria and his wife in Sarajevo. In the wake of that outrage Austria-Hungary presented an ultimatum to Serbia in which it laid out the evidence that the assassins were trained and armed by the Black Hand, a shadowy Serbian organization headed by the chief of Serbian military intelligence. The Black Hand was tolerated or supported by Serbian government officials who arranged safe passage across the border into Bosnia for the seven conspirators in the assassination plot.[9] Accordingly, Austria-Hungary's ultimatum demanded that the Serbs bring those responsible to justice and allow Austro-Hungarian officials to inspect the files to ensure that this had been done properly.

Despite the clear evidence of the involvement of Serbian officials in the crime—evidence that, historians agree, was substantially accurate—the ultimatum Austria-Hungary presented to Serbia was widely condemned in Russia, France, Britain, and the United States. "The most formidable document I have ever seen addressed by one State to another that was independent," the British foreign minister, Sir Edward Grey, called it.[10] The American Legion's official history of the Great War used less diplomatic language, referring to the ultimatum as a "vicious document of unproven accusation and tyrannical demand."[11] Many historians studying the origins of the First World War have condemned the Austro-Hungarian ultimatum, saying that it demanded more than one sovereign state may properly ask of another. They have added that the Austro-Hungarian refusal to negotiate after the Serbian government accepted many, but not all, of its demands is further evidence that Austria-Hungary, together with its backer, Germany, wanted an excuse to declare war on Serbia. Hence they must bear the guilt for the outbreak of the war and the nine million deaths that followed.

Now consider the American response to the 2001 terrorist attacks which were orchestrated by Al Qaeda, then based in Afghanistan. The demands made of the Taliban government of Afghanistan by the Bush administration in 2001 were scarcely less stringent than those put to Serbia in 1914. (The main differ-

ence is that the Austro-Hungarians insisted on the suppression
of hostile nationalist propaganda. Freedom of speech was not so
widely regarded, then, as a human right. The United States, with
its strong constitutional protection of freedom of speech, could
hardly demand that the Taliban do something that would be un-
constitutional in the United States.) Yet the American demands,
far from being condemned as a mere pretext for aggressive war,
were endorsed as reasonable and justifiable by a wide-ranging
coalition of states. When President George W. Bush said, in
speeches and press conferences after September 11, 2001, that he
would not draw a distinction between terrorists and regimes that
harbor terrorists, no ambassadors, foreign ministers, or United
Nations representatives denounced this as a "vicious" doctrine
or a "tyrannical" demand on other sovereign states. The Security
Council broadly endorsed it in its resolution of September 28,
2001.[12] It seems that world leaders now accept that every state has
an obligation to every other state to suppress activities within its
borders that might lead to terrorist attacks carried out in other
countries, and that it is reasonable to go to war with a state that
does not do so. That is a sign of how far the world has moved in
the direction of becoming a global community.

The Bosnian Serb conspirators had only to slip across the border between Serbia and Bosnia in order to reach their target,
but terrorism is no longer local or even regional. The Al Qaeda
terrorists who flew planes into the World Trade Center and the
Pentagon traveled much further (most of them were citizens of
Saudi Arabia), and ISIS has been promoting terrorism over the
internet, encouraging its adherents to carry out attacks in the
countries in which they live. Similarly, in 2015 the civil war in
Syria became a problem for all of Europe, as immigrants crossed
to Greece and made their way up through Europe.

Shortly before the attacks of September 11 a United Nations panel issued a report pointing out that even if there were no altruistic concern among the rich to help the world's poor, their own self-interest should lead them to do so:

In the global village, someone else's poverty very soon becomes one's own problem: of lack of markets for one's products, illegal immigration, pollution, contagious disease, insecurity, fanaticism, terrorism.[13]

Thus the combination of terrorism, mass international travel, and the internet has made our world an integrated community in a new and frightening way. Not merely the activities of our neighbors but also those of the inhabitants of the most remote mountain valleys of the farthest-flung countries of our planet are now potentially threatening, and so have become our concern. We need to extend the reach of the criminal law there and to have the means to bring terrorists to justice without declaring war on an entire country in order to do so. For this we need a sound global system of criminal justice, so justice does not become the victim of national differences of opinion. We also need, though it will be even more difficult to achieve, a sense that we really are one community, that we are people who recognize not only the force of prohibitions against killing each other but also the pull of obligations to assist one another. This may not stop fanatics from carrying out suicide missions, but it will help to isolate them and reduce their support. It was not a coincidence that just two weeks after September 11, 2001, conservative members of the United States Congress abandoned their opposition to the payment of $582 million in back dues that the United States owed to the United Nations.[14] When America was calling for the world to come to its aid to stamp out terrorism, it became apparent that America could no longer flout the rules of the global community to the extent that it had been doing before that fateful September morning.

A New Era for Ethics and Political Theory

Implicit in the term "globalization" rather than the older "internationalization" is the idea that we are moving beyond the era of growing ties between states and are beginning to contemplate something more than the existing conception of state sovereignty. But this change needs to be reflected in all levels of our thought, especially in our thinking about ethics and our political theory.

To see how much our thinking about ethics needs to change, consider the work that, better than any other, represents late twentieth-century thinking on justice in the liberal American establishment: John Rawls's *A Theory of Justice*. When I read it, shortly after its publication in 1971, I was astonished that a book with that title, nearly 600 pages long, could utterly fail to discuss the injustice of the extremes of wealth and poverty that exist between societies. Rawls's method is to seek the nature of justice by asking what principles people would choose if they were choosing in conditions that prevented them from knowing what position they themselves would occupy. That is, they must choose without knowing whether they themselves would be rich or poor, a member of the dominant ethnic majority or of an ethnic minority, a religious believer or an atheist, highly skilled or unskilled, and so on. If we were to apply this method globally rather than for a given society it would immediately be obvious that one fact about which those making the choice should be ignorant is whether they are citizens of a rich country such as the United States or of a poor country such as Haiti. In setting up his original position, however, Rawls simply assumes that the people making the choice all belong to the same society and are choosing principles to achieve justice *within* their society. Hence when he argues that people choosing under the conditions he prescribes would choose a principle that, subject to constraints intended to protect equal liberty and fair equality of opportunity, seeks to improve the position of the worst-off, he limits the conception of worst-off to those within one's own society. If he accepted that to choose justly, people must also be ignorant of their citizenship, his theory would become a forceful argument for improving the prospects of the worst-off people in the world. But in the most influential work on justice written in twentieth-century America, this question *never even arises*.[15] Rawls addressed it, late in his life, in a short book, *The Law of Peoples,* and I shall say something later about what he says there. His approach, however, remains firmly based on the idea that the unit for deciding what is just remains something like today's nation-state.

Rawls's model is that of an international order, not a global order. Most political theorists today still make that assumption, but there is now a growing minority who take a global perspective. Yael Tamir, who, having served in the Israeli parliament and as a government minister, cannot be dismissed as a mere academic remote from political reality, has called for political theorists to dare to ask the fundamental question: "Should the unity and autonomy of the sovereign state be retained, or should the state be transcended for some purposes and divided for others?"[16] Political theorists are now asking that question. As David Held and Pietro Maffettone point out in their preface to a collection of essays by leading scholars working on global political theory, the acceleration of globalization since the 1980s fundamentally challenges the idea that normative political ideas can be confined to the internal life of states. Their volume is evidence that political theory is responding to this challenge and changing its nature as it does so.[17]

Technology Changes (Almost) Everything

For most of the eons of human existence, people living only short distances apart may as well, for all the difference they made to each other's lives, have been living in separate worlds. A river, a mountain range, a stretch of forest or desert, a sea—these were enough to cut people off from each other. Over the past few centuries the isolation has dwindled, slowly at first, then with increasing rapidity. Now people living on opposite sides of the world are linked in ways previously unimaginable.

One hundred and fifty years ago Karl Marx gave a one-sentence summary of his theory of history:

> The handmill gives you society with the feudal lord; the steam mill, society with the industrial capitalist.[18]

Today he might have added:

> The jet plane, the telephone, and the internet give you a global society with the transnational corporation and the World Trade Organization.

Technology changes everything—that was Marx's claim, and if it was a dangerous half truth, it was still an illuminating one. As technology has overcome distance, economic globalization has followed. Planes can bring fresh vegetables from Kenya to compete in London supermarkets alongside those from nearby Kent. In the wrong hands, those planes can also become lethal weapons that bring down tall buildings. Instant digital communication spreads the nature of international trade from physical objects to skilled services. At the end of a day's trading, a bank based in New York may have its accounts balanced by clerks living in India. The increasing degree to which there is a single world economy is reflected in the development of new forms of global governance, the most controversial of which has been the

World Trade Organization, but the WTO is not itself the creator of the global economy.

Global market forces provide incentives for every country to put on what Thomas Friedman has called "a Golden Straitjacket," a set of policies that involve freeing up the private sector of the economy, shrinking the bureaucracy, keeping inflation low, and removing restrictions on foreign investment. If a country refuses to wear the Golden Straitjacket or tries to take it off, then the Electronic Herd—the currency traders, stock and bond traders, and those who make investment decisions for multinational corporations—could gallop off in a different direction, taking with it the investment capital that countries want to keep their economy growing. When capital is internationally mobile, to raise your tax rates is to risk triggering a flight of capital to other countries with comparable investment prospects and lower taxation. The upshot is that as the economy grows and average incomes rise, the scope of politics may shrink—at least as long as no political party is prepared to challenge the assumption that global capitalism is the best economic system. When neither the government nor the opposition is prepared to take the risk of removing the Golden Straitjacket, the differences between the major political parties shrink to differences over minor ways in which the straitjacket might be adjusted.[19] Thus even without the WTO, the growth of the global economy itself marks a decline in the power of the nation-state. (The difficulty of challenging international economic arrangements was vividly demonstrated by the gap between the antiausterity rhetoric used by the Greek leftist party Syriza in its January 2015 election campaign and the actions taken by Syriza in government when faced with an ultimatum from Greece's creditors.)

Marx argued that in the long run we never reject advances in the means by which we satisfy our material needs. Hence history is driven by the growth of productive forces. He would have been contemptuous of the suggestion that globalization is something foisted on the world by a conspiracy of corporate executives meeting at the World Economic Forum in Davos, and he might have agreed with Friedman's remark that the most basic truth about globalization is, "*No one is in charge.*"[20] For Marx, however, the significance of this statement is not that conspiracy theorists are wrong—though he would have agreed that they are wrong—but that we are living in an alienated world in which, instead of ruling ourselves, we are ruled by our own creation, the global economy. For Friedman, on the other hand, all that needs to be said about Marx's alternative—state control of the economy—is that *it doesn't work.*[21]

Marx also believed that a society's ethic is a reflection of the economic structure to which its technology has given rise. Thus a feudal economy in which serfs are tied to their lord's land gives you the ethic of feudal chivalry based on the loyalty of knights and vassals to their lord and the obligations of the lord to protect them in time of war. A capitalist economy requires a mobile labor force able to meet the needs of the market, so it breaks the tie between lord and vassal, substituting an ethic in which the right to buy and sell labor is paramount. Our newly interdependent global society, with its remarkable possibilities for linking people around the planet, gives us the material basis for a new ethic. Marx would have thought that such an ethic will serve the interests of the ruling class, that is, the rich countries and the transnational corporations they have spawned.

Marx wanted to bring our ethical judgments down to earth. They did not, he thought, come from God or from reason but from the economic basis of our society and the means we use to produce the goods we consume. He did not consider a different earthly possibility: that our ethical judgments have a biological basis in our origins as social mammals. The intuitive responses by which we judge many things to be right or wrong have their origins in the behavior and feelings of our human and pre-human ancestors and were suited for life in a small group in which everyone knew everyone else. That is very far from the world in which we live today, but many of our deepest moral intuitions persist.[22] One of the themes of this book will be the way in which they need to change if we are to overcome the problems the world faces.

The fact that many of our moral intuitions stem from our ancestors' need to survive and reproduce in the conditions in which they lived does not mean that our reasoning abilities are powerless to reshape our ethics. If the group to which we must justify ourselves is the tribe or the nation, then our morality is likely to be tribal or national. If, however, the revolution in communications has created a global audience, we may feel a need to justify our behavior to the whole world. That is the approach to ethics that frames the chapters that follow.[23]

It would be naïve to believe that the existence of the internet and the enhanced possibilities of communication across national boundaries that come with it would be sufficient to bring about a new ethic that will serve the interests of all those who live on this planet in a way that, despite much rhetoric, no previous ethic has ever done. The second decade of the twenty-first century has seen a resurgence of nationalism in China, resulting in disputes with Japan, Vietnam, and the Philippines over the ownership of small islands in the East and South China Seas. Similarly, in Russia stronger nationalism led to the occupation of Crimea and support for pro-Russian rebels in eastern Ukraine. Nevertheless, the existence of a global audience and a global discussion would seem to be a necessary, though not sufficient, condition for a truly global ethic.

If this appeal to our need for ethical justification appears to be based on too generous a view of human nature and of the ability of reasoning to influence our ethical judgments and our behavior, there is another consideration of a very different kind that leads in the same direction. The great empires of the past, whether Persian, Roman, Chinese, or British, were, as long as their power lasted, able to keep their major cities safe from the threat of those they considered barbarians on the frontiers of their far-flung realms. The Persians and Romans kept them out by the strength of their armies; the British prevailed by their supremacy on the seas; and the Chinese built the Great Wall. In the twenty-first century the greatest superpower in history was unable to keep the self-appointed warriors of a different world-view from attacking both its financial center and its capital. The thesis of this book is that how well we come through the era of globalization (perhaps whether we come through it at all) will depend on how we respond ethically to the idea that we live in one world. For the rich countries not to take a global ethical viewpoint has long been seriously morally wrong. Now it is also, in the long term, a danger to their security.

2 one atmosphere

The Problem

There can be no clearer illustration of the need for human beings to act globally than the issues raised by the impact of human activity on our atmosphere. That we all share the same planet came to our attention in a particularly pressing way in the 1970s, when scientists discovered that the use of chlorofluorocarbons (CFCs) threatened the ozone layer shielding the surface of our planet from the full force of the sun's ultraviolet radiation. Damage to that protective shield would cause cancer rates to rise sharply and could have other effects, for example, on the growth of algae. The threat to people living in the world's southernmost cities was especially acute, since a large hole in the ozone was found to be opening up each year over Antarctica. In the long term, the entire ozone shield was imperiled. Once the science was accepted, concerted international action followed relatively rapidly with the signing of the Montreal Protocol in 1987. The developed countries phased out virtually all use of CFCs by

1999, and the developing countries, given a ten-year period of grace, achieved the same goal in time for the 25th anniversary of the treaty in 2012.

Getting rid of CFCs turned out to be just the opening act: the main event is climate change. Not to belittle the pioneering achievement of those who brought about the Montreal Protocol, but the problem they faced was not so difficult, for CFCs can be replaced in all their uses at relatively little cost, and the solution to the problem is simply to stop producing them. Climate change is a very different matter.

The scientific evidence that human activities are changing the climate of our planet has been studied by a working group of the Intergovernmental Panel on Climate Change, an international scientific body established to provide policy makers with an authoritative view of climate change and its causes. The group released its *Fifth Assessment Report* in 2014, building on earlier reports and incorporating new evidence accumulated over the five years since the previous report. The report is the work of more than 800 authors. The section on the physical science basis of climate change alone is over 2,000 pages long and draws on 9,200 peer-reviewed scientific publications. Like any scientific document it is open to criticism from other scientists, but it reflects a broad consensus of leading scientific opinion and is by far the most authoritative view available on what is happening to our climate.

The *Fifth Assessment Report* finds that the evidence is unequivocal that, since the 1950s, the atmosphere and oceans have warmed, glaciers have shrunk, the Greenland and Antarctic ice sheets have been losing mass, Arctic sea ice is diminishing, and sea levels are rising at an increasingly rapid rate. At the earth's surface, each of the past three decades has been successively warmer than any preceding decade since 1850.[1] The year 2014 was the hottest until 2015 broke that record too. The ten hottest years on record since reliable global records began in 1880 have occurred since 1998, and thirteen of the fourteen hottest years on record have occurred in the twenty-first century. One way of indicating how the world's climate has changed within the lifespan of people like me, who were born in the mid-twentieth century, is this: if you were born after 1985, you have never experienced even a single month in which the global temperature was below the twentieth-century average for that month.[2]

Paralleling these changes, there has been an increase in concentrations of carbon dioxide, methane, and nitrous oxide in the atmosphere, produced by human activities such as the burning of fossil fuels, the clearing of vegetation, and (in the case of methane) cattle and rice production. These gases are now at levels unprecedented in the last 800,000 years. In addition, the increased amount of carbon dioxide in the atmosphere has caused the oceans to become more acidic.

How much of the change in climate has been produced by human activity, and how much can be explained by natural variation? The *Fifth Assessment Report* finds that it is "*extremely likely*" that human influence has been the dominant cause of the observed warming since the mid-twentieth century." (In the language of the report, "extremely likely" indicates a probability in the range of 95–100 percent.) Those of us who have no expertise in the scientific aspects of assessing climate change and its causes can scarcely disregard the views held by the overwhelming majority of those who do possess that expertise. Even if *all* of them were in agreement, it would still be possible that they are wrong, but in view of what is at stake, to rely on that possibility would be playing Russian roulette with hundreds of millions and possibly billions of lives at stake. Those who are skeptical about the science of climate change must, if they are intellectually honest, admit that there is a significant chance that the overwhelming majority of scientists have got it right; and if that is the case, they should ask themselves whether it is right to take no action and thus to run that risk.[3]

What is likely to happen if we continue on our present course, with increasing amounts of greenhouse gases going into the atmosphere? In the absence of "substantial and sustained" reductions in greenhouse gas emissions we will, according to the *Fifth Assessment Report*, see further warming and other changes in all aspects of our planet's climate. Relative to the period 1986–2005, which was, as we have seen, already warmer than any previous decades since 1850, global mean surface temperatures in the decades 2046–65 (when many readers of this book will still only be middle-aged) are expected to rise between one and two degrees Celsius, with a range of 0.4°C to 2.6°C.

Although these average figures may seem quite small—whether tomorrow is going to be 20°C (69°F) or 22°C (72°F) isn't such a big deal—even a 1°C rise in average temperatures would be greater than any change that has occurred in a single century for the past 10,000 years and would be enough to pose a risk to global and regional food security as well as to threaten to cause the extinction of many species that will be unable to adapt. High temperatures and humidity could make normal human activities, such as growing food and working outdoors, impossible in some now-habitable regions for a part of each year.[4] Moreover, some regional changes will be more extreme and are much more difficult to predict. Northern landmasses, especially North America and Central Asia, will warm more than the oceans or coastal regions. Precipitation will increase overall, but there will be sharp regional variations, with some areas that now receive adequate rainfall becoming arid. There will also be greater year-to-year fluctuations than at present, with more intense El Niño effects in the Pacific Ocean, so we can expect droughts and floods to be more severe. The Asian summer monsoon is likely to become less reliable. It is possible that the changes could be enough to reach critical tipping points at which the weather systems alter or the directions of major ocean currents like the Gulf Stream change. If the Gulf Stream were to disappear, average winter temperatures in Britain would drop about 5°C, and significant drops would occur across Western Europe as well. Finally, warming oceans will cause the melting of ice sheets in Antarctica and Greenland, which will in turn cause sea levels to rise. The *Fifth Assessment Report* predicts a rise in the range of 0.52–0.98 meters (1.5 to 3 feet) by 2100, although, as we shall see, some scientists consider this figure to be too conservative. If warming continues, sea levels are expected to rise by at least 7 meters and possibly as much as 13 meters (that's between 22 and 42 feet), perhaps as soon as 2150.

What will the consequences be for humans? The following impacts are already occurring and will increase in severity during the remainder of the twenty-first century:

- As oceans become warmer, hurricanes and tropical storms that have largely been confined to the tropics are moving further from the equator, hitting large urban areas that have not been built to cope with them.
- Tropical diseases are spreading beyond their previous zones.
- Food production will rise in some regions, especially in the high northern latitudes, and fall in others, including sub-Saharan Africa.
- Rising sea levels are beginning to threaten low-lying coastal regions, including low-lying Pacific islands, fertile delta regions, and some of the world's most densely populated cities.

How much of this change is already happening? Several highly publicized hurricanes, droughts, and floods have been attributed to climate change, but for any individual extreme weather event it is difficult to say that without climate change it would not have occurred. It's like car accidents: if you drive faster, you are more likely to have a serious accident, but any particular accident could be attributed to momentary inattention, a wet road, or a mistake made by another driver rather than to excessive speed. Hurricane Katrina, which hit New Orleans in 2005, killing 1,833 people, and Hurricane Sandy, which hit New York and New Jersey in 2012 and killed 132 people in the United States and Canada and caused at least another 70 deaths in other countries, are examples of the kind of extreme weather events that climate change is likely to make more frequent, even if we cannot say of any one of these events that it would not have happened if there had been no global warming.

Sometimes, however, it is possible to say with a high degree of confidence that climate change caused a particular weather pattern. In 2012–13 Australia experienced its hottest summer on record, with widespread bushfires in the southeast and severe flooding in the northeast, also associated with the high temperatures. Researchers at the University of Melbourne studied this phenomenon against the background of past temperature records. They then applied methods used in population health studies to estimate the impact of particular behaviors, such as smoking, on health. They found, with 90 percent confidence, that climate change caused by human activities resulted in a fivefold increase in the risk of the extreme temperatures Australia experienced that summer.[5] Several Australians died in the bushfires and floods, and some thousands lost their homes. Another study has suggested that the East African drought of 2011 was at least partially attributable to climate change.[6] The human consequences of this event were far more severe than those of the Australian heatwave and bushfires, for it left 9.5 million people in Somalia, Djibouti, Ethiopia, and Kenya in need of assistance, forced 920,000 to become refugees, and caused at least 50,000 deaths.

In coming decades such differences in the impact of climate change on rich and poor countries will be repeated over and over again. Rich countries may be able to cope with these changes without enormous loss of life, though at considerable cost. They are in a better position to store food against the possibility of drought, to move people away from flooded areas, to fight the spread of disease-carrying insects, and to build walls to keep out the rising seas. Poor countries will be unable to do such things. Bangladesh, the world's most densely populated large country, has the world's largest system of deltas and mudflats, where mighty rivers like the Ganges and the Brahmaputra reach the sea. Living on such low-lying land is risky. In 1991 a cyclone hit the coast of Bangladesh, coinciding with high tides that made ten million people homeless and killed 139,000. Most of these people were living on mudflats in the deltas. People continue to live there in large numbers because the soil is fertile and they have nowhere else to go. But if sea levels continue to rise, 70 million people could have to leave. In Egypt and Vietnam millions of peasant farmers on the Nile and Mekong deltas also stand to lose their land. On a smaller scale, Pacific island countries that consist of atolls no more than a meter or two above sea level face even more drastic losses. High tides are already causing erosion and polluting fragile sources of freshwater, and some uninhabited islands have been submerged. Some countries may disappear entirely.

Global warming will lead to an increase in summer deaths due to heat stress, but these will be offset by a reduced death toll from winter cold. Much more dangerous than either of these effects, however, will be the spread of tropical diseases, including diseases carried by insects that need warmth to survive. A study by the World Health Organization estimates that an additional 250,000 deaths per year between 2030 and 2050 will result from heat exposure, diarrhea, malaria, and childhood undernutrition.[7] The study does not attempt to estimate deaths or health impacts of major disasters such as flooding or increases in migration or violent conflict caused by climate change.

If the Asian monsoon weakens and its life-giving rains become less reliable, as some models of global warming predict, hundreds of millions of peasant farmers in India and other countries will go hungry, for they have no other way of obtaining the water they need to grow their crops. In general, less reliable rainfall patterns will cause immense hardship among the large proportion of the world's population who must grow their own food if they want to eat and depend on rainfall to grow it.

The consequences for nonhuman animals and for biodiversity will also be severe. In some regions plant and animal communities will gradually move further from the equator or to higher altitudes, chasing the kind of climate in which in which they do well; but that option is not always available. Australia's unique alpine plants and animals already survive only on the country's highest alpine plains and peaks, which are barely over 2,000 meters. If snow ceases to fall on their territory they will become extinct. Coastal ecosystems will change dramatically, and warmer waters may destroy coral reefs. These predictions look ahead only as far as 2100, but even if greenhouse gas emissions have been stabilized by that time, changes in climate will persist for hundreds, perhaps thousands, of years.

The Greenland ice cap is visibly melting, with new offshore islands being discovered as the ice sheet retreats from over the ocean. As oceans warm, there is a risk that the much larger Antarctic ice sheets that extend over the ocean will begin to break up. The ice would then float to warmer waters and melt. A study led by James Hansen, with researchers from the United States, France, Germany, and China, suggests that in as little as 50 years such melting could cause a rise in sea level of between 5 and 9 meters. Such a rise would be sufficient to inundate large parts of almost every major coastal city in the world as well as intensively farmed low-lying areas of Bangladesh, the European lowlands, and large areas of the U.S. East Coast and China's northern plains. Hundreds of millions of people would be displaced.[8]

Ethics for the Anthropocene

Our current geological epoch is, at the time of writing, still officially known as the Holocene. It began 11,700 years ago, and during almost all of this period earth's systems have been unusually stable. One thing that has not been at all stable during this period, however, is the human population and its impact. At the beginning of the Holocene there may have been about six million humans, mostly hunter-gatherers. In thinking about these earlier humans, we should not be deceived by the myth of noble savages living in perfect harmony with their environments. Even those small, low-tech societies were able to transform the flora and fauna of the regions they inhabited—one has only to look at the way in which the first humans to reach Australia about 40,000 years ago brought about the extinction of the megafauna they found there, and then by firestick farming caused the original forests to be replaced by fire-resistant eucalypts. In much more recent times, the arrival of the Maori in New Zealand was soon followed by the extinction of the moa, a giant flightless bird. But the impact of the more than seven billion people now present on the earth, many of them living in industrialized economies based on energy from fossil fuels and subsisting on diets that demand a vastly increased global herd of methane-producing cattle, is far more all-encompassing than anything our ancestors could achieve, extending beyond species extinction to deforestation, desertification, pollution in the most remote regions of the planet, ozone depletion, ocean acidification, and climate change. Hence the suggestion, first made in the 1980s by the biologist Eugene Stoermer, that we are living in a new epoch, the Anthropocene. The idea has slowly caught on, and at the time of writing a formal proposal to declare this new epoch in our planet's history is under review by the International Commission on Stratigraphy, the authoritative scientific body that makes such decisions.[9]

All of this forces us to think differently about our ethics. Our moral attitudes were formed in circumstances in which the atmosphere and oceans seemed so limitless that we took it for granted that they were able to absorb our wastes without noticeable ill consequences. Under such circumstances, responsibilities and harms were generally visible and well defined. If someone hit someone else, it was clear who had done what and why it was wrong. Now the twin problems of the ozone hole and climate change have revealed bizarre new ways of harming people. Before CFCs were phased out you could, by spraying deodorant at your armpit in your New York apartment, be contributing to skin cancer deaths many years later in Punta Arenas, Chile. Today, by driving your car you could be releasing carbon dioxide that is part of a causal chain leading to lethal floods in Bangladesh.

Does this mean it is wrong to drive a car unnecessarily or, for that matter, to eat beef, since cattle emit such large quantities of methane? To live an ethical life, is it essential that we minimize our carbon footprint by, for example, installing solar panels on our roof, avoiding meat, and whenever possible riding a bike or taking public transport rather than driving a car? By doing these things we minimize the harm we are causing to others, and that is commendable. We are also setting an example to others—and if enough of us do it, to our leaders—about our willingness to live sustainably. So these are good things to do, but we should not fool ourselves into believing that the problem of climate change can be solved by individual actions of this kind. There need to be changes on a larger scale, including changes in how we generate electricity, power our vehicles, and produce the foods we eat. For these changes to occur, the price of carbon will have to be increased to reflect the true cost of emitting it—as economists would say, to internalize the costs that are currently externalities, which means they are imposed on others who are not part of the transactions between us and the power company, the gas station, or the supermarket. We will need all of the major greenhouse gas–emitting countries, present and future, to agree to reduce their emissions drastically enough to avoid disaster. Our overriding obligation, as individuals, is therefore to be activist citizens and to do our best to persuade our government to come together with other governments and find a global solution to a global problem.

From Rio to Paris, Via Kyoto and Copenhagen

Climate change entered the international political arena in 1988, when the United Nations Environment Program and the World Meteorological Office jointly set up the Intergovernmental Panel on Climate Change. In 1990 the IPCC reported that the threat of climate change was real and that a global treaty was needed to deal with it. The United Nations General Assembly resolved to proceed with such a treaty. The United Nations Framework Convention on Climate Change was agreed to in 1992 and opened for signature at the Earth Summit or, more formally, the

UN Conference on Environment and Development, which was held in Rio de Janeiro in the same year. This framework convention has been accepted by more than 190 governments. It is, as its name suggests, no more than a framework for further action, but it calls for greenhouse gases to be stabilized "at a level that would prevent dangerous anthropogenic interference with the climate system." The parties to the convention should do this, the convention states, "on the basis of equity and in accordance with their common but differentiated responsibilities and respective capabilities." Developed countries should "take the lead in combating climate change and the adverse effects thereof." The developed countries committed themselves to 1990 levels of emissions by the year 2000, but this commitment was not legally binding.[10] For the United States and several other countries that was just as well because they came nowhere near meeting it. In the United States, for example, by 2000 carbon dioxide emissions were 14 percent higher than they were in 1990.[11]

The Framework Convention builds in what is sometimes termed the precautionary principle, calling on the parties to act to avoid the risk of serious, irreversible damage even in the absence of full scientific certainty. The convention also recognizes a "right to sustainable development," asserting that economic development is essential to addressing climate change. Accordingly, the Rio Earth Summit did not set any emissions reduction targets for developing countries to meet.

The Framework Convention set up a procedure for holding Conferences of the Parties to assess progress. In 1995 this conference decided that more binding targets were needed. The result, after two years of negotiations, was the 1997 Kyoto Protocol, which set targets for 39 developed countries to limit or reduce their greenhouse gas emissions by 2012. The limits and reductions were designed to reduce total emissions from the developed countries to a level at least 5 percent below 1990 levels. The national targets varied, however, with the European Union countries and the United States having targets of 8 percent and 7 percent, respectively, below 1990 levels and other countries, such as Australia, being allowed to go over their 1990 levels. These targets were arrived at through negotiations with government leaders and were not based on any general principles of fairness, nor much else that can be defended on any terms other than the need to get agreement.[12] Flexibility in these negotiations was necessary since under the prevailing conception of state sovereignty, countries cannot be bound to meet their targets unless they decide to sign the treaty that commits them to do so. To assist countries in reaching their targets the Kyoto Protocol accepted the principle of emissions trading, by which one country can buy emissions credits from another country that can reach its target with something to spare.

The Kyoto conference did not settle the details of how countries could meet their targets—for example, whether they would be allowed credits for planting forests that soak up carbon dioxide from the atmosphere—and how emissions trading was to operate. These issues were resolved at further meetings held in Bonn and Marrakech in 2001. There, 178 countries reached a historic agreement that made it possible to put the Kyoto Protocol into effect. The problem was that under the leadership of George W. Bush the United States, at the time the world's largest emitter of greenhouse gases, was no longer a party to the agreement, and China, which would become the world's largest emitter during the period of the Kyoto agreement, was classed as a developing country and not given a target for its emissions. No wonder, therefore, that the Kyoto agreement did not solve the problem of the impact of human activity on the world's climate.

Years passed, global greenhouse gas emissions kept increasing, and the 2012 date by which countries were supposed to meet their targets was fast approaching. What would happen after that? In 2009 representatives of 192 parties to the Framework Convention met in Copenhagen with the aim of deciding on the principles of a treaty to replace the Kyoto Protocol when it expired in 2012. Barack Obama had replaced Bush as president of the United States, but that was not enough to prevent the meeting disappointing the hopes of most observers. Instead of agreeing on a new treaty, the participants agreed only to "take note of" a nonbinding "Copenhagen Accord" that asked member states to send in pledges for future reductions in emissions. Obama made his frustration clear. He later described the negotiations as chaotic.[13] With the benefit of hindsight, however, it may have been fortunate that the Copenhagen meeting did *not* achieve a binding treaty, for Obama would have had to submit such a treaty to the Senate, which—judging by its defeat, shortly after the Copenhagen meeting, of a climate change bill put forward by Senator John Kerry—would probably have refused to ratify it. Although Obama was reelected in 2012, conservative Republicans, many of whom denied the reality of human-caused climate change, increased their strength in Congress. Obama therefore embarked on a different strategy, using his executive powers as president to reduce carbon emissions from power plants and reaching an emissions reduction agreement with President Xi Jinping of China that spurred many other states to set emission reduction targets of their own, thus giving new life to the Copenhagen accord that each state would set itself a target and pledge to meet it. What looked initially like a woefully inadequate strategy adopted only to draw a veil over the conference's failure to achieve a binding treaty was thus transformed into something that, if still insufficient, as it stands, to avert an unacceptably high risk of catastrophic climate change, did at least provide a framework that is, in Obama's words, "the best chance we've had to save the one planet we've got."[14]

Prior to the Paris meeting 195 states submitted pledges, officially termed Intended Nationally Determined Contributions, to reduce their greenhouse gas emissions. The underlying idea was to keep global warming to 2°C or less, compared to pre-industrial times. That figure is the absolute maximum that most scientists believe is compatible with avoiding the "dangerous anthropogenic climate change" that all of the signatories to the Framework Convention on Climate Change agreed, back in 1992, to avoid. In Paris, at the insistence of some of the countries most at risk from climate change, the wording was strengthened to commit the signatories to holding the increase to "well below" 2°C and "to pursue efforts to limit the temperature increase to 1.5°C." The lower the increase, the agreement recognized, the greater the chance of avoiding some of the tipping points that could lead to catastrophe, like the breakup of the Antarctic ice sheets.[15]

Because the Paris agreement is not, for the reasons we have seen, a legally binding treaty, there is no way of binding countries to meet their Intended Nationally Determined Contributions. What will happen if they do not? First, a country that fails to meet its pledge will not be able to hide. The agreement includes measures designed to ensure transparency (although no doubt there will be gray areas). The approach is sometimes called pledge and review or, more bluntly, naming and shaming. It has been used, with some success, to get states to honor their signatories on various human rights documents, like the Geneva Convention and the Helsinki Accords, and to encourage political leaders to meet their pledges to provide aid to meet the Millennium Development Goals. Moreover, as Jennifer Jacquet and Dale Jamieson point out, international law is difficult to enforce even when there are legally binding treaties. The European Union has yet to sanction any of its member states for violating their legally binding commitments to keep budget deficits at no more than 3 percent of gross domestic product.[16]

Let's be optimistic and imagine that all the parties to the Paris agreement do reduce their emissions by the full amount pledged. Unfortunately, even that will not suffice to prevent catastrophic climate change. The Grantham Institute at the London School of Economics reviewed the pledges and found that "the most optimistic estimate of global emissions in 2030 resulting from the intended nationally determined contributions is about half-way between hypothetical 'business as usual' and a pathway that is consistent with the 2°C limit."[17] In other words, just to stay within the not-very-safe 2°C safety barrier, the world needs cuts about twice as deep as those currently pledged. To achieve the somewhat safer (but, given the very high stakes, arguably still too risky) 1.5°C limit the cuts will need to be deeper still. The Paris agreement does, however, require all signatories to renew their emission reduction targets every five years and to be given a "global stocktake" that will show whether the world is on track to meet its stated goals. Inevitably, for the reasons we have just noted, even if all signatories keep the pledges they made in 2015, the first stocktake will indicate that global warming is likely to exceed 2°C. The key question therefore is, Will the signatories then commit themselves to reducing their emissions beyond their own 2015 pledges? For that to happen, some major emitting countries will have to take the lead. Which ones should it be? That leads to a further question.

What Is an Equitable Distribution?

In the second of the three televised debates held during the United States presidential election in 2000, the candidates were asked what they would do about global warming. George W. Bush said,

I'll tell you one thing I'm not going to do is I'm not going to let the United States carry the burden for cleaning up the world's air, like the Kyoto treaty would have done. China and India were exempted from that treaty. I think we need to be more even-handed.

A sense of fairness appears to be universal among human beings, although conceptions of what is fair in particular situations vary across cultures and times. In political philosophy it is common to follow Robert Nozick in distinguishing between "historical" principles and "time-slice" principles.[18] A historical principle is one that says, We can't decide, merely by looking at the present situation, whether a given distribution of goods is just or unjust. We must also ask how the situation came about; we must know its history. Are the parties entitled, by an originally justifiable acquisition and a chain of legitimate transfers, to the holdings they now have? If so, the present distribution is just. If not, rectification or compensation will be needed to produce a just distribution. In contrast, a time-slice principle looks at the existing distribution at a particular moment and asks if that distribution satisfies some principles of fairness, irrespective of any preceding sequence of events. I shall look at both of these approaches in turn.

A Historical Principle: "The Polluter Pays," or "You Broke It, You Fix It"

Imagine that we live in a village in which we all put our wastes down a giant sink. No one quite knows what happens to the wastes after they go down the sink, but since they disappear and have no adverse impact on anyone, no one worries about it. Some people consume a lot and so have a lot of waste, while others, with more limited means, have barely any, but the capacity of the sink to dispose of our wastes seems so limitless that no one worries about the difference. As long as that situation continues, it is reasonable to believe that, in putting waste down the sink, we are leaving "enough and as good" for others because no matter how much we put down it, others can also put as much as they want, without the sink overflowing. This phrase "enough and as good" comes from John Locke's justification of private property in his *Second Treatise on Civil Government,* published in 1690. In that work Locke says, "The earth and all that is therein is given to men for the support and comfort of their being." The earth and its contents "belong to mankind in common." How, then, can there be private property? Because our labor is our own, and hence when we mix our own labor with the land and its products we make them our own. But why does mixing my labor with the common property of all humankind mean that I have gained property in what belongs to all humankind rather than lost property in my own labor? It has this effect, Locke says, as long as the appropriation of what is held in common does not prevent there being "enough and as good left in common for others."[19] Locke's justification of the acquisition of private property is the classic historical account of how property can be legitimately acquired, and it has served as the starting point for many more recent discussions. Its significance here is that, if it is valid and the sink is or appears to be of limitless capacity, it would justify allowing everyone to put what he or she wants down the sink, even if some put much more than others down it.

Now imagine that conditions change, so that the sink's capacity to carry away our wastes is used to the full, and there is already some unpleasant seepage that seems to be the result of the sink being used too much. This seepage causes occasional problems. When the weather is warm it smells. A nearby waterhole where our children swim now has algae blooms that make it unusable. Several respected figures in the village warn that unless usage of the sink is cut down, all the village water supplies will be polluted. At this point, when we continue to throw our usual wastes down the sink we are no longer leaving "enough and as good" for others, and hence our right to unchecked waste disposal becomes questionable. For the sink belongs to us all in common, and by using it without restriction now, we are depriving others of their right to use the sink in the same way without bringing about results none of us want. We have an example of the well-known "tragedy of the commons."[20] The use of the sink is a limited resource that needs to be shared in some equitable way. But how? A problem of distributive justice has arisen.

Think of the atmosphere as a giant global sink into which we can pour our waste gases. Then once we have used up the capacity of the atmosphere to absorb our gases without harmful consequences, it becomes impossible to justify our usage of this asset by the claim that we are leaving "enough and as good" for others. The atmosphere's capacity to absorb our gases has become a finite resource on which various parties have competing claims. The problem is to allocate those claims justly.

Are there any other arguments that justify taking something that has, for all of human history, belonged to human beings in common and turning it into private property? Locke has a further argument—one that is arguably inconsistent with his first argument—defending the continued unequal distribution of property even when there is no longer "enough and as good" for others. Comparing the situation of American Indians, where there is no private ownership of land and hence the land is not cultivated, with that of England, where some landowners hold vast estates and many laborers have no land at all, he claims that "a king of a large and fruitful territory there [i.e., in America] feeds, lodges, and is clad worse than a day laborer in England."[21]

Therefore, Locke suggests, even the landless laborer is better off because of the private, though unequal, appropriation of the common asset and hence should consent to it. The factual basis of Locke's comparison between English laborers and American Indians is evidently dubious, as is its failure to consider other, more equitable ways of ensuring that the land is used productively. But even if the argument worked for the landless English laborer, we cannot defend the private appropriation of the global sink in the same way. The landless laborer who no longer has the opportunity to have a share of what was formerly owned in common should not complain, Locke seems to think, because he is better off than he would have been if private property in land had not been recognized. The parallel argument to this in relation to the use of the global sink would be that even the world's poorest people have benefited from the increased productivity that has come from the use of the global sink by the industrialized countries. But the argument does not work because many of the world's poorest people, whose shares of the atmosphere's capacity have been appropriated by the industrialized countries, are not able to partake in the benefits of this increased productivity in the industrialized countries—they cannot afford to buy its products—and if shifting rainfall patterns leave them unable to grow their crops or rising sea levels inundate their farmlands or cyclones destroy their homes, they will be much worse off than they would otherwise have been.

Apart from Locke, the thinker most often quoted in justifying the right of the rich to their wealth is probably Adam Smith. Smith argued that the rich did not deprive the poor of their share of the world's wealth because

the rich only select from the heap what is most precious and agreeable. They consume little more than the poor,

and in spite of their natural selfishness and rapacity,
though they mean only their own conveniency, though
the sole end which they propose from the labours of
all the thousands whom they employ, be the gratification
of their own vain and insatiable desires, they divide with
the poor the produce of all their improvements.[22]

How can this be? It is, Smith tells us, as if an "invisible hand"
brings about a distribution of the necessaries of life that is "nearly
the same" as it would have been if the world had been divided
up equally among all its inhabitants. By that Smith meant that
in order to obtain what they want, the rich spread their wealth
throughout the entire economy. But while Smith knew that the
rich could be selfish and rapacious, he did not imagine that the
rich could, far from consuming "little more" than the poor, consume many times as much of a scarce resource than the poor do.
The average American, by driving a car, eating meat and other
animal products, keeping cool in summer and warm in winter,
and consuming products at a hitherto unknown rate, uses ten
times as much of the global atmospheric sink as the average Indian.[23] Thus Americans, along with Australians, Canadians, and
to a lesser degree Europeans, effectively deprive the poor of the
opportunity to develop along the lines that the rich themselves
have taken. If the poor were to behave as the rich now do, we
would undoubtedly exceed the level of greenhouse gas emissions
that is likely to cause catastrophic warming and sea level rise.

The putatively historical grounds given for justifying private
property put forward by its most philosophically eminent defenders—writing at a time when capitalism was only beginning
its rise to dominance over the world's economy—cannot apply
to the current use of the atmosphere. Neither Locke nor Smith
provides any justification for the rich having more than their

fair share of the finite capacity of the global atmospheric sink. In fact, just the contrary is true. Their arguments imply that this appropriation of a resource once common to all humankind is not justifiable. And since the wealth of the developed countries is inextricably tied to their prodigious use of fossil fuels (a use that began more than two hundred years ago and continues today) it is a small step from here to the conclusion that the present global distribution of wealth is the result of the wrongful expropriation by a small fraction of the world's population of a resource that belongs to all human beings in common.

For those whose principles of justice focus on historical processes, a wrongful expropriation is grounds for rectification or compensation. What sort of rectification or compensation should take place in this situation?

One advantage of sharing a house with someone whose hair is different in color or length from your own is that when a clump of hair blocks the bath outlet, it's easy to tell whose hair it is. "Get your own hair out of the tub" is a fair and reasonable household rule, and if the blockage is too far down the pipe for anyone but a plumber to reach, then it would also seem fair and reasonable (if a little too mucky) to settle the plumber's bill by dividing it up proportionately to the amount of hair from each person that has built up over the period that people have been using the tub and has caused the present blockage.

Carbon dioxide in the atmosphere is harder to see than hair in the bathtub, and it lasts longer. Much of the carbon emitted a century ago is still in the atmosphere, contributing to climate change, and unless we develop some new technology for removing it, about a quarter of what we emit today will still be warming the planet a thousand years from now.[24]

Developing states, including China, India, and Brazil, have advanced a view of fairness in relation to climate change that closely resembles the view that the bill for the plumber should be divided up in proportion to the contribution that people have made to blocking the sink. Those countries that industrialized earlier and still use energy more intensely than countries that are still developing have done most to cause the problem of climate change. If the developed countries had, since the preindustrial era, emitted greenhouse gases at the same per capita levels as the developing countries, we would not be facing an urgent need to reduce emissions. Instead we would have an ample window of opportunity to do something before greenhouse gas levels in the atmosphere reached a level sufficient to cause a problem. To put this argument in terms a child could understand, as far as the atmosphere is concerned, the developed countries broke it. If we believe that people should contribute to fixing something in proportion to their responsibility for breaking it, then the developed countries owe it to the rest of the world to fix the problem with the atmosphere.

The "you broke it, you fix it" view of fairness puts a heavy burden on the developed countries. In their defense, it might be argued that at the time when the developed countries put most of their cumulative contributions of greenhouse gases into the atmosphere, they could not have known about the limits to the capacity of the atmosphere to absorb those gases. Although the Swedish scientist Svante Arrhenius predicted as long ago as 1895 that increasing amounts of carbon dioxide in the atmosphere would cause the planet to warm, that view was not sufficiently well understood to justify taking strong action until the 1980s. It would therefore be fairer, it may be claimed, to make a fresh start now and set standards that look to the future rather than to the past.

There can be circumstances in which we are right to wipe the slate clean and start again. A case can be made for doing so in respect of cumulative emissions that occurred before governments could reasonably be expected to have known that these emissions might harm people in other countries. At least since 1990, however, when the Intergovernmental Panel on Climate Change published its first report, solid evidence about the hazards associated with emissions has existed, and in 1992 the developed countries themselves (including the United States under President George H. W. Bush) agreed, at the Earth Summit, to reduce emissions so as to prevent dangerous anthropogenic climate change.[25] To wipe the slate clean on what happened since 1990 seems unduly favorable to the industrialized countries that have, despite that evidence, continued to emit a disproportionate share of greenhouse gases.

A group of Chinese scientists led by Teng Fei from Tsinghua University has attempted to spell out the implications of the historical view of responsibility in a way that focuses on the unfairness of an unequal division of a common resource rather than on blaming the developed countries for moral turpitude. They suggest that one understanding of fairness in greenhouse gas emissions is equal per capita emissions over time. We can calculate the total amount of greenhouse gases that could safely be emitted during the period 1850–2050 without risking the dangerous anthropogenic climate change that the parties to the Framework Convention agreed to avoid—that is, without global warming exceeding 2°C over preindustrial levels. Think of this as the carbon budget—that is, the amount of carbon available for everyone in the world to spend. Then think of each person on the planet during that period as entitled to spend an equal share of that budget. Now consider these individuals as citizens of countries that have spent different amounts of the world's carbon budget and have benefited from those expenditures. Those countries that industrialized early, like the United States and the European countries, especially in northern Europe, have already used a large share of that budget. The average resident of the United States, for example, has used more than ten times as much as the average resident of China. The cumulative emissions of the United States since 1850 amount to 30 percent of the world's total cumulative emissions. If the United States and other countries that industrialized early do not cut their emissions very soon and very sharply, it will be impossible for residents of developing countries to emit amounts that are in any way comparable to those emitted by American residents—or at least impossible for them to do so without a grave risk of climate change becoming dangerous. Because burning fossil fuels has been and largely still is a path to a high standard of living, this is unfair.[26]

This way of putting the argument from historical responsibility does not imply that it was morally wrong for some countries to industrialize when they did or to use fossil fuels to provide the energy they required. Rather, the claim is that those countries have, by taking more than their fair share of the global carbon budget, achieved a higher standard of living than developing countries while at the same time preventing people in developing countries from taking a similar path, one in which they make use of cheap fossil fuels to improve their own standard of living. Fairness in dividing up a common resource demands that we take into account not only how much everyone is using now but also how much everyone used in the past.

Time-Slice Principles

The argument for taking account of historical responsibility for emissions is strong, especially when put in terms of fairness rather than blameworthiness. Nevertheless, in order to see whether there are widely held principles of justice that do not impose such stringent requirements on the long-developed countries, let us assume that the still developing and recently developed countries generously overlook the past. We would then need to look for a time-slice principle to decide how much each country should be allowed to emit. What would such a principle look like, and what would it require of the developed countries?

An Equal Share for Everyone

If we forget about the past, we can still ask why, of people alive today, anyone should have a greater claim to part of the global atmospheric sink than anyone else. The first and simplest response is that there is no reason why anyone should. Everyone has the same claim to common resources like the atmosphere and so should have an equal share of it. This kind of equality seems fair, at least as a starting point for discussion, and perhaps, if no good reasons can be found for moving from it, as an end-point as well.

If we take this view, then we need to ask how much carbon dioxide or other greenhouse gases we can add to the atmosphere and still avoid dangerous anthropogenic climate change. If we know that amount, then we can divide it by the population of the world to yield the amount that each person would be allowed to emit, and we could then in turn multiply this individual allowance by the population of any country to obtain the level for each country to emit, given equal per capita shares. To decide upon the first of these figures, however, we need to make two distinct judgments: What rise in global temperature is dangerous? And what degree of risk are we prepared to run that we will exceed that temperature rise?

The first of these questions, as we have seen, has been answered by the 2°C limit, although with an acknowledgment in the Paris agreement that it is desirable to stay well below that threshold and that efforts should be made to avoid exceeding

1.5°C above preindustrial levels. In discussion of this question the 1.5°C limit was strongly advocated by small island states facing the inundation of large parts of their territory and by many of the 48 developing countries, mostly from sub-Saharan Africa. The lower limit has been opposed by all the major economies of the world, including the developed countries as well as India and China. They argue that to hold the temperature rise to 1.5°C would be extraordinarily difficult—and costly—because it would require not merely stabilizing the amount of carbon in the atmosphere at present levels of around 400 parts per million (ppm), as it then was, but reducing it to 350ppm.[27] In Paris the developed countries did more to show that they were listening to the proponents of the 1.5°C limit but would not commit themselves to it. The reasons for that refusal were political rather than scientific. Most of those negotiating at climate change conferences think it is simply unrealistic to aim for a lower target. The challenge of holding the rise in temperature to 2°C will be difficult enough.

One reason for the uncertainty about what is a safe limit is that global warming can trigger feedback loops that bring about more warming. For example, less ice in the arctic ocean means that less of the sun's warmth is reflected back and more is absorbed by the ocean. More thawing of the Siberian permafrost will release more methane, a potent greenhouse gas. There could also be negative feedback loops that slow warming. Our knowledge is incomplete, and so even if we specify a level of carbon in the atmosphere that we believe will not take warming above 2°C, we could be wrong. Another factor determining the acceptable level of carbon in the atmosphere is therefore the degree of probability we are willing to settle for that the temperature rise will stay below 2°C. The IPCC's *Fifth Assessment Report*, in its "Summary for Policymakers," calculates how much carbon dioxide can be emitted if we accept a probability of greater than 33 percent, greater than 50 percent, or greater than 66 percent.

Even the *lowest* risk scenario leaves a one in three chance that we will have a rise beyond 2°C, and hence climate change will become dangerous. "Dangerous" here means we do not really know what will happen. We cannot exclude that powerful feedback loops will make large sections of our planet uninhabitable. Once again, the reason the "Summary for Policymakers" does not tell us what limit on emissions would be necessary to reduce the risk to 10 percent or 1 percent or zero appears to be that no one thinks such a limit practicable. Think about this for a moment. If you are crazy enough to play Russian roulette in the traditional way—loading a single bullet into the cylinder of a revolver that can carry six bullets, spinning the cylinder, putting the muzzle to your head, and pulling the trigger—you are taking a one in six chance of killing yourself. Compare that with the *Fifth Assessment Report,* a document issued by the world's most authoritative intergovernmental body considering climate change, written by the world's leading experts in sciences related to climate change, and vetted by representatives of the governments that have signed the Framework Convention, and what does its "Summary for Policymakers" offer us? Nothing better than running a one in three risk of climate change getting completely out of control. Do we really want to load the cylinder of our six-chamber revolver with not one but two bullets before we put the muzzle to the head of our planet?

If reducing the risk to 33 percent is the best we can hope for, then the *Fifth Assessment Report* tells us we must limit cumulative emissions since 1861 to 790 gigatons of carbon, which is equivalent to 2,900 gigatons of carbon dioxide ($GtCO_2$). Of that total, 1,890 $GtCO_2$ had already been emitted by 2011, leaving only 1,010 $GtCO_2$ to be emitted.[28] Given that emissions in

2010 (including greenhouse gases like methane and nitrous oxide) were the equivalent of 49 $GtCO_2$ and rising, we can assume that by the end of 2015 no more than 910 $GtCO_2$ can be emitted in coming decades. If the world continues on its present course, we have no more than 18 years before emissions have to be cut to zero; but it isn't going to be possible to cut emissions to zero by 2033. Optimistically, some scientists believe that alternative energy sources and new technologies may develop rapidly enough to get to zero emissions by 2050. We also have to be optimistic enough to assume that the livestock industry will either vanish or discover how to stop ruminants like cattle and sheep from belching and farting methane, because a report by the United Nations Food and Agriculture Organization shows that the livestock industry makes a larger contribution to global warming than the entire transport sector—all the cars, trucks, buses, trains, ships, and planes combined.[29] Let's assume, nevertheless, that we do have until 2050 to get to zero emissions. That would mean we can emit 910 $GtCO_2$ over the next 35 years, or 26 $GtCO_2$ each year, and still have a 66 percent chance of avoiding dangerous anthropogenic climate change. If we take the world's population as seven billion and divide the 26 $GtCO_2$ equally among them, that gives each of them an annual allowance of 3.7 tons of CO_2 equivalent.

Now compare actual per capita emissions for some key countries. Small Persian Gulf states top the list, with Kuwait at 64 tons and Qatar at 43. Outside that region, Australia's per capita emissions are among the highest, at almost 27 tons. The United States and Canada produce more than 20 tons of carbon dioxide per person per year. Russia emits almost 15 tons per capita, Germany just over 10, the United Kingdom 9.3, and the European Union as a whole, across its 28 member states, 8.7 tons, which is similar to Japan and, more surprisingly, to Indonesia, where changes in land use, especially forest clearance, contribute more than half of all emissions. China's per capita emissions are 7 tons, and Brazil's and Mexico's both just below 6. In contrast, India and Pakistan have per capita emissions of only 1.9 tons, Ethiopia 1.7, Uganda and Burkina Faso 1.3, and Bangladesh just 1.[30]

On these figures, the equal per capita share view of equality is only a little less demanding for the affluent industrial countries than the historical responsibility view. To avoid exceeding its share, Australia would have to cut its emissions by 85 percent and the United States and Canada by 80 percent, while Germany, the United Kingdom, and the European Union would need to reduce emissions to below half of their present levels. China would have to make sizable cuts too. This is not, it is important to understand, a target to be reached by some distant future date: it is what emissions would have to average up to 2050, if that is the date we have chosen as the time when it is reasonable to hope that new technologies will enable us to cease adding carbon dioxide to the atmosphere.

We can therefore also calculate in how many years, at present rates of emission, a country will use up its share of the greenhouse gases that it can, under the equal per capita share principle, emit up to 2050. All we have to do is multiply the fair share (3.7 tons) by 35 (the number of years remaining to 2050) and divide by the present rate of emissions. If the United States continues with business as usual, that will happen in 2022, less than seven years away, and for Australia even sooner, in 2020. The European Union will exhaust its allocation in 2030. On the other hand, India and Pakistan could almost double their per capita emissions without exceeding their share, and Bangladesh could more than treble its emissions.

One objection to this approach is that allowing countries to have allocations based on their population gives them insufficient incentive to do anything about population growth. But if the global population increases, the per capita amount of carbon that each country is allocated will diminish, for the aim is to keep total carbon emissions below a given level. Therefore a country that increases its population would be imposing additional burdens on other countries. Even countries with zero population growth would have to decrease their carbon outputs to meet the new, reduced per capita allocation.

We can meet this objection by setting state allocations that are tied to a specified population rather than allowing allocations to increase with an increase in a state's population. We could fix a state's allocation on its predicted population in a given year, such as the year that a new agreement on reducing emissions comes into force. But since different countries have different proportions of young people about to reach reproductive age, this might produce greater hardship in those countries that have younger populations than in those that have older ones. To overcome this, the per capita allocation could be based on an estimate of a country's likely population at some given future dates. For example, the estimates of each country's population size in 2050, which are already compiled by the United Nations, might be used.[31] Countries would then be rewarded (in terms of an increased emission quota per citizen) if they achieve lower-than-expected population growth and penalized (in terms of a reduced emission quota per citizen) if they exceeded the population forecast—and there would be no impact on other countries.

Aiding the Worst-Off

Some of the best-known accounts of fairness hold that fairness requires that we seek to improve the prospects of those who are worst-off. Some take the view that we should assist the worst-off only if their poverty is due to circumstances for which they are not responsible, like the family or country into which they were born or the abilities they have inherited. Others think we should help the worst-off irrespective of how they have come to be so badly off. Among the various accounts that pay special attention to the situation of the worst-off, by far the most widely discussed is that of Rawls. Rawls holds that, when we distribute goods, we can justify giving more to those who are already well off only if this will bring about "the greatest benefit of the least advantaged members of society."[32] This approach allows us to depart from equality, but only when doing so is the best thing we can do for the worst-off.

Whereas the strict egalitarian is vulnerable to the objection that equality can be achieved by "leveling down," that is, by bringing the rich down to the level of the poor without improving the position of the poor, Rawls's account is immune to this objection. For example, if allowing some entrepreneurs to become very rich—and thus increasing inequality within the society—will give them incentives to work hard and set up industries that provide employment for the worst-off, and there is no other way to provide that employment or any similar benefit to the worst-off, then that inequality would be permissible.

That there are today very great differences in wealth and income between people living in different countries is glaringly obvious. Equally evident is the fact that these differences depend largely on the fact that people are born into diverse circumstances, not that they have failed to take advantage of opportunities open to them. Hence if, in distributing the atmosphere's capacity to absorb our waste gases without harmful consequences, we were to reject any distribution that fails to improve the situation of those who, through no fault of their own, are at the bottom of the heap, we would not allow the living standard in poor countries to be reduced while rich countries remain much better off.[33] To put this more concretely: if, to meet the limits set for the United States, taxes or other disincentives are used that go no further than providing incentives for Americans to drive more fuel-efficient cars, it would not be right to set limits on China that prevent most Chinese from driving cars at all.

In accordance with Rawls's principle, the only grounds on which one could argue against rich countries bearing *all* the costs of reducing emissions would be that to do so would make the poor countries even worse off than they would have been if the rich countries were not bearing all the costs. Is this plausible? President George W. Bush defended his refusal to curb U.S. greenhouse gas emissions by saying that his administration was adopting a "greenhouse gas intensity approach" which seeks to reduce the amount of greenhouse gases the United States emits per unit of economic activity. Bush added that "economic growth is the solution, not the problem," and "the United States wants to foster economic growth in the developing world, including the world's poorest countries."[34]

Allowing countries to emit in proportion to their economic activity—in effect, in proportion to their gross domestic product—can be seen as encouraging efficiency, in the sense of leading to the lowest possible level of emissions for the goods and services produced. But it is also compatible with the United States continuing to increase its greenhouse gases emissions because it is producing more goods. That will mean that other countries, including countries with far lower per capita emissions than the United States, must decrease their emissions if catastrophic climate change is to be averted. Hence for this defense of the present high per capita level of U.S. emissions to be compatible with Rawls's theory of justice, it would be necessary to show that the country's high level of productivity not only makes the world as a whole better off but also provides the greatest benefit to those who are worst-off, which in this situation would be the poorest people in the poorest countries.

The major flaw in this argument is that the primary beneficiaries of U.S. production are the residents of the United States itself. The vast majority of the goods and services the country produces—more than 85 percent of them—are consumed in the United States.[35] Even if we focus on the relatively small fraction of goods produced in the United States that are sold abroad, U.S. residents benefit from the employment that is created, and, of course, U.S. producers receive payment for the goods they sell abroad. Many residents of other countries, especially of the poorest countries, cannot afford to buy goods produced in the United States, and it isn't clear that they benefit from U.S. production.

The factual basis of the argument has another flaw: the United States does not produce more efficiently, in terms of carbon dioxide emissions, than other countries. Figures published by the International Energy Agency show that the United States is about average in the quantity of emissions it produces in proportion to its GDP. It is less efficient than many developed countries like Germany, France, Italy, Singapore, Spain, or the United Kingdom and also less efficient than many developing countries in Africa, Asia, and Central and South America.[36]

Since the efficiency argument fails, we must conclude that a principle that requires us to distribute resources so as to improve the level of the worst-off would still, given the huge resource gap between rich and poor countries, make the rich countries bear all of the costs of the required changes.

The Greatest Happiness Principle

Classical utilitarians would not support any of the principles of fairness discussed so far. They would ask what proposal would lead to the greatest net happiness for all affected—net happiness being what you have left when you deduct the amount of suffering the proposal causes from the amount of happiness it brings about. An advocate of preference utilitarianism would instead ask what proposal would lead to the greatest net satisfaction of preferences for all concerned. In this context, the difference between the two forms of utilitarianism is not very meaningful. What is much more of a problem, for either of these views, is to indicate how one might do such a calculation. Evidently, there are good utilitarian reasons for capping the emission of greenhouse gases, but what way of doing it will lead to the greatest net benefits?

In considering what we need to do to bring about the greatest net benefits, it is important that we look at this question impartially across time as well as across space—so not only between, say, Americans and citizens of Nigeria or India, but also between people living now and people who will be living on our planet a century or more hence. Some economists, when estimating the costs or benefits of long-term projects, discount the future. Bjorn Lomborg achieved considerable publicity for his claim that money spent reducing greenhouse gas emissions would do more good if spent in other ways to help the global poor.[37] His figures were based on discounting future costs of climate change at an annual rate of 5 percent. Since the costs of reducing greenhouse gas emissions will come soon whereas most of the costs of not doing so fall several decades into the future, this makes a huge difference to the cost/benefit equation. Assume that unchecked global warming will lead to rising sea levels and that, as a result, in forty years many areas of valuable land, from Manhattan to the delta regions of Bangladesh, will be inundated. With an annual discount rate of 5 percent, every $1,000 that the flooding will cost in 40 years is equivalent to only $142 today. Losses that will occur in the further future—say, a century or more hence—dwindle to virtually nothing. This is not because of inflation—we are talking about costs expressed in dollars already adjusted for inflation. Lomborg justified his discount by arguing that if we invest $142 today, we can get a (completely safe) return of 5 percent on it, and so it will grow to $1,000 in 40 years. That figure may have looked reasonable before the global financial crisis hit in 2008, but, as events have shown, it was unwarranted. Assuming different interest rates or even acknowledging uncertainty about interest rates would lead to very different cost/benefit ratios.[38] More important, however, there is an ethical issue about discounting the kind of future goods that are threatened by climate change. True, our investments may increase in value over time, and we will become richer, but the price we are prepared to pay to save human lives or endangered species may go up just as much. These values are not consumer goods, like TVs or dishwashers, which, if our earnings rise, will drop in cost as a proportion of our earnings. They are more like health, something that the richer we get, the more we are willing to spend to preserve. An ethical, not an economic, justification would be needed for discounting suffering and death or the extinction of species because these losses will not occur for forty years. No such justification has been offered.

Because it is so difficult to estimate what will maximize utility in the long run, utilitarians may appeal to other principles of fair or just distribution, like the ones we have been discussing. These principles give you easier answers and are likely to lead to an outcome that approximates the best consequences (or is at least as likely to do so as any calculation we could make without using those principles). The principles discussed above can be justified in utilitarian terms, although each for somewhat different reasons. To go through them in turn:

1. The principle that "the polluter pays" or, more generally "you broke it, you fix it," provides a strong incentive to be careful about causing pollution, or breaking things. So if it is upheld as a general rule, there will be less pollution, and people will be more careful in situations where they might break something, all of which will be to the general benefit.

2. The equal per capita shares principle will not, in general, be what utilitarians with perfect knowledge of all the consequences of their actions would choose. Where there is no other clear criterion for allocating shares, however, it can be defended as a compromise that leads to a peaceful solution rather than to no change at all. Arguably, that is the best basis for defending one person, one vote as a rule of democracy against claims that those with more education, or who pay more taxes, or who have served in the military, or who believe in the one true God, or who are worse off should have additional votes because of their particular attributes.[39]

3. In practice, utilitarians can often support the principle of distributing resources to those who are worst-off because when you already have a lot, giving you more does not increase your utility as much as when you have only a little. One of the 700 million people in the world living on $1.90 per day will get much more benefit from an additional $100 than will someone living on $100,000 per year. Similarly, if we have to take $100 from someone, we will cause much less suffering if we take it from the person earning $100,000

than if we take it from the person earning $700 a year. This is known as diminishing marginal utility. When compared with giving resources to meet someone's core needs, giving further resources at the margin to someone else whose core needs have already been satisfied will lead to less utility. Hence a utilitarian will generally favor the worst-off when it comes to distributing resources. In contrast to Rawls, however, a utilitarian does not consider this principle to be absolute. The utilitarian always seeks the greatest overall benefit, and it is only a rule of thumb that this will generally be obtained by adding to the stock of resources of those who have the least.

Utilitarians would also have to take into account the greater hardship that might be imposed on people living in countries that have difficulty in complying with strict emission standards because their geography or climate compels their citizens to use a greater amount of energy to achieve a given level of comfort than do people living elsewhere. Canadians, for example, could argue that it would simply not be possible to live in many parts of their country without using above average quantities of energy to keep warm. Residents of rich countries might even advance the bolder claim that, since their affluent residents have become used to traveling by car and keeping their houses cool in hot weather, they would suffer more if they have to give up their energy-intensive lifestyle than poorer people will suffer if they never get the chance to experience such comforts.

Utilitarians cannot refuse to consider such claims of hardship, even when the claims come from those who are already far better off than most of the world's people. As we shall see, however, these claims can be taken into account in a way that is compatible with the general conclusion to which the utilitarian view would otherwise lead: that the rich countries should bear much more of the burden of reducing greenhouse gas emissions than the poor countries—perhaps even the entire burden.

Fairness: A Proposal

Each of the four principles of fairness I have considered could be defended as the best one to take, or we could take some in combination. I propose, both because of its simplicity and hence its suitability as a political compromise and because it seems likely to increase global welfare, that we support the second principle, that of equal per capita future entitlements to a share of the capacity of the atmospheric sink, tied to the current United Nations projection of population growth per country in 2050.

Some will say that this is excessively harsh on industrialized countries like the United States, which will have to cut back the most on their output of greenhouse gases. But we have now seen that equal per capita shares is much more indulgent to the United States and other developed countries than other principles for which there are strong arguments. If, for example, we accepted the principle that equal per capita shares should include a state's previous emissions as well, then, as we saw earlier in this chapter, we would hold that the emissions of the countries that industrialized early ought to be held down to much *less* than an equal per capita share for future emissions. As things stand now, even on the basis of an equal per capita share of future emissions, the developing countries are going to have to accept lower outputs of greenhouse gases than they would have had to if the industrialized countries had kept to an equal per capita share in the past. So by saying, "Forget about the past, let's start anew," the equal per capita share of future emissions principle is a lot more favorable to the developed countries than a timeless equal per capita share principle would be.

This proposal has an immediate practical implication: for the five-yearly reviews of emission reduction targets envisaged by the 2015 Paris agreement, countries with high per capita emissions—starting with Australia, the United States, Canada, and European Union members like France, Germany, and the United Kingdom—should take the lead in adjusting their emission targets sharply downward, thus setting an example of what can be and needs to be done. For all the moral reasons we have now examined, they should not use the reluctance of developing countries to take similarly strong action as an excuse for doing nothing themselves.

Emissions Trading

The ethical principles I have been discussing all imply that the rich nations should dramatically reduce their greenhouse gas emissions. One might doubt whether any such drastic reductions are politically feasible. In response, it has been suggested that allowing emissions trading between nations that are above their emissions targets and those that are below their targets would make the transition easier. Emissions trading works on the same simple economic principle as trade in general: if you can buy something from someone else more cheaply than you can produce it yourself, you are better off buying it than making it. A country like the United States that is already producing more gases than its fair share could buy a permit to emit greenhouse gases from a country like Bangladesh that has emissions below its fair share. Such a trade would make it easier for the United States to reach its target and would give Bangladesh an incentive to maintain its low levels of greenhouse gas emissions in order to maximize the amount of quota it can sell. Thus emissions trading, it is claimed, will produce the best outcome for everyone. A given amount of carbon dioxide added to the atmosphere makes the same contribution to global warming whether it comes from the United States or from Bangladesh. Moreover, global emissions trading would give the world's poorest countries something they can trade in exchange for the resources that will help them to meet their needs. This would be, on most principles of justice or utility, a very good thing indeed. It may also make developing countries more willing to be part of a binding agreement on emissions because without binding quotas they would have nothing to sell.

Although the 2015 Paris agreement did not allocate quotas to each state and so does not envisage emissions trading, local, regional, and—in the case of the European Union Emission Trading Scheme—multinational emission trading schemes are already in operation in Europe, North America, Latin America, and Asia, and they are growing in number and scope. China is developing a national scheme that will grow to twice the size of the European Union scheme. To curb its rising emissions, China plans a carbon price of around $18, which is, at the time of writing, more than double the going rate in the European Union scheme, although European Union officials have acknowledged that the carbon price in their scheme needs boosting.[40] It is possible that in future some form of global emissions trading will come under consideration.

Emissions trading would answer two objections to allocating greenhouse gas emissions quotas on the basis of a principle such as equal per capita shares. First, it would answer the objection raised when discussing a utilitarian approach to these problems, namely, that countries like Canada might suffer undue hardship if forced to limit emissions to the same per capita amount as, say, Mexico because Canadians need to use more energy to survive their winters. But global emissions trading means that Canada would be able to buy the quota it requires from other countries that do not need their full quota. Thus the market would provide a measure of the additional burden put on the world's atmosphere by keeping one's house at a pleasant temperature when it is too cold or too hot outside. Citizens of rich countries could choose to pay that price. They would not, however, be claiming a benefit for themselves that they were not prepared to allow poor countries to have because the poor countries would benefit by having emission quotas to sell. The claim of undue hardship therefore does not justify allowing rich countries to have a higher per capita emissions quota than poor countries.

Second, global emissions trading would answer the objection that equal per capita shares would lead to inefficient production because countries with little industrialization would be able to continue to manufacture goods even though they emit more greenhouse gases per unit of economic activity than highly industrialized countries, while the highly industrialized countries would have to cut back on their manufacturing capacity, even though they produce fewer emissions per unit of economic activity. The present laissez-faire system is, of course, even worse than that—it allows emitters to reap economic benefits for themselves while imposing costs on third parties who may or may not share in the benefits of the polluters' high productivity. That is recognized by economists as a form of market failure, and it is neither a fair nor an efficient outcome. A well-regulated system of per capita entitlements combined with global emissions trading would be both fair and, in economic terms, efficient.

There are three serious objections, one scientific and two ethical, to global emissions trading. The scientific objection is that we do not have the means to measure emissions accurately in all countries. Hence it would not be possible to know how much quota these countries have to sell or need to buy. This is something that needs more research, but it should not prove an insuperable obstacle in the long run. Estimates do not need to be accurate to the last ton of carbon.

Pope Francis objected to emissions trading in his 2015 encyclical on the environment, *Laudato Si:*

> The strategy of buying and selling "carbon credits" can lead to a new form of speculation which would not help reduce the emission of polluting gases worldwide. This system seems to provide a quick and easy solution under the guise of a certain commitment to the environment, but in no way does it allow for the radical change which present circumstances require. Rather, it may simply become a ploy which permits maintaining the excessive consumption of some countries and sectors.[41]

If emissions trading were to be a mere "ploy"—that is, if it did not lead to real reductions in emissions made at the lowest possible cost—then it would indeed be unethical to engage in emissions trading. Perhaps Francis is doing no more than warning that an emissions trading scheme could be distorted in this way; but if he is going beyond that warning and rejecting emissions trading even when the cuts that are paid for can be verified as having been made, it is difficult to see what the objection is. It is true that the rich countries, by buying up emissions quotas from countries that are not using their per capita share, will not have to reduce their emissions as much as they otherwise would have to do; but is that wrong? They will be paying for their emissions above their equal per capita share, and those countries that are selling part of their quota will have chosen to accept the price they were offered. It isn't easy to see why such an exchange is unethical, especially when the alternative to reducing emissions as efficiently as possible is likely to be that the reductions made are lower, with a correspondingly greater risk of catastrophe. As

Joseph Heath has put it, the pope's objection to emissions trading overlooks the fact that "efficiency, in this context, is a moral principle."[42]

A second, more pragmatic ethical objection is that while emissions trading would benefit poor countries if the governments of those countries used it for the benefit of their people, some countries are run by corrupt dictators more interested in increasing their military spending or adding to their Swiss bank accounts. Emissions trading would simply give them a new way of raising money for these purposes. This objection is similar to a problem discussed at the end of the next chapter, and my proposed solution may be clearer after a reading of that section. It is to refuse to recognize a corrupt dictatorial regime, one interested only in self-preservation and self-enrichment, as the legitimate government of the country that has excess quota to sell. In the absence of any legitimate government that can receive payments for quota, the sale of quota could be managed by an international authority answerable to the United Nations. That authority could hold the money it receives in trust until the country has a government able to make a credible claim that the money will be used to benefit the people as a whole.

Down from the Clouds?

To cynical observers of the negotiations on climate change, some of this ethical argument may seem lacking in political realism. There appears to be little real prospect of the United States, Canada, or Australia committing themselves to emission reduction targets based on a principle such as equal per capita shares. So what is the point of even discussing such a principle?

One aim of the preceding discussion is to help us to see that there is no *ethical* basis for the present distribution of the atmosphere's capacity to absorb greenhouse gases without drastic climate change. If high-emitting countries choose to retain this distribution or to use it as the starting point for setting targets that are limited to small percentage reductions of their emissions, they are standing simply on their presumed rights as sovereign states. That and the raw military power they yield make it difficult for anyone else to impose a more ethically defensible solution on them. If we, as citizens of the industrialized countries, do not understand what would be a fair solution to global warming, then we cannot understand how flagrantly self-serving such a stance would be. If, on the other hand, we can convey to our fellow citizens a sense of what would be a fair solution to the problem, it may be possible to change the policies that are now leading the world to a situation in which we are risking an irreversible catastrophe of unknown dimensions.

Today there is broad agreement that greenhouse gas emissions should be reduced to a level that will keep global warming below 2°C, but even many states that accept this position are continuing to emit amounts that cannot be defended on any reasonable ethical principle. If the naming and shaming process initiated in Paris in 2015 fails, we will need to consider whether there are other possible institutions or principles of international law that could help. The fact that seemingly harmless, trivial human actions can affect people in distant countries makes a significant difference to the sovereignty of states. Even without any new international agreements, the principles of international law make states responsible for ensuring that activities within their jurisdiction do not cause damage to the environment of other states or of areas beyond the limits of national jurisdiction, such as the atmosphere or the sea. In the 1970s it became clear that sulfur dioxide emitted by industries in the United States was causing acid rain in Canada, and similarly emissions from continental Europe were causing acidification in Scandinavia.

When water systems become acid, forests can die and other plants and animals are affected also. Acid rain damages buildings as well, including older stone buildings that are of cultural significance, and fine particles of sulfur dioxide in the air have a harmful effect on human health, causing asthma and bronchitis. There are now treaties between the United States and Canada and between European states aimed at reducing air emissions that cause acid rain,[43] but if there were not, it would seem that the states harmed by the sulfur dioxide emitted by other states would have been able to sue for damages in the International Court of Justice.

The science linking greenhouse gas emissions with global warming is more complex than the science linking sulfur dioxide emissions with acid rain, and the consequences of global warming are more diverse than those of acid rain, but the underlying principle is the same. If the United States allows large quantities of carbon dioxide to be emitted into the atmosphere, causing damage to villagers farming the deltas of Bangladesh, Bangladesh should have the same grounds for seeking action under international law to restrain U.S. emissions as Canada would have had if the United States had done nothing to reduce its sulfur dioxide emissions.

Another possibility worth considering is sanctions. There have been several occasions on which the United Nations has used sanctions against states that have been seen as doing something gravely wrong. Perhaps one day a reformed and strengthened United Nations will invoke sanctions against states that do not play their part in global measures for the protection of the environment. The problem is that by the time that day comes, it is likely to be too late, for the world will have already emitted more than enough greenhouse gases to cross the threshold beyond which dangerous climate change can no longer be prevented.

Some scientists believe it is already too late to prevent climate change getting out of control and making parts of our planet uninhabitable;[44] but even if they are mistaken, we should not forget that climate change is harming people who bear little or no responsibility for it. They can expect more extreme weather events, like hurricanes, heat waves, and droughts, and sea levels will continue to rise.

The United Nations Framework Convention on Climate Change recognized that developed countries have, historically, made the largest contribution to the greenhouse gases in the atmosphere that are causing climate change and that developing countries have made a smaller contribution. The convention also states that developed countries will "assist the developing country Parties that are particularly vulnerable to the adverse effects of climate change in meeting costs of adaptation to those adverse effects." Developed countries have therefore accepted that they have some responsibility to help developing countries respond to climate change. In 2010 the World Bank completed a major report on the cost of adapting to a world that is 2°C warmer and reached an estimate of $70-$100 billion per year between 2010 and 2050, an amount roughly comparable to the amount of aid that is given to developing countries each year but small in relation to the roughly $60-trillion income the world earns each year—it is, in fact, only 0.17 percent, or $0.17 in every $100 earned.[45] The study also confirms that, as we have already noted, it is the poor who are most vulnerable to the effects of climate change. Yet the amount that is currently going into the international funds set up to help poor countries adapt to climate change is nowhere near the level that the World Bank estimates is required. Between 2010 and 2012 developed countries committed a total of only $30 billion.[46] At Paris in 2015 the developed countries agreed to "take the lead in mobilizing climate finance" to meet the needs of developing countries and to draw on both public and private funds for that purpose. The preamble to the agreement mentions the sum of $100 billion per year for this purpose, but to the disappointment of many developing countries there is no binding commitment to any specific amount.[47]

When it comes to paying for the costs of adapting to climate change, the case for the historical principle—you broke it, you fix it—is very strong. Most legal systems make people or corporations liable for harm they deliberately, recklessly, or negligently cause to others. This is sometimes called fault liability because it relies on the causer of the harm being at fault in some way. On that basis, liability for paying for adaptation would be limited to the period when climate science had developed to the point at which the developed countries knew their greenhouse emissions were likely to cause harm but recklessly did nothing about it; or were negligent in not ascertaining whether or not they were likely to cause harm. As I mentioned when discussing historical responsibility, this would, at a minimum, apply to the emissions from developed countries since 1992, when the Framework Convention was accepted.

The alternative legal form of liability, strict liability, does not require any fault, not even negligence, on the part of the causer of the harm. It is usually applied to inherently dangerous activities but is also often invoked to hold manufacturers of products liable for faults in them, irrespective of any negligence or other misconduct by the manufacturer. As Paul Baer has pointed out, strict liability is often applied to environmental pollution, not only in court cases but also in legislation. The United States Superfund legislation or, to give it its full title, the Comprehensive Environmental Response, Compensation, and Liability Act of 1980, a federal law, holds those who have dumped hazardous wastes liable for the cost of cleaning up contaminated sites, even if the contaminants were not known to be hazardous when they were dumped.[48]

Although the principle of historical responsibility offers a strong answer to the question of who should pay for adaptation —and one that is, at least if limited to fault liability, in accord with widely accepted moral principles—it is not the only possible way of deciding who should pay for adaptation. As is the case with the principles that can be applied to allocate greenhouse gas emission quotas between states, however, all the plausible principles point in the same direction. Rawls's view that inequalities should benefit the worst-off also suggests that the developed countries should meet the developing country's costs of adaptation, and so does the principle of utilitarianism.

Geoengineering

When Mount Pinatubo in the Philippines erupted in 1991, it injected 20 million tons of tiny sulfur particles into the stratosphere. The particles reflected some of the sun's rays back into space, thus causing a reduction of temperatures of about half a degree Celsius for the next one to three years. If a volcano can do that, some scientists have said, so could we, in order to counteract the effects of greenhouse gases. Technically, it would not be difficult to do. Other scientists have suggested more complicated ways of cooling the planet, like putting large solar mirrors into space to reflect sunlight or finding economically viable methods for removing carbon from the atmosphere and storing it underground. This and other large-scale techniques for changing the climate of the planet are popularly referred to as geoengineering, a term defined in a Royal Society report as "the deliberate, large-scale manipulation of the Earth's climate system in order to counteract climate change."[49] Geoengineering has been described as Plan B for climate change, which suggests, Dale Jamieson has quipped, that it's a morning-after pill for societies that do not practice safe consumption.[50]

If climate change is a paradigm example of a problem in need of a global solution, then geoengineering is a paradigm example of a proposed solution in need of global decision making. Until recently, geoengineering has been viewed by both climate scientists and environmentalists with either suspicion or outright hostility. Jamieson, after finding a lack of coherence in the options that are and are not included under the label "geoengineering," has suggested we use it not to mark a specific type of response to climate change but "as an attitudinal marker of suspicion" that alerts us to the fact that what is being proposed is "viewed as novel, weird, exotic, unfamiliar, or untested."[51]

It is certainly true that we are very far from having any safe method of changing the climate of our planet on a scale sufficient to counteract the climate change that is likely to result from our greenhouse gas emissions. One might see the Mount Pinatubo eruption as a natural experiment, but if so, the results were decidedly mixed. If we have learned anything about trying to manage local environmental problems, it is that it is difficult to do only one thing because most interventions have unpredicted further effects. When we are intervening on a global scale it is hard to imagine how we could predict all of these further effects, and some of them might be disastrous. It has been suggested, for example, that injecting sulfur particles into the stratosphere could cause the disruption of the monsoon that brings India 75 percent of its rainfall and is critical for the survival of its agricultural sector, which employs more than half its population.[52] (On the other hand, as we saw earlier, it has also been suggested that continued climate change could weaken the monsoon.) In the case of the Mount Pinatubo eruption, other impacts include a drop in precipitation over land and, more specifically, drought in the tropics.[53]

Nor would the injection of sulfate particles into the atmosphere have any impact on the fact that the additional carbon dioxide we are putting into the atmosphere is making the oceans more acidic. The National Oceanic and Atmospheric Administration, part of the U.S. Department of Commerce, refers to this as "the other carbon dioxide problem." We are still discovering how ocean acidification affects marine life and the overall ocean ecology, but one known consequence is that it inhibits the growth of shells, which imperils shellfish such as oysters.[54]

Despite the very significant known and unknown risks of geoengineering, there is some plausibility to the idea that we ought to have it in our back pocket as a Plan B in case we fail to reduce greenhouse gas emissions sufficiently to prevent catastrophic climate change. To make it even a halfway plausible Plan B, however, we would need to start doing research directed at finding out what might work and how to reduce the risks. In 2015 a U.S. government–sponsored panel of the National Academy of Sciences brought geoengineering research a step closer when it said that if proper governance and other safeguards could be developed it would be acceptable to carry out some small-scale outdoor experiments that would help scientists understand whether geoengineering would work.[55] Therein, however, lies a problem that is familiar in the insurance industry, where it is known as moral hazard. If people insure their property, they have less incentive to prevent fire or theft. If we come to believe that geoengineering will enable us to avoid catastrophic climate change, we will have less incentive to reduce our greenhouse gas emissions and, in the absence of sufficiently strong incentives, we are unlikely to do so. When a Californian businessman, Russ George, used a chartered fishing boat to spread 120 tons of iron dust over the ocean in an unregulated experiment to cause an algae bloom that would soak up carbon dioxide, Silvia Ribeiro, speaking for the ETC group, an environmental watchdog, called for geoengineering experiments to be banned on the grounds that they are "a dangerous distraction providing governments and industry with an excuse to avoid reducing fossil-fuel emissions."[56] Jamieson agrees that we "will avert our eyes from reality as long as a simple solution seems just over the horizon." The hope that a simple, inexpensive solution will be found has been, he says, "a constant if ghostly presence in the climate change debate for the last half century," and it may have already, in his view, reduced our willingness to change the fossil-fuel-intensive lifestyle to which we have become accustomed.[57]

Yet the problem remains, because even if we agree with those who think it would be better to reduce our greenhouse gas emissions than to attempt something as hazardous as geoengineering, there is, as we have seen, a very real risk that we will not reduce our greenhouse gas emissions sufficiently to avoid catastrophic climate change. If that happens, and the next generation stands faced with the catastrophe we have brought upon them, our refusal to evaluate the likelihood of some form of geoengineering averting such a catastrophe could be seen as a well-motivated but nevertheless tragic excess of caution.

If doing research on geoengineering is defensible, that raises the question of how a decision to use it would be taken. At present any state or group of states could act unilaterally and maintain that it had not violated international law. A state might see such action as being in its own interests because its scientists believe that climate change would have devastating consequences for its people, whereas the major risks of geoengineering would fall on other countries. We can imagine, for example, that after a period of severe droughts across the Midwest and Western parts of the United States, the country would unilaterally engage in geoengineering despite the risk this would present to the monsoon on which, as we have seen, Indian agriculture relies. Another possible scenario is that a country that has reduced its own emissions might argue that, because the rest of the world has not done so, geoengineering is necessary and, in the absence of any United Nations agreement to undertake it, unilateral action is morally required. (In chapter 4 I will consider a situation that might be regarded as comparable: when the United Nations Security Council is unwilling to act to prevent an ongoing genocide in one part of the world, one state may justifiably take unilateral military action.)

Any use of geoengineering would affect the entire world, so its use should require a decision taken by an international body. On these grounds, a case can be made for developing a global body that could say no to geoengineering.[58] The problem is that to make such a decision credible, the global body would also need to have the option of saying yes, should the evidence for some particular form of climate management become compelling. Then the problem of moral hazard once again rears its ugly head. Nevertheless, on balance it seems better to have such a body than not to have it.

3 one economy

What This Chapter Is Not About

If you are among those who believe that the solution to the world's economic problems is to end capitalism, this chapter is not for you. I assume that, like it or not, capitalism will be the dominant economic system for the foreseeable future. To challenge that assumption, opponents of capitalism would have to establish two claims. First, they would need to show that there is an alternative economic system that will, in a world like ours and given what we have learned about human nature, do a better job of providing people with food, clothing, shelter, health care, education, and the other things that are central to our well-being. Second, they need to tell a believable story about how that alternative economic system could come to replace contemporary capitalism. I've yet to be convinced by any attempt to persuade me of the truth of either of these claims.

Until we have an answer to these two questions, to talk about getting rid of capitalism is a distraction from the many ways in which, within the constraints of a capitalist economy, we can make the world a better place. Saying that doesn't make me a starry-eyed enthusiast for the global capitalist system we have today. There are serious ethical questions about how far economic globalization should go, and the purpose of this chapter is to discuss those questions. As we shall see, global capitalism as currently practiced is flawed in important ways, and we ought to seek remedies for these flaws. To hardheaded realists, some of my suggestions will seem idealistic, but at least they have the merit of being achievable without overthrowing capitalism itself.

The World Trade Organization: Protest and Response

The raison d'être of the World Trade Organization, or the WTO, is the view that free trade makes people better off on average and in the long run. In 1999 the WTO was planning to hold its third ministerial conference in Seattle. Prior to the meeting, if the popular media mentioned the WTO at all it was to describe, in glowing terms, the economic benefits flowing from the expansion of world trade under its auspices. Since, as the prevalent metaphor put it, a rising tide lifts all boats, these benefits were supposed to be sure to reach the poorest countries as well. Most members of the public and many politicians and corporate leaders as well had little idea that there was serious opposition to economic globalization or to the WTO's program of removing barriers to world trade. They were startled when 40,000 people filled the streets of Seattle. The protestors included American unionists and human rights activists marching against cheap imports made by child labor; consumer groups worried about the safety of imported products; environmentalists dressed as sea turtles protesting WTO decisions that had struck down bans on imports of prawns caught in ways that also killed endangered turtles; and anarchists in black tights throwing rocks at the windows of stores like Nike and Starbucks, which they saw as representing global capitalism. When the protestors unexpectedly proved capable of disrupting the schedules of presidents and prime ministers they immediately became front-page news. Their impact was reinforced when the new round of trade negotiations expected to begin in Seattle failed to get started.

The initial response of media commentators was bewilderment, incomprehension, and ridicule. The *New York Times* columnist Thomas Friedman wrote an intemperate column that began by asking, "Is there anything more ridiculous in the news today than the protests against the World Trade Organization in Seattle?" He went on to call the protestors "a Noah's ark of flat-earth advocates, protectionist trade unions and yuppies looking for their 1960's fix."[1] They may have been an odd collection of people with very diverse views, but they succeeded in generating a whole new debate about the impact of world trade and the role of the WTO.

Has any noncriminal organization ever been so vehemently condemned on such wide-ranging grounds by critics from so many countries as the WTO? Here are some of the hostile comments made about the WTO at the time. According to Victor Menotti, the director of the Environment Program of the U.S.-based International Forum on Globalization, the regime of trade and investment fostered by the WTO has "unleashed global economic forces that systematically punish ecologically sound forestry while rewarding destructive practices that accelerate forest degradation."[2] From the standpoint of Compassion in World Farming, a leading British campaigner for farm animals, the WTO is "the Biggest Threat Facing Animal Welfare Today."[3] Martin Khor, the Malaysia-based leader of the Third World Network, claims that the WTO is "an instrument to govern the South."[4] Vandana Shiva, the founder and president of India's

Research Foundation for Science, Technology and Ecology and the author of a book called *Biopiracy: The Plunder of Nature and Knowledge,* writes that the rules of the WTO are "primarily rules of robbery, camouflaged by arithmetic and legalese" and that global free trade in food and agriculture is "the biggest refugee creation program in the world." It is, not to put too fine a point on it, "leading to slavery."[5] All in all, many of these critics would agree with the summary judgment attributed to the Zapatistas, an organization of Mexican peasants, that the WTO is simply "the biggest enemy of mankind."[6]

A few weeks after the failure of the Seattle meeting I found myself in Davos as an invited speaker at the annual meeting of the World Economic Forum. Bafflement about the protests was evident. I heard politicians like President Ernesto Zedillo of Mexico and corporate leaders like Lewis Campbell, the chief executive of Textron, a corporation with a turnover of $10 billion a year, swiftly dismiss the protestors as falling into one of two groups: those who were well intentioned in their concern to protect the environment and help the world's poorest people but were naïve and misled by their emotions; and those who, under the cynical guise of defending human rights and the environment, were seeking to protect their own well-paid jobs in inefficient industries by high tariff barriers that raise costs for domestic consumers and leave workers in less developed countries stuck in dire poverty.

There were dissenting voices at Davos. The U.S. labor leader John Sweeney and Khor spoke against the dominant view. Prime Minister Tony Blair of Great Britain and President Bill Clinton, quick learners both, said that genuine issues had been raised, and they needed serious consideration. Nevertheless, there was no real discussion of what those issues might be or of how they might be resolved. It was as if everyone already knew that globalization was economically beneficial, and "good for the economy" was identical in meaning to "good all things considered." So the real question was how to brush off the vexing opposition and make faster headway toward the goal of a single world economy, free of all barriers to trade or investment between different states. The alternative was, in Zedillo's word, just "globaphobia."[7]

For the next decade bodies like the WTO, the International Monetary Fund, the World Bank, and the G8 group of the major economic powers had to contend with large and sometimes violent protests at their major meetings, whether they took place in Washington, Prague, Melbourne, Quebec City, Gothenburg, Genoa, Cancún, Geneva, or Bali. The repeated rituals of street theater did not do much to advance the kind of discussion that is needed if we are to decide whether movement toward a single global economy is or is not a good thing. There are complicated questions of fact to be sorted out, and even if we could get agreement on the factual issues, the debate about economic globalization raises important questions of value. Unfortunately economists tend to be too focused on markets to give sufficient weight to values that are not dealt with well by the market.

Four Charges Against Economic Globalization

Among the many charges commonly made against economic globalization, and more specifically against the WTO as the leading agent for eliminating barriers to trade, four are central to any assessment of the desirability of building a global economy that is very different from anything that existed until quite recently:

1. Economic globalization places economic considerations ahead of concerns for the environment, animal welfare, and even human rights.
2. Economic globalization erodes state sovereignty.

3. Economic globalization affects everyone, but a small group of rich countries dominate trade negotiations and push through the trade deals that favor them.
4. Economic globalization increases inequality; or (a stronger charge) it makes the rich richer and leaves the world's poorest people even worse off than they would otherwise have been.

Before we can consider these charges, we need some background. The WTO was created by the Uruguay Round of talks held by member states of the General Agreement on Tariffs and Trade, or GATT. It came into existence in January 1995, and at the time of writing has about 160 member states, accounting for more than 95 percent of world trade.[8] The WTO claims that the result of its work is a "more prosperous, peaceful and accountable economic world."[9] This belief is based on the usual rationale of the market, that if two people have different abilities to make products they both desire, they will do better if they each work in the areas of production where they are most efficient relative to the other person and then exchange, rather than if they both try to make the full range of products they want. This will be true, it is claimed, whether the people are neighbors or live on opposite sides of the world, as long as the transaction costs involved in making the exchange are less than the differences in their costs of production. Moreover, this exchange should be particularly good for countries with low labor costs because they should be able to produce goods more cheaply than countries with high labor costs. Hence we can expect the demand for labor in those countries to rise, and, once the supply of labor begins to tighten, wages should rise too. Thus a free market should have the effect not only of making the world as a whole more prosperous but also, more specifically, of assisting the poorest countries.

The agreement by which the WTO was set up gives it the power to enforce a set of rules and agreements relating to free trade that now total about 30,000 pages.[10] If one member state believes it is disadvantaged by actions taken by another member state that are in breach of these rules, the first state can make a complaint. If efforts to mediate the dispute fail, a Dispute Panel consisting of experts in trade and law is set up to hear it. Dispute Panels are the most distinctive difference between the old GATT and the new WTO. In formal terms, the Dispute Panel does not decide the dispute but recommends a decision to the membership. In practice the decision of the Dispute Panel is invariably adopted. If the complaint is upheld and the member state continues to act in breach of WTO rules, it can be subjected to severe penalties, including tariffs against its own goods.

The protests in Seattle occurred at a time when the WTO was in the ascendant. It seemed to have the ability to reshape the world in the direction that the major developed countries wanted it to go. Today, that has changed. The negotiations that failed to get under way in Seattle began at the WTO's next ministerial conference, in Doha in 2001, when the Doha Round was launched with considerable fanfare. It was also known as the Doha Development Agenda because one of its stated objectives was to improve the trading prospects of developing countries. Over the next 14 years, seemingly endless negotiations failed to reach a successful conclusion. That occurred in large part because the developed countries no longer had it their own way. Instead, developing countries like Brazil and India stood up more strongly for their own interests. Agriculture is one area in which developing countries often produce more economically than developed countries; but because both the United States and the European Union subsidize their farmers, developing countries cannot sell their products on the world market. The developing countries therefore demanded that the United States and the European Union cut their agricultural subsidies. Although most economists in the United States and the European Union agree that agricultural subsidies are a waste of taxpayers' funds and a barrier to free trade, political considerations have prevented them from being rolled back. Thus no agreement could be reached on a new round of cuts to trade barriers. Each of the next five ministerial conferences revealed a deep division between developing and developed countries but nevertheless ended by "reaffirming" the Doha agenda. Finally, at the ministerial conference held in Nairobi in 2015, this ritual ceased: there was no expression of support for a round of negotiations that many regarded as dead. In future the WTO seems likely to aim at narrowly focused agreements on specific issues rather than at a global agreement to cut trade barriers. In the meantime many states are entering into bilateral and regional free trade agreements that bypass the WTO.

The influence of the WTO in reshaping the global economy may be waning, but its rules continue to determine the conditions of international trade, and so in the course of our discussion of the four charges against economic globalization, we still need to examine the impact of those rules.

The First Charge: Economics as Trumps

Much of the opposition to economic globalization in general and to the WTO in particular has been based on the claim that free trade makes it harder for states to protect the environment, promote high standards of animal welfare, and advance human rights. At first glance it is not obvious why removing barriers to trade should interfere with these three objectives. Indeed, the WTO claims this is all a misunderstanding. In a publication called *10 Things the WTO Can Do,* clearly aimed at a broad audience, the WTO confronts the following issue:

> An often-heard accusation is that the WTO system treats trade as the priority, at the expense of environmental and humanitarian objectives.
> This is untrue.[11]

In explaining why this is untrue, the publication points out that in the sea turtle case, mentioned above, the WTO Appellate Body stressed that WTO members "can, should and do take measures to protect endangered species and to protect the environment in other ways." The publication explains that when a dispute ruling says that a measure designed to protect the environment is illegal under WTO rules, this does not mean that the WTO is putting trade ahead of the environment but rather that the measure "violates trade rules," typically because it discriminates against products coming from some countries or is tougher on products from other countries than on products made by domestic producers. In the words of the publication, "If it were equally tough (or equally lenient) on goods from all sources, it would be legal."[12]

That sounds like a very reasonable principle. The WTO allows member states to protect endangered species as long as they do so fairly and do not, under the guise of environmental protection, favor their own industries. Presumably, then, the United States could, for example, prohibit the import of tuna caught by methods that drown dolphins, as long as it also prohibits the sale of tuna caught by American ships that catch tuna by this method. If this is correct, then the critics of the WTO seem wrong in their allegations that the organization is opposed to measures to protect the environment. The WTO only opposes, it seems, measures that use environmental protection as a disguise for the protection of domestic industries against foreign competition. If the WTO struck down U.S. laws to protect dolphins or sea turtles for those reasons, the fault must lie not with the WTO but with the United States for drafting laws that favor its producers.

This is indeed consistent with the wording of several WTO documents, including Article XX of the General Agreement on Tariffs and Trade, and the Preamble to the Agreement on Technical Barriers to Trade, which came into force with the founding of the WTO in 1994 and states in its preamble,

> *Recognizing* that no country should be prevented from taking measures necessary to ensure the quality of its exports, or for the protection of human, animal or plant life or health, of the environment, or for the prevention of deceptive practices, at the levels it considers appropriate, subject to the requirement that they are not applied in a manner which would constitute a means of arbitrary or unjustifiable discrimination between countries where the same conditions prevail or a disguised restriction on international trade . . .[13]

This is not, however, how the WTO Dispute Panels have always reached their decisions. Consider, for example, the tuna–dolphin dispute, which, although decided under GATT rather than the WTO, sets out principles the WTO uses. Here is an account of the dispute given in the WTO publication *Trading into the Future* (which provides a rather less simplistic account of how the WTO works than *10 Things the WTO Can Do*):

> The US Marine Mammal Protection Act sets dolphin protection standards for the domestic American fishing

fleet and for countries whose fishing boats catch yellowfin tuna in that part of the Pacific Ocean [where schools of dolphin swim over schools of tuna]. If a country exporting tuna to the United States cannot prove to the U.S. authorities that it meets the dolphin protection standards set out in U.S. law, the U.S. government must embargo all imports of fish from that country. In this case Mexico was the exporting country concerned. Its exports of yellowfin tuna to the U.S. were banned.[14]

In other words, the U.S. Marine Mammal Protection Act was not lenient toward U.S. domestic producers while being strict to foreign producers. It applied the same standards to everyone. In effect, Congress had said, "We think it wrong to trap and drown dolphins unnecessarily while catching tuna, and we are not going to allow any tuna caught in that way to be sold in the U.S." So if the WTO were to exclude only environmental protection laws when they favor one's own country, presumably when Mexico complained to GATT about the U.S. embargo, its complaint would have been thrown out? But the GATT panel concluded, as *Trading into the Future* notes,

> that the U.S. could not embargo imports of tuna products from Mexico simply because Mexican regulations on the way the tuna was produced did not satisfy U.S. regulations. (But the U.S. could apply its regulations on the quality or content of the tuna imported.) This has become known as a "product" versus "process" issue.[15]

The Misuse of the Product/Process Distinction

This product/process distinction is crucial to understanding the impact of WTO rules in many areas. As the tuna–dolphin case exemplifies, the WTO has operated on the basis that a country cannot ban a product on the basis of the process by which the product was made but only by showing that the banned product is different in its inherent nature from other products. But what does the product / process distinction have to do with the rejection of discriminatory trading practices that, according to *10 Things the WTO Can Do,* is the reason the WTO prohibits some forms of environmental protection? At first glance, nothing at all. But *Trading into the Future* suggests the following link:

> What was the reason behind . . . [the tuna–dolphin] ruling? If the US arguments were accepted, then any country could ban imports of a product from another country merely because the exporting country has different environmental, health and social policies from its own. This would create a virtually open-ended route for any country to apply trade restrictions unilaterally. . . . [T]he door would be opened to a possible flood of protectionist abuses.[16]

Whereas *10 Things the WTO Can Do* defends WTO dispute decisions on the grounds that they prohibit environmental protection measures only if foreign producers are treated more harshly than domestic producers, what really happens when the WTO considers a case where the law is being applied fairly to both domestic and foreign producers is that the issue becomes not whether foreign producers were in fact treated more harshly than domestic producers, but whether allowing a country to prohibit a product because of the way in which it was produced could open the door to "a . . . flood of protectionist abuses." Even if it is true that this would occur, the argument assumes that the value of preventing such a flood of protectionist abuses is greater than the value of protecting the environment, animals, and community peace of mind—greater, for example, than the value of protecting millions of dolphins from cruel and premature death or of providing the public with the peace of mind they seek in respect to their concerns about these needless deaths. And these are just two among the countless things we value that our governments might, but for WTO rulings, see fit to protect by prohibiting the import of products produced in ways we consider objectionable. Import prohibitions against goods produced in ways that violate human rights—for example, by using forced labor or pushing indigenous people off their land—would also fail to pass the test of being applied to a product rather than a process. If any form of protection, no matter how fair it is in the way it treats domestic and foreign enterprises, is ruled out by the fact that it targets a process rather than a product, the means by which a country can protect its values have been drastically curtailed.

In any case, there is no solid ground for believing that the product / process distinction is the only way to stop a flood of protectionist legislation. There are more finely grained ways in which Dispute Panels—made up, the WTO tells us, of experts in trade and law—can distinguish disguised or unjustifiable protectionism from reasonable measures to protect the environment. The first test should be, as the preamble to the Agreement on Technical Barriers to Trade suggests, whether the measure taken to protect the environment or animal welfare or whatever other legitimate objectives a state may have deals evenhandedly with the state's own producers and with foreign producers. If it does, then the measure is prima facie acceptable, and any state seeking to have it invalidated should be required to show that the environmental or other objectives the measure purports to aim at could reasonably have been achieved without restricting trade to the extent that the measure does restrict it.

Trading into the Future claims, in the passage just quoted, that if the U.S. argument in the tuna–dolphin case had been accepted, "any country could ban imports of a product from another country merely because the exporting country has different environmental, health and social policies from its own." The use of the word "merely" here is noteworthy, for the "different . . . policies" in the exporting countries might be ones permitting the dumping of toxic wastes into the ocean, extreme cruelty to animals, or denying workers the right to unionize. The implication is that these are somehow less important reasons for banning a product than those that are concerned with the inherent qualities of a product, which the WTO would unhesitatingly accept, as long as the bans did not discriminate between domestic and foreign producers. There is, however, no reason to think that our support for the environment, for animals, and for human rights is any less important than the desire to protect one's citizens from products that are of inferior quality.

In any case, the suggestion that the importing country is, by banning the product made in ways harmful to the environment or to animals or to workers, trying to exercise extraterritorial powers over the exporting country is misleading. This may be the case, and it would not necessarily be wrong—as we shall see in the next chapter, it is sometimes justifiable to intervene militarily to prevent flagrant human rights abuses in other countries, so it can hardly always be wrong to try to prevent such abuses by trade measures—but it is not true that any prohibition of a product made in another country because of the process by which that product is made *must* be an attempt to exercise extraterritorial powers. Just as a country might ban the sale of a pesticide, whether of domestic or foreign origin, because it is toxic to wildlife—and to that the WTO would not object—so a country might ban the sale of a product, whether domestic or foreign, because the process by which it is made is toxic to wildlife. Wild animals need not be seen as the property of one country. The process by which the product is made might kill migratory birds or, as in the dolphin and sea turtle cases, animals living in the oceans. Even when the animals killed live entirely within the borders of the country making the product, however, the country seeking to ban the product may think it is wrong to be indifferent to the death and suffering of animals and may find it morally objectionable for a product made in a way that displays such indifference to be sold within its jurisdiction. The ethical argument that motivates the other chapters of this book is relevant here too: just as there is no sound reason why the citizens of a state should be concerned solely with the interests of their fellow citizens rather than with the interests of people everywhere, so there is no sound reason why the citizens of a state should be concerned with the well-being of animals only when those animals are living within the boundaries of their own state. Given this, if a state decides that catching tuna by methods that trap and drown dolphins is cruel and immoral, and it prohibits the marketing, within its own borders, of tuna caught in that manner, this comes squarely within the conventionally accepted powers of sovereignty over its own territory. If preventing the sale of morally objectionable products within one's own borders is contrary to WTO trade rules, then how could a country be justified in prohibiting the import of films that display acts of real, nonconsensual sexual violence, even sexual violence resulting in death (as in so-called snuff movies)? No one regards prohibiting such films as objectionable because it is an attempt by one state to prevent the "extraterritorial" rape and murder of women and children. Yet here too it is the "process" that is the reason for the prohibition. The final product may be indistinguishable from a film in which skilled actors who are not harmed perform the same scenes. As far as claims of extraterritoriality are concerned, it is hard to discern a difference of principle between the prohibition of snuff movies and the prohibition of tuna that has been caught in nets that trap dolphins.

It would, of course, be both possible and consistent with the overall argument of this book to favor a reduction in the significance of state sovereignty and to hold that global or transnational bodies should decide what is acceptable in respect of issues like environmental protection, animal welfare, and human rights. But that cannot happen until there are such bodies, with procedures, hopefully ones that are democratic and responsive to public opinion, by which these questions can be decided.

Protecting Public Morals

Notwithstanding the use that the WTO Dispute Panels have made of the product / process distinction, one article of the General Agreement on Tariffs and Trade appears to give explicit blessing to import bans undertaken for various purposes, including the protection of the environment and animal welfare. Article XX reads, in its relevant sections, as follows:

General Exceptions
Subject to the requirement that such measures are
not applied in a manner which would constitute a means
of arbitrary or unjustifiable discrimination between
countries where the same conditions prevail, or a
disguised restriction on international trade, nothing in
this Agreement shall be construed to prevent the adoption
or enforcement by any contracting party of measures:
(a) necessary to protect public morals;
(b) necessary to protect human, animal or plant life or
health;

. . .

(g) relating to the conservation of exhaustible natural resources if such measures are made effective in conjunction with restrictions on domestic production or consumption.

The most natural reading of this article would give a country several grounds on which it could prohibit the importation of goods obtained in ways that threaten dolphins or cause great suffering to animals. Clause (b) allows exceptions to protect animal life, and clause (g) allows an exception to conserve "exhaustible natural resources." A prohibition on importing products produced by unethical methods of fishing or by the use of cruel traps could also be justified by clause (a), which refers to the protection of "public morals." If this means the morals people actually have, then there are many countries in which the unnecessary killing of animals, especially those of endangered species, offends against moral standards widely held by the general public. The sale of products that result from such killing is as offensive to public morals as, say, nudity would be in some countries. If, on the other hand, the clause referring to the protection of public morals is intended to refer to sound moral values, irrespective of how widely they are held, then the case against products obtained by cruel methods is much *stronger* than the case against mere nudity.

In the sea turtle case the United States argued that its prohibition on the importation of shrimp caught by fishing fleets not using devices to exclude sea turtles was allowable under clauses (b) and (g) of Article XX. After this argument was rejected by the Dispute Panel on grounds consistent with the tuna–dolphin case, the United States appealed, but the appeal was again rejected. This time the WTO's Appellate Body did accept that a measure to protect endangered species could fall under the exemptions. It nevertheless rejected the U.S. shrimp prohibition on the grounds that it required essentially the same methods of excluding turtles used by domestic vessels to be used by other countries, instead of allowing other methods of avoiding the killing of turtles that may be more appropriate for their local conditions. This was, the Appellate Body said, discriminatory, as were some other aspects of the manner in which the United States had applied the ban. Hence the Appellate Body found that the United States had failed to pass the test stated in the opening proviso of Article XX which makes the exemptions subject to the proviso that the "measures are not applied in a manner which would constitute a means of arbitrary or unjustifiable discrimination between countries where the same conditions prevail."

The Appellate Body concluded its judgment with these words:

> 185. In reaching these conclusions, we wish to underscore what we have not decided in this appeal. We have not decided that the protection and preservation of the environment is of no significance to the Members of the WTO. Clearly, it is. We have not decided that the sovereign states that are Members of the WTO cannot adopt effective measures to protect endangered species, such as sea turtles. Clearly, they can and should. And we have not decided that sovereign states should not act together bilaterally, plurilaterally or multilaterally, either within the WTO or in other international fora, to protect endangered species or to otherwise protect the environment. Clearly, they should and do.
>
> 186. What we have decided in this appeal is simply this: although the measure of the United States in dispute

in this appeal serves an environmental objective that is recognized as legitimate under paragraph (g) of Article XX of the GATT 1994, this measure has been applied by the United States in a manner which constitutes arbitrary and unjustifiable discrimination between Members of the WTO.[17]

That sounds fine, but the nature of the decision showed that it was going to be extremely difficult for any trade prohibition to pass the scrutiny of the Appellate Body. At one point in its judgment the Appellate Body remarked, "It is relevant to observe that an import prohibition is, ordinarily, the heaviest 'weapon' in a Member's armoury of trade measures" [par. 171], an observation that apparently leads it to take the view that all other avenues of achieving the desired objective must have been exhausted before an import prohibition can be adopted.

Following the decision of the Appellate Body, the United States entered into negotiations with other countries to reach a multilateral agreement on the use of turtle-excluding devices. Meanwhile, it retained its ban on the importation of shrimp caught by ships not using such devices. Again a dispute arose about the ban, and finally, in November 2001, the Appellate Body accepted that the United States was doing enough. As long as the United States was engaging in "ongoing, serious good faith efforts" to reach a multilateral agreement on the protection of sea turtles, the import ban could remain in place.[18]

Perhaps the final decision in the sea turtle case—the first time in the entire history of both GATT and the WTO that a unilateral, extraterritorial national measure involving trade restrictions has been upheld on environmental grounds—is evidence that the Seattle protests had an impact, leading the WTO to become more sensitive to criticism of its environmental record.

Observers had to wait several years for further decisions to see whether there had been a real shift in WTO jurisprudence. The clearest indication came in 2014 in a case involving a European Union prohibition on the import of products such as fur, meat, and oil derived from seal hunting. Animal welfare organizations have for many years objected to the Canadian seal hunt, showing videos of seal pups being clubbed to death on the ice. The proposal for a ban became a popular issue in the European elections of 2009 and was subsequently adopted by the European Parliament. The ban has limited exceptions for seal products derived from hunts by indigenous communities and from seals killed for purposes of marine resource management. Canada and Norway challenged the ban, claiming it was a barrier to trade and contrary to WTO rules. The European Union defended the ban as falling under Article XX (a), that is, that it was "necessary to protect public morals."

Although there is no doubt that the treatment of animals raises moral issues, and animal welfare is a public moral concern in many countries, including the states that make up the European Union, it was difficult to be confident that the WTO would look favorably on the European Union's claim, given the nature of WTO rulings up to that time. Surprisingly, the Dispute Panel accepted the European Union's defense of its ban. It held that the protection of public moral concerns with regard to animal welfare is "an important value or interest."[19] Although the Dispute Panel found some problems with the ways in which the framing of exceptions for indigenous communities was drawn up, it largely upheld the ban on seal products. Canada and Norway appealed the decision. The Canadian representative argued that the Dispute Panel had erred in finding that the ban was "necessary to protect public morals" without identifying a risk against which the ban was seeking to protect public morals. If accepted, this contention would have limited the use of Article XX in consequential ways. The Appellate Body rejected it, holding that the requirement that the ban be necessary to protect public morals does not require the identification of a specific risk against which it is necessary to provide protection. Moreover, member states should, the Appellate Body held, "be given some scope to define and apply for themselves the concept of public morals according to their own systems and scales of values."[20]

Fifteen years after the protests in Seattle, it seems that the WTO has listened to the concerns of the protestors and of at least some of its member states. The verdict in the seal product case, by interpreting the need to protect public morals broadly, shifts the balance significantly away from the goal of promoting free trade and avoiding any step that could lead to "a flood of protectionist abuses" and toward allowing member states to decide how best to promote the values most important to them, as long as they do so in a manner that does not discriminate between different producers, domestic or foreign.

The Second Charge: Interference with State Sovereignty

The standard response by WTO supporters to the claim that the organization overrides state sovereignty is that it is no more than the administrative framework for a set of agreements or treaties freely entered into by sovereign governments. Every member nation of the WTO is a member because its government has decided to join and has not subsequently decided to leave. Moreover, decisions on matters other than the resolution of disputes are generally reached by consensus. Since the WTO is an expression of the decisions of sovereign governments, it is not something that can interfere with state sovereignty.

This account of the WTO as being merely the administrator of a set of multilateral agreements may be true in formal terms, but it leaves out some crucial practical details. Once a government joins the WTO, it and its successors come under considerable pressure to remain a member. Export industries based on free trade develop, employing substantial numbers of people, and the threat that these industries will collapse if the state withdraws from the treaties administered by the WTO becomes so potent that going one's own way becomes almost unthinkable. The WTO argues that this is a good thing. In *10 Things the WTO Can Do,* the fifth item is "encourage good governance." Governments need, the argument goes, "to be armed against pressure from narrow interest groups, and the WTO system can help." These narrow interest groups might seek protection for local industries that produce for the domestic market, but protection means higher prices for consumers and can lead to trade wars that disadvantage local industries producing for export. Once the government has become a WTO member it can point to the overall benefits of belonging and demonstrate that the benefits that would flow for the protected industry would be outweighed by the losses inflicted on others.[21]

While it is true that states are free—at a price—to stay outside the WTO or to leave it, when states are members they can have their sovereignty seriously curtailed. This is far from a trivial matter. The battle over the availability of generic drugs for the treatment of AIDS in Africa indicates the crucial importance of getting these matters right. In South Africa alone, at the end of 2001, more than four million people, or 20 percent of the adult population, were infected with HIV, the virus that causes AIDS. By that time, if one lived in one of the rich countries, having the virus was no longer a death sentence because the antiretroviral drugs that effectively suppress the infection were available. But costing about $10,000 a year, these drugs were out of the reach of almost all infected Africans. Finding itself in this desperate situation, the South African government floated the idea of licensing manufacture of the drugs in South Africa, a procedure known as compulsory licensing and a recognized means of dealing with a health emergency. Local manufacture would mean that the drugs could be produced at a cost of about $350 a year. Even this was too much for many Africans who live in countries in which the annual per capita spending on health care is about $10. But $350 a year is a realistic amount for some, especially South Africans.

When the South African government began to consider the possibility of licensing local drug manufacture, the United States responded with the threat of trade sanctions to defend the intellectual property rights of the drug manufacturers. After pressure from AIDS activists, the Clinton administration dropped this threat. The world's major pharmaceutical corporations then went to court to stop South Africa from providing lifesaving treatment for its people at a price they could afford. In April 2001 public outrage led the companies to abandon their case and enter into arrangements to supply their products to African countries free or at greatly reduced prices. In October of the same year the issue took a new turn because of an incident of bioterrorism in the United States: letters containing anthrax spores were sent to several news media outlets and to two U.S. senators. Five people died as a result of inhaling the spores. In the panic that followed, the Canadian government announced it would compulsorily license the manufacture of Cipro, the antibiotic most effective against anthrax. With some American politicians calling on the U.S. government to follow Canada's lead, the U.S. secretary for health and human services instead persuaded Bayer, the pharmaceutical corporation that holds the patent for Cipro, to slash the drug's price. If they were not willing to do so, he made it clear, the United States would buy a cheaper generic version.

Not surprisingly, since the U.S. government was still trying to restrict the ways in which African countries could obtain generic anti-AIDS drugs, this demand led to an immediate outcry that the administration was using one standard for Americans, only a handful of whom had been infected with anthrax, and another for the estimated 25 million Africans who had been infected with the AIDS virus.[22]

Though the anthrax outbreak was a tragedy for the unlucky few who were its victims, its timing could not have been better for the millions of people needing cheaper drugs because it came just before the Doha WTO ministerial meeting in November 2001. The developed countries, embarrassed by the accusation of double standards, agreed to a declaration that the WTO Agreement on Trade-Related Aspects of Intellectual Property Rights (known as the TRIPS Agreement) "does not and should not prevent Members from taking measures to protect public health." The declaration added that each member "has the right to determine what constitutes a national emergency or other circumstances of extreme urgency" and specifically included "HIV / AIDS, tuberculosis, malaria and other epidemics" as representing a situation in which compulsory licensing of necessary drugs is permissible.[23]

Despite this positive outcome, the issue shows how sharply trade agreements can intrude into the most vital decisions a government can face. Granted, South Africa, as a free and sovereign state, did not have to take part in the original TRIPS agreement. But there may have been substantial economic costs in refusing to do so. If states, once they join the WTO, can lose state sovereignty in important areas and if they are under constant pressure to remain in the organization, the view that the WTO is no threat to sovereignty is simplistic.

If we conclude that a state under pressure to remain a member of the WTO has diminished sovereignty, that is not in itself grounds for condemning the WTO. The loss of sovereignty might be a price worth paying for the benefits the organization brings. The choice is either to enter the agreement or not, and presumably those governments that decide to enter the agreement judge it to be better to do so, both for their own generation and for future generations. Before we criticize the WTO for eroding state sovereignty, then, we should ask, Is there any alternative means by which states and their citizens could gain these benefits?

Traditionally, those on the left have been cosmopolitans, whereas conservatives have been nationalists, opposing any constraints on state sovereignty. It is because the WTO appears to put free trade above both environmental values and state sovereignty that opposition to the WTO brings together people from both left and right. The alliance would split if the WTO were to be reformed in a way that enabled it to protect workers' rights and the environment because such modifications would give it more, rather than fewer, of the powers of global governance. Thus it would satisfy some critics on the left but would further inflame the nationalists on the right. The WTO's critics on the left support the supremacy of national legislatures and defend their right to make laws to protect the environment because they believe that the legislators are at least answerable to the people. Global corporations are not, and the WTO, in the eyes of the left, makes it too easy for global corporations to do as they please. This suggests that the WTO could meet the criticisms from the left—but not those from the right—by claiming that it provides the possibility of bringing global corporations under democratic rule. Then, just as, in the philosophy of social contract theorists like Jean-Jacques Rousseau, people forming a political community give up some of their individual freedom in order to gain a voice in the running of the whole community, so states entering the WTO would give up some of their sovereignty in order to gain a voice in the running of the global economy.

The Third Charge: The WTO Makes Decisions Affecting Everyone, But It Is Dominated by a Small Group of Countries

Making decisions by consensus can be a very difficult process. In practice, until the Seattle protests the WTO agenda was set by informal meetings of the major trading powers, a group known as the Quad: the United States, the European Union, Japan, and Canada. On major questions, once these powers reached agreement, the results were presented to the formal meeting, but they were often a fait accompli.[24] According to John Weekes, a former Canadian ambassador to the General Agreement on Tariffs and Trade and subsequently to the WTO, it was not until 2003 that a proposal agreed to by the United States and the European Union was rejected by other members of the WTO.[25] The opposition to that proposal, which concerned trade in agricultural products, came from a group of developing countries led by Brazil. The increasing willingness of states like Brazil, India, and China (which was not a member until 2001) to assert themselves in negotiations has broken the power of the Quad while at the same time making it much more difficult for the WTO to negotiate a new round of cuts to trade barriers.

Yet it remains difficult for the poorest states to have an equal voice in the WTO. It is difficult for them even to maintain an office in Geneva, one of the world's most expensive cities, where the WTO has its headquarters, and if they can afford to do that, their staff must also be aware of what is happening in the many United Nations agencies based there doing work that affects their country. In recognition of the importance of this problem, the WTO offers some technical assistance and training for officials from developing countries.

Another step in the same direction was the establishment of the independent Geneva-based Advisory Centre on WTO Law, which was set up in 2001 to provide developing countries with low-cost legal advice and to support them in WTO dispute settlement procedures. (Although proposals for such an Advisory Centre had been discussed earlier, this was another positive initiative that did not become a reality until after the Seattle protests.) After the Advisory Centre had been operating for ten years, the WTO's director, Pascal Lamy, acknowledged that its existence was essential to the achievement of fairness and impartiality in the dispute resolution procedure. He noted that the "daunting volume" of WTO rules and the "ever-increasing complexity" of cases had led many member states to hire private law firms to assist with their cases. Lamy conceded that the poorer states were unable to afford to do so and that the least developed countries, in particular, had not, with one exception, been involved in dispute settlement procedures. His proposed solution was to urge the Advisory Centre to do more to reach out to the least developed countries—easy to say, but elsewhere in the same speech Lamy recognized that funding for the Advisory Centre comes from only a few countries and is fragile. Effectively, therefore, the fairness and impartiality of the WTO's dispute resolution procedure as it applies to the least developed countries is left up to an independent organization that has no guarantee of adequate funding.[26]

In summary, the WTO is no longer dominated by the Quad, but it remains a constant struggle to ensure that developing countries, and especially the least developed countries, can protect their interests as adequately as richer states can.

The Fourth Charge: Taking from the Poor and Giving to the Rich

President George W. Bush expressed the line taken by most advocates of global free trade when he said, "Those who protest free trade are no friends of the poor. Those who protest free trade seek to deny them their best hope for escaping poverty."[27] On the other hand, critics of economic globalization say that it leads to the rich getting richer and the poor getting poorer. Which view is right?

The facts are not easy to sort out, and on some aspects of this question leading opponents of economic globalization do not speak with one voice. Some say the rich countries do not offer a level playing field to the poor countries, and so free trade does not benefit the poor, while others—like the American unionists who protested against the WTO in Seattle—object that free trade means that jobs shift from developed countries to places like China and India, where wages are much lower. If jobs do flow from rich countries to poor ones, that can be expected to raise the income of people who are, on average, much less well off than the workers in rich countries who lose their jobs. Those who favor reducing poverty globally, rather than only in their own country, should see this as a good thing.

Another relevant question is whether free trade means cheaper goods, and whether this is good for the poor. Vandana Shiva, one of the best-known WTO opponents from a developing country, India, writes in an essay that the liberalization of trade in India means that more food is exported, and as a result "food prices have doubled and the poor have had to cut their consumption in half." To anyone familiar with poverty in India before trade liberalization, it is difficult to believe that India's poor would be able to survive at all if they had to cut their food consumption in half, so such claims may well provoke skepticism. That skepticism is not allayed when one reads, on the very next page, that Indian farmers have lost markets and mills have had to close because "cheap, subsidized imports of soybeans are dumped on the Indian market . . . thus worsening the country's balance of payments situation."[28] If the lowering of trade barriers has meant that soybeans are now cheaper than they were before, it is strange that this same lowering of trade barriers should have caused food prices as a whole to double. Moreover, the large quantities of food that Shiva claims are exported because of trade liberalization should have raised the prices farmers receive for their crops and improved the country's balance of payments. There may be an explanation of such apparently conflicting claims, but if there is, Shiva does not offer it.

In trying to assess the impact of recent trade reforms, it is useful to distinguish two questions:

* Has inequality increased during the period of global economic liberalization?
* Have the poor become worse off?

The questions are distinct because it would be possible for the situation of the poor to improve in absolute terms—that is, they might eat better and have safer water, greater access to education and health care, and so on—while the situation of the rich improves even more, so that the gap in income and wealth between the rich and the poor is greater than before. (In what follows, unless otherwise specified, I will use "rich" and "poor" to refer to people on high and low incomes, respectively, rather than to the value of their possessions. Needless to say, those with a high income often tend to be wealthy, and vice versa. But the correlation is not perfect.) We will also, of course, need to ask whether the changes that can be observed are the result of economic globalization or merely happen to have coincided with it.

Since 1990 the World Bank has been monitoring the state of poverty in the world. It does so by calculating how much income a person needs to meet basic needs, such as food, shelter, and clothing. The initial figure was about $1.00 per day, but it has since been revised to keep pace with price changes, and as of September 2015 it stood at $1.90 per day. This figure needs to be explained. We may think that the purchasing power of a U.S. dollar in, say, rural India is vastly greater than the purchasing power of a U.S. dollar in New York. So perhaps these people, though poor, are not as desperately poor as we may at first imagine. But the figure already takes the difference in purchasing power into account—it is what is known as a purchasing power parity figure. That means that it is the amount, in local currency, that would purchase as much as $1.90 would purchase in the United States. On the other hand, the World Bank's figures are in 2011 dollars, and when we allow for inflation, that takes the extreme poverty line to the purchasing power equivalent of $2.03 in 2015 U.S. dollars. This, however, is the upper bound of those in extreme poverty. The *average* income of people living in extreme poverty will be significantly lower.[29]

The good news is that the number of people in extreme poverty has been declining since 1990 (when it was 1.95 billion) and the rate of decline has increased since 2000, so that by the end of 2015, the number was estimated at 702 million. That change appears even more remarkable when put in terms of the percentage of the world's population living in extreme poverty: in 1990, nearly 37 percent of the world's population lived in extreme poverty; by the end of 2015, that proportion was, for the first time, below 10 percent.[30] If the proportion of people living in extreme poverty had remained unchanged, there would be 2.7 billion people in that situation, or almost 2 billion more than there are today. Conversely, the working middle class of developing countries, defined as people living on more than $4 per day, has grown from only 18 percent of the workforce in developing regions in 1991 to half the workforce of those regions today. In the same period, the proportion of people in developing regions who are undernourished has been cut from 23 percent to 13 percent.[31]

In 1990, following dissatisfaction with the narrow economic view that judges the progress a country is making by its per capita income alone, the United Nations Development Programme developed its Human Development Index, which includes measures of health and education as well as income. That in turn led, in 2010, to the Multidimensional Poverty Index, again designed to take into account health and education as well as income, not to rank countries but to assess the extent and severity of poverty. In 2013, according to this new way of assessing poverty—not extreme poverty—1.5 billion people were living in poverty and another 800 million in near-poverty.[32]

Poverty in developing countries is measured by an absolute standard related to basic needs. It is not the relative poverty that is often used as a measure in affluent countries—the kind of poverty that is compatible with having safe drinking water, sanitation, health care, electricity, enough to eat, and appliances like a television set, a car, and an air conditioner. Worldwide, despite the positive trends, 795 million people are chronically undernourished or hungry, 2.5 billion lack access to improved sanitation (with 1 billion of them defecating in the open), 1.8 billion drink water from a source contaminated with faeces, and hundreds of millions have no access to soap and water to wash their hands. In rich countries fewer than one child in a hundred dies before the age of five; in the poorest countries, one in twelve does. That is 16,000 young children dying every day from preventable causes. In the poorest countries more than one child in three is moderately or severely stunted, a result of poor nutrition or sanitation. In rich countries stunting is virtually unknown. Rich countries have 28 physicians for every 10,000 people; poor countries have fewer than two. Life expectancy at birth in rich countries is around 80, whereas in the poorest countries it is 58.[33]

Poverty of this kind has been described as "a condition of life so characterized by malnutrition, illiteracy, disease, squalid surroundings, high infant mortality and low life expectancy as to be beneath any reasonable definition of human decency."[34] The question we are considering is, however, not whether the existence of extreme poverty on a large scale is a bad thing—of course it is—but whether it supports the charge against economic globalization that we are considering. Has economic globalization caused or increased the poverty just described?

In 2014 Oxfam reported that the 80 wealthiest people in the world own almost as much as the poorest 3.5 billion people, and the richest 1 percent of the world own 48 percent of the world's wealth.[35] These figures seem shocking. They show that the richest billionaires could and—as I will argue in chapter 5—*should* do more to help the poorest people. Stark as this inequality in wealth is, however, it does not show either that the world is becoming more unequal or that economic globalization has caused the poor to become or to remain poor.

Is the world becoming more unequal? It is tempting to answer this question by looking at whether the gap between rich countries and poor countries is growing or shrinking. But that can be misleading. The strong economic growth experienced by China has, since 1981, lifted 753 million people out of extreme poverty and hence done a lot to reduce global inequality.[36] The economic growth of Singapore, which has a population of 5.4 million people, obviously has less impact on global inequality. This implies that in assessing whether global inequality has increased, we should weight the shifts in the wealth of countries by their population. If everyone in each country had the same average income, that would yield the right answer; but this is not the case. If we are asking whether inequality in the world as a whole increased in the era of economic globalization, it makes a big difference whether the benefits of economic growth in China went predominantly to the poor in that countries or predominantly to the rich or were distributed in some other way.

We therefore need information on what happened to the incomes of individuals, not of countries, during the era of economic globalization. That information does not exist for all countries, especially before the mid-1980s, but the available data have been carefully gathered and examined by Branko Milanovic and his research team at the World Bank. Milanovic's best guess is that global inequality rose steadily from the industrial revolution until the middle of the twentieth century and then remained at a high level until the late 1980s, when the better data that became available show that during these decades of economic globalization the incomes of the richest 1 percent rose by 60 percent. The richest 1 percent did not, however, make the biggest percentage gains. The incomes of those around and just below the median income—to be specific, those between the 50th and 60th percentiles of the global income distribution—increased by 70–80 percent. (They include 200 million Chinese, 90 million Indians, and 30 million each in Indonesia, Brazil, and Egypt.) Even more meaningfully, from the perspective of global equality, the incomes of the bottom third of the world's population rose by 40–70 percent. This good news is marred, however, by the fact that the incomes of the very poorest, the bottom 5 percent, remained flat.[37]

Consistently with these income figures, other indicators of human development have improved. Between 1990 and 2012, global average life expectancy at birth increased by six years, the biggest increases occurring in low-income countries. There the increase averaged nine years, with dramatic gains in Liberia (20 years) and Ethiopia (19 years).[38] These gains happened in large part because the child mortality rate has been halved during this period, from 90 per 1,000 births to 43, saving the lives of about 18,000 children every day. The greatest reductions in child deaths have been among the poorest households.[39] The proportion of people in the world who suffer from hunger has been cut in half between 1990 and 2015.[40] More children in developing regions are going to school. In 2000 enrollment was at 83 percent, and in 2010 it reached 91 percent.[41]

We have now answered our first question. Whether you judge that economic globalization, at least over the past two decades, has increased global inequality will depend on what you understand by the term, but it is at least arguable that it has not. Economic globalization has made the rich richer, but it has helped the poor too. Especially if we focus on indicators other than money, inequality has diminished because the poor have seen bigger gains in measures of health and quality of life, for example, in life expectancy, than the rich have. The fact that the bottom third of the world's people have had substantial increases in their income during the past two decades of economic globalization also suggests an answer to our second question. During the period of economic globalization for which we have the required data, the poor have not become poorer. With the exception of the poorest 5 percent, they have become less poor.

It would seem that we can, therefore, reject the fourth charge against economic globalization. Economic globalization may give to the rich, but it does not do so by taking from the poor. It does so by increasing the size of the pie. The rising tide of economic globalization has lifted all boats.

This may, however, be too quick. First, what about the poorest 5 percent of the world's people, whose boats have not been lifted by the rising tide (no doubt they are too poor to own boats)? Second, even if the bottom third has, as a whole, become better off, many of them—not only the bottom 5 percent—still live in extreme poverty. Isn't it possible that if the rich had not tilted the playing field to their own advantage more of those who are extremely poor could have escaped from extreme poverty?

Let's begin our consideration of these questions by reminding ourselves of what we have just learned about the outcome of the period of economic globalization from 1988 to 2008:

- The incomes of the bottom 5 percent of the world's people (about 360 million people) have remained the same.
- The incomes of the bottom third of the world's people (about 2.4 billion people) have risen by 40–70 percent.
- The incomes of people at or slightly below the median income (about 380 million people) have risen by 70–80 percent.
- The incomes of the top 1 percent (about 72 million people) have risen by 60 percent.

If our overriding priority is the welfare of everyone affected by economic globalization we should think of this as good news. To focus on inequality in itself as the key value would be a mistake. A society in which almost everyone was living at the standard of the average Norwegian and the remainder were billionaires would, other things being equal, be much better than an egalitarian society in which absolutely everyone was at the level of the average Eritrean. We could argue about whether we should be equally concerned with promoting the welfare of all members of society, or whether we should give some kind of priority to promoting the welfare of society's poorest members, but whatever we decide, what matters is people's welfare, not the size of the gap between rich and poor.

It is true that greater inequality can mean a decrease in overall welfare. Not surprisingly, a given percentage of economic growth will lead to a greater amount of poverty reduction in a relatively equal society than in a highly unequal one.[42] In addition, there is evidence that inequality hampers economic growth, whereas a moderate amount of redistribution does not have a negative impact on growth.[43]

Inequality has other undesirable consequences. When a few individuals can use their great wealth to help their favored candidates win elections, then one person, one vote becomes irrelevant. Democracy is undermined. Politicians will be far more sensitive to the wishes of their wealthy backers than to those of the much larger number of voters on below-average incomes. As the U.S. Supreme Court justice Louis Brandeis is often quoted as having said, "We may have democracy, or we may have wealth concentrated in the hands of a few, but we can't have both."[44] That might not be true if money were taken out of the election cycle, but there is no sign of that happening in the United States, and in many developing countries there are even fewer restrictions on how money may be used to gain power.

Inequality can undermine the self-esteem of those on the lower levels of society and make them feel worse off than if they were living on the same income in a more egalitarian society. Here, because people tend to compare themselves with those around them, inequality within countries matters more than inequality between countries.

Other factors, however, can shrink the importance of inequality. For those who are desperately struggling to get enough to eat and to house and clothe their children, the need to keep up with one's neighbors is less significant than it is for those who have no difficulty in meeting their basic needs. For people near the bare minimum on which they can survive, a small addition to their income may make a large difference to their welfare, even if their neighbors' incomes grow by much more in dollar terms. And the society they live in may not be a democracy anyway, so inequalities of income may not add much to the inequalities of power under which they must live.

The WTO Grade: "Can Do Better"

In *The Communist Manifesto,* Marx and Engels described the impact of the capitalist class in terms that might today be applied to the global expansion of trade:

> It has resolved personal worth into exchange value, and in place of the numberless indefeasible chartered freedoms, has set up that single, unconscionable freedom—Free Trade. . . . All fixed, fast-frozen relations, with their train of ancient and venerable prejudices and opinions are swept away, all new-formed ones become antiquated before they can ossify. All that is solid melts into air, all that is holy is profaned.[45]

Defenders of free trade would reject loaded words like "unconscionable," but they might agree that a global free market will sweep away "ancient and venerable prejudices." They would see this as a good thing because such prejudices restrict the use of individual creativity that benefits both the innovative producer and the consumers who can choose to take advantage of it. Economic globalization is revolutionary in its impact on traditional societies. Whether or not we think this is a good thing, we can ask if there are ways of making it work better or at least less badly. Even those who accept the general argument for the economic benefits of a global free market should ask themselves how well a global free market can work in the absence of any global authority to set minimum standards on issues like child labor, worker safety, the right to form a union, and environmental and animal welfare protection.

According to standard economic models, if various assumptions hold—including the assumptions that people always act fully rationally and on the basis of perfect information—free trade within a single, well-governed country can be expected to create a state of affairs that is "Pareto efficient"—in other words, a state of affairs where no one's welfare can be improved without reducing the welfare of at least one other person. This is because the government will have legislated so that the private costs of production are brought into line with their costs to society overall. A corporation that pollutes a river into which it discharges wastes will be made to clean it up and to compensate those who have been harmed. Thus the costs of keeping the environment clean become part of the costs of production, and producers who try to save money by not cleaning up their wastes gain no economic advantages over their competitors. But as we saw in the previous chapter when considering greenhouse gas emissions, global free trade in the absence of any global authority to regulate pollution or of any international civil law that mandates effective remedies to the victims of pollution is different. A state government may have little interest in forcing a producer to internalize damage done to the global environment, for example, to the oceans or the atmosphere or to stocks of cetaceans, fish, or migrating birds. Even though all countries share the global environment, the tragedy of the commons rules here, and a country may benefit more by allowing its fishing fleet to catch as much as it can than by restraining the fleet so that the fleets of other countries can catch more. Thus, judged strictly in economic terms, without global environmental protection there is no reason to expect free trade to be Pareto efficient, let alone to maximize overall welfare.

Even if we ignore goods like the oceans and the atmosphere that belong to no state and focus on the quality of life within each state, since governments are imperfect, unconstrained globalization is likely to lead to economic inefficiencies. If a ruling elite does not care about the working classes or about the people of a particular region of its territory, it may not take into account the cost to them of air or water pollution or for that matter of being forced to work long hours for little pay. Countries governed by such elites can then out-compete countries that provide some minimal standards for their workers, and, as Herman Daly puts it, "more of world production shifts to countries that do the poorest job of counting costs—a sure recipe for reducing the efficiency of global production."[46] The result is that the nexus between human welfare and the growth of the global economy, incomplete at the best of times, will be further eroded.

The desirability of uniform global environmental and labor standards is a point on which advocates of free trade from the poorer countries often clash with labor and environmental activists from the rich countries. The fear is that the rich countries will use high standards to keep out goods from the poor countries. Shiva claims, "Social clauses make bed-fellows of Northern trade unions and their corporations to jointly police and undermine social movements in the South."[47] This can and does happen, but what is the alternative?

In 2013 the collapse of Rana Plaza, an eight-story building in Bangladesh, provided a graphic illustration of the need for international standards for labor rights and occupational health and safety. The building housed clothing factories making well-known international brands, employing a total of 5,000 workers. On the day before the disaster, cracks had appeared in the building, and an engineer had warned that the building should be evacuated. Banks and shops on lower floors closed, but the garment workers, who were not unionized, were told to go to work and, according to some reports, threatened with the loss of a month's pay if they refused. When the building fell the next day, 1,136 workers were killed and more than 2,000 injured. Some reports said that a permit to construct the upper four floors of the building had been granted because of the owner's political influence. Bangladeshi unions demonstrated for reforms of labor law to make it easier for workers to unionize and demand better health and safety conditions. The International Labor Organization sent a mission to Bangladesh to try to improve safety standards for buildings and occupational safety and health.[48]

Against this background, moves in developed countries by unionists and organizations seeking greater corporate social responsibility don't seem like an attempt to "undermine" social movements in developing countries. On the contrary, they are attempts to bolster the efforts of those seeking better working conditions in developing countries. The problem is that if garment workers in Bangladesh had the same working conditions and the same wages as workers in the rich countries, most of them would not have jobs because clothes would be made in the rich countries.

It is therefore important to distinguish those rights that we believe all workers should have—for example, the right to join a union and minimum standards for occupational health and safety—and other matters that can and should vary with the standard of living in a country, such as rates of pay. In the end, just as state laws and regulations were eventually seen as essential to prevent the inhuman harshness of nineteenth-century laissez-faire capitalism in the industrialized countries, so in future some basic global labor standards will be the only way to deal with what would otherwise be an equally inhuman form of uncontrolled global capitalism.

The WTO accepts this idea, at least in theory. At its ministerial meeting in Singapore in 1996, the WTO ministers renewed an earlier commitment "to the observance of internationally recognized core labor standards" and affirmed its support for the International Labor Organization as the body to set these standards. In Doha in 2001 the ministers reaffirmed that declaration and noted the "work under way in the International Labor Organization (ILO) on the social dimension of globalization."[49] Unfortunately, nothing concrete had happened in the five years between those statements, and very little has happened since. The WTO's website says, "The WTO agreements do not deal with labour standards as such" and then notes that some countries would like to change this in order to give member states an incentive to improve working conditions, while other countries believe that efforts to bring labor standards into the WTO trade negotiations are "a smokescreen for protectionism."[50]

The WTO has, at least until recently, been dominated by neo-liberal economic thinking. There are some signs that the WTO is willing to rethink this approach, and it is possible to imagine a reformed WTO in which the overwhelming commitment to free trade is replaced by a commitment to more fundamental goals. The WTO could then become a tool for pursuing these objectives. There are clauses even in the GATT agreement that could become the basis for affirmative action in trade, designed to help the least developed states. In article XXXVI (3) the contracting parties agree that there is a "need for positive efforts designed to ensure that less-developed contracting parties secure a share in the growth in international trade commensurate with the needs of their economic development." Yet the Doha Development Agenda has made little progress since 2001, at least in part because rich countries, especially the United States and the European Union, have failed to reduce their own trade barriers in those areas that would do the most good for the less developed countries. As the *New York Times* has put it, several protectionist measures in the richest countries "mock those countries' rhetorical support for free trade."[51] The WTO itself has pointed out that the rich countries subsidize their agricultural producers at a rate of $1 billion a day, or more than six times the level of development aid they give to poor countries.[52] In 2014 agricultural subsidies again became a sticking point when India threatened to block a WTO agreement to simplify trade procedures that would, many hoped, revive the stalled Doha Round. The agreement was likely to benefit rich countries more than poor ones, and India wanted, in return, progress on a proposal supported by many developing countries to ensure that government programs that buy food from local farmers and distribute it to the poor are not considered illegal agricultural subsidies. India's commerce minister, Nirmala Sitharaman, described it as regrettable that the WTO could not agree on how to treat India's efforts to provide food for its poor "while the rich world can continue to subsidize their farmers unabatedly."[53] The trade facilitation agreement was eventually approved when, in an arrangement seen as a victory for the Indian government, the United States agreed not to challenge India's food security program, and India withdrew its opposition.[54] At the 2015 WTO ministerial conference, however, developing countries were unable to make any substantial progress against the agricultural subsidies that rich countries pay to their farmers. If the judgments that the Doha Round is now dead prove to be accurate, then it seems the Doha Development Agenda will have been nothing more than empty words.

There may still be other ways of using the WTO to benefit developing countries. As we have already noted, there have been signs, from the November 2001 ministerial meeting in Doha to the 2014 decision of the Appellate Body on the European Union's ban on seal products, that some people at the WTO are reconsidering the priority that had previously been given to free trade. If the WTO begins to take seriously Article XX on the protection of public morals and human and animal life and Article XXXVI (3) regarding assistance for developing countries, we could in time come to see the WTO as a platform from which a policy of laissez-faire in global trade could be replaced by a global system of regulation that promotes minimum standards for environmental protection, worker safety, union rights, and animal welfare. If the WTO cannot respond to these influences, it would be best for its scope to be curtailed by a different body willing to take on the challenges of setting global environmental and labor standards and making them stick.

To avoid the frustrations of the WTO negotiating process, we should also consider the scope for action by nongovernment organizations. Oxfam International, for example, has launched Behind the Brands, a campaign to inform consumers how the world's ten largest food and beverage companies—firms like Nestlé, Pepsico, Unilever, Mondelez, Coca-Cola, and Mars—perform on several issues, including the treatment of agricultural workers and smaller producers in their supply chain. The campaign has already had some success in persuading these huge corporations to take responsibility for the workplace practices of their suppliers.[55] Strengthening ideas about corporate social responsibility can, if combined with consumer awareness, transform labor practices.

Are We Buying Stolen Goods?

One might expect that the discovery of oil or minerals in a developing country would increase its prosperity and raise its standard of living. Such development is, however, so often the very opposite of this that it has become known as the resource curse. In a study of the impact of extractive industries on the poor, Michael Ross, a political scientist at the University of California, Los Angeles, found that the living standards and quality of life experienced by the general population in countries dependent on selling minerals and oil tend to be much lower than one would expect them to be given the countries' per capita income.

Mineral dependence correlated strongly with high levels of poverty and with unusually high levels of corruption, authoritarian government, military spending, and civil war. Ross's findings are in accord with those of an earlier, influential study of natural resources and economic growth by Jeffrey Sachs and Andrew Warner.[56]

Angola, the second largest African oil producer south of the Sahara, is an example of a country suffering from the resource curse. Nicholas Kristof describes Angola as "laden with oil, diamonds, Porsche-driving millionaires and toddlers starving to death." The United Nations Children's Fund, or UNICEF, ranks Angola as the worst country in the world for the rate at which its children die before the age of five. Angola is the home of Isabel dos Santos, Africa's wealthiest woman, whose assets amount to $3 billion. She is the daughter of the country's autocratic ruler, José Eduardo dos Santos, and, according to *Forbes* magazine, "Every major Angolan investment held by [Isabel] Dos Santos stems either from taking a chunk of a company that wants to do business in the country or from a stroke of the president's pen that cut her into the action."[57] That means there is a large ethical question mark hanging over any oil company that buys the country's valuable resources from the state-owned oil company.

After Angola, Equatorial Guinea is the next largest oil producer in sub-Saharan Africa, and because it has a population of only 730,000 people it has the highest per capita gross domestic product in Africa. Yet Equatorial Guinea is another victim of the resource curse, ranking 136 out of 187 countries on the Human Development Index and having a high proportion of its population living in extreme poverty.[58] Since 1979 the country has been ruled by Teodoro Obiang Nguema Mbasogo, whom the prodemocracy organization Freedom House has described as one of the world's "most kleptocratic living autocrats." Obiang seized power in a military coup and has tortured and executed many of his political opponents. Elections he has held have been described by international observers as falling well short of democratic standards.[59] Obiang and his son and heir apparent, Teodorin Obiang, own several private planes, luxury cars like Lamborghinis, Ferraris, and Bentleys, and luxurious homes in places like Malibu, Potomac, Madrid, and the Canary Islands. Between 2005 and 2007 Teodorin Obiang deposited $75 million in a U.S. bank that later paid $25 million to settle charges that it violated regulations to prevent money laundering. Among companies doing business with the elder Obiang's government were Chevron Texaco, Exxon Mobil, Hess, and Marathon Oil.[60]

Democratic governments often trade with countries while disapproving of their regimes. Only in extreme cases, such as South Africa under apartheid, is this neutrality challenged. The United States has attacked China for its human rights record while at the same time expanding its trade with that country, and it continued to trade with Russia while condemning Russian intervention to assist separatists in eastern Ukraine. Trade, we usually assume, is ethically and politically neutral. Sometimes, however, trading with a country implies an ethical judgment that needs to be held up to public scrutiny.

When corporations trade with governments like those of Dos Santos and Obiang, they are implicitly accepting the government's right to sell the resources that lie within its borders. They do not stop to ask, What gives someone the moral right to sell the resources of the country over which he or she rules? Philosophers like Thomas Pogge and Leif Wenar have begun asking that question, and not only in academic journals. Pogge is a professor at Yale University, where he directs the Global Justice Program. He is also the founder of Academics Stand Against Poverty, an organization trying to do something about global poverty, and the author of *World Poverty and Human Rights*.[61] Wenar, who holds the Chair of Ethics at King's College, London, is the author of *Blood Oil* and the founder of Clean Trade, a nonpartisan effort to change the international trade rules that lead to consumers' unwitting financing of repression, conflict, and even genocide.[62] As Wenar describes the present situation, "Consumers buy stolen goods every day" because the raw materials in products from gasoline to cell phones have been taken "sometimes by stealth, sometimes by force" from some of the poorest people in the world. After that, the stolen goods "flow through the system of global commerce under cover of a rule that is little more than a cloak for larceny."[63]

Countries rich in resources like oil and minerals have high levels of corruption and dictatorship. This is not a coincidence. The possibility of gaining control of such vast wealth is a constant temptation to military officers and others who have the means to overthrow civilian governments. If overthrowing the government did not bring with it control of the huge revenues that come from oil or mineral exports, the temptation to do so would be that much less.[64]

"Clean Trade in Natural Resources," a policy brief on the website of Clean Trade, sets out concrete steps that individual countries can take.[65] First, they should identify the worst regimes among those states afflicted by the resource curse. Then they should pass a Clean Trade Act, prohibiting all those over whom they have jurisdiction from doing business with the resource exporters of those countries. It may seem idealistic to expect any country to take the first move on an issue like this since that would be likely to increase the cost of the resources it buys, and until other countries passed similar legislation it would achieve little; but in *Blood Oil* Wenar gives examples of equally idealistic campaigns that have succeeded. They include the British decision to abolish the slave trade and, more recently, the international movement against bribery, which led to the U.S. Congress passing the Foreign Corrupt Practices Act in 1977 and subsequently to other states passing similar or stronger legislation. This legislation has not eliminated bribery, but by making the practice much more risky for individuals and corporations based in developed countries it has reduced the size of the problem.

A refusal to buy resources from countries ruled by rapacious dictatorial regimes is not the same as the imposition of a total trade boycott on that country. Such boycotts can be very harmful to individual citizens in the country boycotted. Renewable resources like agricultural produce and manufactured goods might still be traded. But when a corporation or a state accepts the right of dictators to sell the nonrenewable natural resources of the country over which they hold sway, it is accepting the dictators' claims to legitimate authority over those resources. To do so is, Wenar argues, to be complicit in the violation of the people's right to ownership of their country's resources.[66]

One obvious objection to the Clean Trade proposal is that it will involve discrimination against products from some countries and therefore will be contrary to the WTO rules that we examined earlier in this chapter. Lorand Bartels, who teaches WTO law at the University of Cambridge, has argued that this may not be so. His argument draws in part on the case previously mentioned in this chapter in which the European Union prohibition on the import of products derived from seal hunting was upheld as being within the WTO rule that allows states to prohibit imports where that is necessary to protect public morals.[67] As we saw earlier, the Appellate Body held that members should "be given some scope to define and apply for themselves the concept of public morals according to their own systems and scales of values." It would not be difficult for a state to argue that public morals are threatened by the open acceptance of trade with a corrupt dictator who keeps most of the profits for personal enrichment rather than using them for the benefit of the country's people. Once people know that this is how the goods they purchase are obtained, there is a real danger they will become more cynical and more tolerant of parallel forms of conduct, like taking bribes and receiving stolen goods in their own society.

Democracy and Legitimacy

The core of the problem we have been discussing is that once a government is recognized as legitimate, that legitimacy automatically confers the right to trade in the country's resources. In popular parlance, the term "legitimate" appears to express an ethical judgment—for example, in discussing whether a soccer player should have been awarded a penalty kick, a fan may say, "Yes, that was a legitimate penalty because his opponent deliberately tripped him when he was about to shoot at goal." That is not, however, the way in which "legitimate" is used when a government is recognized as legitimate. There the standard view has long been that the recognition of a government as being legitimate has nothing to do with how that government came to power or, for that matter, with how it governs. The sole test of whether a government is legitimate is whether it is in effective control of the territory. Brad Roth puts it this way:

> In such a conception, the international system regards
> ruling apparatuses as self-sufficient sources of authority
> —or rather deems their authority to derive from their
> characteristic ability to secure the acquiescence of their
> populaces, by whatever means . . . a government is
> recognized simply because its existence is a fact of life.[68]

International bodies, including the United Nations and the WTO, use this concept of legitimacy when they accept governments as the representatives of member states.

The dominance of this conception makes alternatives seem unrealistic. There is, however, an alternative view with strong ethical credentials. In November 1792, in the wake of the French National Convention's declaration of a republic, Thomas Jefferson, the U.S. secretary of state, wrote to the representative of the United States in France: "It accords with our principles to acknowledge any government to be rightful which is formed by the will of the people, substantially declared."[69] Now it is true that we cannot assume, from this statement, that Jefferson also intended the converse: that a government that cannot show it has been formed by the declared will of the people is not rightfully the government of the country. There may well be other grounds on which a government could be considered legitimate, perhaps by ruling unopposed for a long period without employing repressive measures to stifle dissent. Jefferson's principle does seem to imply, however, that some governments would *not* be regarded as legitimate—for example, one that had seized power by force of arms, dismissed democratically elected rulers, and killed those who spoke out against it.

The claim that there is a fundamental human right to take part in deciding who governs us is one reason for denying the legitimacy of a government that cannot show that it represents the will of the people. We could reach the same conclusion by invoking the classical utilitarian argument for democracy: democratic governments can be expected to have more concern for the people over whom they rule than governments that do not have to answer, at regular intervals, to an electorate. In international law this view of legitimacy has been gathering support in recent years, although it cannot yet be said to be the majority view.

In support of it, its defenders can point to many international documents, beginning with the opening words of the United Nations Charter, "We the peoples . . ." The signatories of the Charter apparently regarded themselves as representatives of and deriving their authority from the peoples they governed. Also relevant is the Universal Declaration of Human Rights, which in Article 21 (3) states,

> The will of the people shall be the basis of the authority of government; this will shall be expressed in periodic and genuine elections which shall be by universal and equal suffrage and shall be held by secret vote or by equivalent free voting procedures.

The Universal Declaration of Human Rights is not a treaty with explicit legal force, but the International Covenant on Civil and Political Rights is. Its first article states,

> All peoples have the right of self-determination. By virtue of that right they freely determine their political status and freely pursue their economic, social and cultural development.

In the second article, the parties to the Covenant undertake to ensure that each individual in its territory has the rights it contains, "without distinction of any kind, such as race, color, sex, language, religion, political or other opinion, national or social origin, property, birth or other status." The inclusion of "political or other opinion" is noteworthy here, since Article 25 reads,

> Every citizen shall have the right and the opportunity, without any of the distinctions mentioned in article 2 and without unreasonable restrictions:

(a) To take part in the conduct of public affairs, directly or through freely chosen representatives; (b) To vote and to be elected at genuine periodic elections which shall be by universal and equal suffrage and shall be held by secret ballot, guaranteeing the free expression of the will of the electors.

If we were to take these statements seriously we would have to develop an entirely new concept of legitimate government, with far-reaching implications not only for trade but also for issues like the use of military intervention for humanitarian purposes, a topic to which I turn in the next chapter. And surely we should take these statements seriously. But how would we decide when a government is sufficiently democratic to be recognized as being legitimate? During the counting and recounting of votes in the United States presidential election between George W. Bush and Al Gore in November 2000, jokes circulated to the effect that the United Nations was about to send in a team of observers to ensure that the elections were fair and democratic. The jokes had a serious point to make. Put aside the many allegations of irregularities in voting and counting and the refusal of the U.S. Supreme Court to allow a proper count of all votes. Forget about the fact that, in the United States, candidates must raise hundreds of millions of dollars to have any chance of success, thus ensuring that the rich have far more influence on the political process than the poor. Even without any of those blemishes, the use of the electoral college rather than the popular vote to elect the president of the United States gives greater value to the votes of people living in states with small populations than to those living in states with large populations and hence fails the basic "one vote, one value" requirement of democracy as well as the "equal suffrage" stipulation of Article 25 (b) of the Universal

Declaration of Human Rights.[70] Nevertheless, the evident im-
perfections of democracy in the United States are not of the kind
that should lead us to withdraw our recognition of the legitimacy
of the U.S. government. A minimalist concept of democracy is
needed, for otherwise there will be few legitimate governments
left. It may be useful to distinguish between governments that,
although not democratic, can claim a traditional, long-standing
authority that enables them to rule with the apparent acquies-
cence of the population and without severe restrictions on basic
civil liberties; and other regimes that, having seized power by
force, use repressive measures to maintain themselves in power.
A traditional absolute monarchy might be an example of the first
form of government; a military regime that has come to power
through a successful coup, does not hold free elections, and kills
or jails its opponents is an example of the second.

There are already international organizations that have to
face the question of when a regime is sufficiently democratic to
count as a democracy. At the inaugural meeting of the Community of Democracies in Warsaw in June 2000, representatives
of the governments of 106 countries signed the Warsaw Declaration, recognizing "the universality of democratic values." They
agreed to "collaborate on democracy-related issues in existing
international and regional institutions, forming coalitions and
caucuses to support resolutions and other international activities aimed at the promotion of democratic governance" in order to "create an external environment conducive to democratic
development."[71] Since the Warsaw meeting, the Community of
Democracies has held ministerial conferences approximately
every two years. Before each conference a decision is taken on
which countries are eligible to participate; those that do not fully
meet the criteria for being a democracy may attend, but only as
observers.[72]

A change in the concept of what is a legitimate government will not come soon. There are solid practical reasons for recognizing and being able to deal with governments that are in effective control of their territories. We might, however, move to a two-stage system, in which some governments are recognized simply for their ability to control their territories and others are recognized as legitimate, that is, justified in holding their power. At present, in the absence of any such distinction, organizations like the WTO automatically use the former, and lower, standard to determine which governments are acceptable as negotiating partners for membership and trade negotiations. Given the high moral value that international declarations and covenants place on democracy, however, it is not impossible that in the long run this could change. The WTO would then become the appropriate international forum for deciding which governments are entitled to sell the national resources of the country over which they rule.

4 one law

The Need for Intervention

In chapter 2 we saw that our increased awareness of our dependence on the vulnerable atmosphere of our planet has put pressure on traditional ideas of state sovereignty. The movement toward a single global economy that I discussed in chapter 3 also pushes us in that direction. Now I turn to an area in which the traditional idea of state sovereignty has been more directly confronted—and overridden. Progress toward an effective universal prohibition on genocide, ethnic cleansing, war crimes, and crimes against humanity shows more clearly than any other issue how our conception of the sovereign rights of states has changed over the past fifty years. This chapter examines the ethical basis of that change.

Genocide is not a new phenomenon, as anyone who has read the Bible would know. The book of Numbers tells of a time when Israelite men were succumbing to the charms of the women of a neighboring tribe, the Midianites. Worse still, it seems that these women succeeded in persuading their Israelite lovers to follow the Midianite religion. Here is what happened next:

> And the LORD spake unto Moses, saying, Avenge the children of Israel of the Midianites. . . . And Moses spake unto the people, saying, Arm some of yourselves unto the war, and let them go against the Midianites, and avenge the LORD of Midian. Of every tribe a thousand, throughout all the tribes of Israel, shall ye send to the war. So there were delivered out of the thousands of Israel, a thousand of every tribe, twelve thousand armed for war. . . . And they warred against the Midianites, as the LORD commanded Moses; and they slew all the males. . . . And the children of Israel took all the women of Midian captives, and their little ones, and took the spoil of all their cattle, and all their flocks, and all their goods. And they burnt all their cities wherein they dwelt, and all their goodly castles, with fire. And they took all the spoil, and all the prey, both of men and of beasts. And they brought the captives, and the prey, and the spoil, unto Moses, and Eleazar the priest, and unto the congregation of the children of Israel, unto the camp at the plains of Moab, which are by Jordan near Jericho. And Moses, and Eleazar the priest, and all the princes of the congregation, went forth to meet them without the camp. And Moses was wroth with the officers of the host, with the captains over thousands, and captains over hundreds, which came from the battle. And Moses said unto them, Have ye saved all the women alive? Behold, these caused the children of Israel . . . to commit trespass

against the LORD . . . and there was a plague among
the congregation of the LORD. Now therefore kill every
male among the little ones, and kill every woman that
hath known man by lying with him. But all the women
children, that have not known a man by lying with him,
keep alive for yourselves.[1]

For much of the past century it has been widely believed that
people commit crimes of violence because they are poor, ignorant, oppressed, abused, or exploited; or if none of the above
applies to them at the time they commit these crimes, then one
or more of them must have applied to them when they were
children. This was supposed to be true not only of people who
commit individual crimes but also of those who take part in
crimes on a larger scale. It follows that trying to prevent crimes
by more effective policing is treating the symptoms, not the
causes. To get at the roots of the problem we must end injustice
and exploitation, reform education so that it teaches the importance of respecting all human beings, prevent the corruption of
the democratic process by the arms manufacturers who profit
from war and genocide, and ensure that no child is brought up
in poverty or by abusive parents.

We would, I hope, all like to end injustice and exploitation
and see that no child lives in poverty or is abused. Nor would
I disagree with those who would like to see our schools do whatever they can to encourage an attitude of respect for others. We
ought to do these things even if it does nothing to reduce violence. But would doing them be enough to put an end to violence, and make other measures unnecessary? I do not think so,
and the passage from the book of Numbers that I have quoted
suggests three reasons why it will not.

First, that text—especially if read alongside other biblical passages describing other slaughters no less ruthless[2]—shows that the horrific mass killings of the twentieth century were not a new phenomenon, except insofar as modern technology and communications enabled the killers to murder far more people in a relatively brief period of time than had ever happened before. As Lawrence Keeley has shown in *War Before Civilization*, war has been a regular part of the existence of the overwhelming majority of human cultures, and male prisoners were usually not taken, although women and children sometimes were. Massacres of entire groups seem not to have been unusual. The mass graves of Europe—burial pits containing people of all ages who have met violent deaths—go back at least 7,000 years to the Neolithic grave at Talheim in Germany. At Crow Creek, in South Dakota, more than a century before Columbus sailed for America, 500 men, women, and children were scalped and mutilated before being thrown into a ditch. It is a sobering thought that in many tribal societies, despite the absence of machine guns and high explosives, the percentage of the population killed annually in warfare far exceeds that of any modern society, including Germany and Russia in the twentieth century.[3] Despite the impression one could easily get from watching the evening news on television that the world is becoming ever more violent, what is true of killing in war is also true of individual acts of homicide. For the average person living today, his or her chances of meeting a violent death at the hands of another human being are lower now than they have been for the average person living in any other period of history or prehistory. The evidence for this surprising but cheering fact can be found in the impressive body of research Steven Pinker has drawn together in *The Better Angels of Our Nature*, in which he argues that our era is less violent, less cruel, and more peaceful than all of the millennia of human existence that have preceded it.[4]

Notwithstanding the progress that has been made over the long arc of human history, the quotation from the book of Numbers offers a second reason why reducing poverty and injustice will not be enough to end violence. As the text indicates, the Israelites' motivation for wiping out the Midianites had nothing to do with their own poverty or with any injustice they had suffered at the hands of the people they attacked. In fact, the Midianites appear to have committed no crime at all except consenting to sexual relations—to which, presumably, the Israelite men also consented—and having a religion that was, at least to some Israelites, more attractive than that followed by Moses.

A third reason for thinking it will take more to stop violence than social reformers tend to think is the striking resemblance between what the book of Numbers tells us that the Lord commanded Moses to do and the course of action one might take if one were seeking to maximize the number of Israelite descendants in the light of our modern understanding of genetics. Since women can have only a limited number of children and the Israelite men were capable of providing the Midianite women with all the sperm they needed for that purpose, Midianite males were potential competitors and of no genetic use to the Israelites. So Moses ruthlessly eliminated them, men and boys alike. Killing all the Midianite women who are not virgins ensured that there were no pregnant women who might carry Midianite children. This meant that there would be no one of full Midianite descent in the next generation and guaranteed the complete success of the genocide against the Midianites. Allowing the captains to keep the young Midianite females for themselves increased the number of their own descendants. The genetic advantage to the perpetrators is as clear as anything can be.

What does this mean for us? We are all the descendants of men who succeeded in leaving their genes in subsequent generations, while many other men did not. Killing rival males with whom one does not share any genes and mating with their wives or daughters is one way in which men can enhance their prospects of leaving their genes in subsequent generations. Don't be misled by the thought that the killing of some humans by others cannot be good for the species. Species come in and out of existence too slowly to be the dominant unit of evolution. It is better to think of evolution as a competition more between genes, individuals, and perhaps small, genetically related groups than between species. That, presumably, has something to do with the central part that war and massacre have played in human history and prehistory.

Indeed, the capacity to commit massacres probably goes back even further than our distinct identity as human beings. Chimpanzees, who, together with bonobos, are our closest nonhuman relatives, go on raiding parties across the borders of their territory to deliberately—if you doubt that word, read a description of how they go about it—seek out and kill vulnerable chimpanzees, usually males, from another group. In one instance the chimpanzees that Jane Goodall was observing at Gombe completely wiped out a neighboring group over a three-year period, killing at least four adult and adolescent males and one adult female, driving away all the other adults, and "keeping alive for themselves," if I may here use the biblical expression, the two young daughters of the adult female they had killed. Similar behavior has been observed in other chimpanzee groups widely dispersed across Africa.[5]

Are we, then, all potential perpetrators of genocide? That goes too far. There are many ways in which one can do better than others in leaving one's genes in later generations. One of them is being particularly good at forming mutually beneficial cooperative relationships.[6] Amazingly, humans can do this even when they are divided into warring nations. In World War I the British and French opposed the Germans on the battlefields of France. After being subjected to all kinds of nationalist propaganda about the evil of the enemy, the soldiers of both sides were marched into trenches facing each other, given a rifle, and told to kill the soldiers in the opposite trenches. Instead of doing so, in what became known as the live and let live system, the French and British shot over the heads of the enemy troops, and the Germans did the same. It took considerable efforts and threats by the commanders to break this system.[7] The circumstances in which the forming of cooperative relationships is likely to be advantageous are more common than the circumstances in which genocide is likely to be advantageous. Thus we could say that we are all potential cooperators. But that a sizable number of human males have the potential to be perpetrators of genocide is, in view of the evidence from ethology, anthropology, and history, highly plausible. It is also plausible to believe that although this potential may be more likely to be acted upon in the presence of poverty, injustice, exploitation, or a lack of education, it will sometimes be acted upon without these factors.

If we bring our gaze forward from biblical times to the twentieth century, we find terrible confirmation of that bleak statement. In 1915–17 Turks massacred perhaps 1.5 million Armenians. In the 1930s Stalin ordered the deaths of somewhere between seven and ten million people. The figure of six million is usually assigned to the Nazi genocide against Jews, and the Nazis also murdered many Roma, homosexuals, and other civilians in the territories they occupied. Then came the killings in Cambodia, in Rwanda, and, as the century neared its end, in Bosnia, Kosovo, and East Timor. Some of these killings were perpetrated by people who were poor and uneducated, but others were not.

Germany in the 1920s was among the most highly educated countries in the world. Yugoslavia had, since 1918, been striving to educate its citizens to think of themselves as Yugoslavs, not as Croats, Serbs, or members of other nationalities or ethnic groups. Timothy Garton Ash asks, in his *History of the Present*, what we have learned from the events in that region during the last decade of the twentieth century. He answers, "We have learned that human nature has not changed. That Europe at the end of the twentieth century is quite as capable of barbarism as it was in the Holocaust of mid-century."[8] He might have also said, ". . . and for millennia before that, and not only in Europe."

So although overcoming poverty, eliminating injustice, and improving education may make genocide less likely, we cannot rely on these policies alone to prevent it. What else can be done? Developing mechanisms to promote peace and reduce the risk of war between countries is vital, for the mentality of war breaks down inhibitions and makes people more prone to kill noncombatants as well as the enemy's armed forces. But in the end we need to be able to do something that will make potential perpetrators of genocide fear the consequences of their actions. Despite the fact that when nation-states go to war, they often inflict violent death on a large scale, Pinker argues that the rise of the state saw a sharp decline in the risk of violent death.[9] Just as, at the domestic level, the last line of defense against individual crimes of murder, rape, and assault is law enforcement, so the last line of defense against genocide and similar crimes must be law enforcement, at a global level and, where other methods of achieving that fail, the method of last resort will be military intervention.

The Rise of International Criminal Law

The charter of the International Military Tribunal set up by the Allies to try the leading Nazi war criminals at Nuremberg gave it jurisdiction over three kinds of crimes: crimes against peace, war crimes, and crimes against humanity. In promulgating this charter, the Allies declared it a "crime against peace" to initiate a war of aggression; a "war crime" to murder, ill-treat, or deport either civilians or prisoners of war; and a "crime against humanity" to murder, exterminate, enslave, or deport any civilian population or to persecute them on political, racial, or religious grounds. These acts, the charter of the tribunal stated, are crimes "whether or not in violation of the domestic law of the country where perpetrated."[10]

Though the Allies were able to draw on earlier precedents and conventions to justify their claim that crimes against humanity were already recognized in international law, the Nuremberg Tribunal gave new impetus to the idea that certain acts are so horrendous that they are crimes no matter what the prevailing law at the time in the country in which they are perpetrated. Subsequently, the United Nations General Assembly asked the International Law Commission to formulate principles of international law relating to crimes such as those dealt with by the Nuremberg Tribunal, and the commission recommended that there should be international criminal responsibility for crimes against humanity committed at the instigation of, or with the toleration of, state authorities. The 1984 Convention against Torture, signed by 110 states, accepted this principle. That convention was central to the House of Lords decision on whether the United Kingdom government could extradite Senator Augusto Pinochet to Spain, to be tried there for crimes he was alleged to have committed in Chile. Chile had ratified the Convention against Torture, and this was sufficient for the law lords to find that Pinochet could be extradited to Spain.[11] But that case also raised the question of what is called universal jurisdiction, that is, the right of any country to try a person who has committed crimes against humanity irrespective of whether the country in which the crime was committed is a signatory to a convention that provides for international criminal responsibility in respect of that crime.

At the time of the Pinochet hearing, Amnesty International made a strong case that international law already recognizes universal jurisdiction for crimes against humanity.[12] The prosecution of Adolf Eichmann in Israel is often cited as a precedent for this view.[13] Eichmann was, under Heinrich Himmler and Reinhard Heydrich, in charge of the implementation of the murder of European Jews under Nazi rule. He was kidnapped in Argentina and flown to Israel, where he was tried and subsequently executed. Though the method by which he was brought to Israel was of doubtful legality, there has been general acceptance that Israel had the right to assert jurisdiction over offenses committed in Germany. Moreover, the Supreme Court of Israel claimed this jurisdiction not on the ground that Israel was the legal representative of Eichmann's victims but on the ground of universal jurisdiction over crimes against humanity. Eichmann's crimes against non-Jewish Roma, Poles, and others were thus also germane to the proceedings in Israel.[14]

In 2016 the first African court based on the principle of universal jurisdiction, the Extraordinary African Chambers, set up by Senegal and the African Union, sentenced Hissène Habré to life in prison for crimes against humanity, torture, and sex crimes. The verdict was the culmination of a 20-year campaign to hold Habré accountable for the deaths and suffering of tens of thousands of people during his presidency of Chad from 1982–1990. (The trial was held in Senegal because he had been in exile there prior to the decision to put him on trial.)[15]

In the Pinochet case, Lord Phillips of Worth Matravers discussed the question of universal jurisdiction and concluded,

> I believe that it is still an open question whether international law recognises universal jurisdiction in respect

of international crimes—that is the right, under international law, of the courts of any state to prosecute for such crimes wherever they occur. In relation to war crimes, such a jurisdiction has been asserted by the State of Israel, notably in the prosecution of Adolf Eichmann, but this assertion of jurisdiction does not reflect any general state practice in relation to international crimes. Rather, states have tended to agree, or to attempt to agree, on the creation of international tribunals to try international crimes. They have however, on occasion, agreed by conventions, that their national courts should enjoy jurisdiction to prosecute for a particular category of international crime wherever occurring.[16]

In January 2001, at the initiative of the International Commission of Jurists, an international group of 30 scholars and jurists meeting at Princeton University attempted to reach consensus on a desirable direction for universal jurisdiction. They came very close: the Princeton Principles on Universal Jurisdiction were agreed to with only a single dissent among those assembled. The principles endorse the idea of criminal jurisdiction exercised by any state "based solely on the nature of the crime, without regard to where the crime was committed, the nationality of the alleged or convicted perpetrator, the nationality of the victim, or any other connection to the state exercising such jurisdiction." The crimes specified include piracy, slavery, war crimes, crimes against peace, crimes against humanity, genocide, and torture. Subsequent principles require adherence to international norms of due process, reject the idea of immunity for those in official positions such as head of state, and deny the efficacy of a grant of amnesty by a state to the accused.[17] The Princeton Principles seek to establish a truly global jurisdiction for the crimes they cover.

Yet it would be a mistake to disregard why the lone dissenter at the Princeton meeting, Lord Browne-Wilkinson, did not join the consensus. Like Lord Phillips of Worth Matravers, Lord Browne-Wilkinson is a distinguished judge of Britain's highest court. He was the senior judge in the Pinochet case. In his dissenting statement, Lord Browne-Wilkinson warns that universal jurisdiction could lead to states hostile to other states seizing their officials and staging show trials for alleged international crimes. As examples he suggests—and this was written before the terrorist attacks on the World Trade Center and the Pentagon—that states hostile to the Western powers might put Western officials on trial or Western zealots might seek to prosecute Islamic extremists for terrorist activities. The state of which the accused is a citizen might then resort to force in order to protect its subjects. The result "would be more likely to damage than to advance chances of international peace."[18]

In 2001, the year in which the Princeton Principles were published, the fears Lord Browne-Wilkinson had expressed came a step closer to reality. Ironically, in view of the role that the Eichmann case has played in establishing the principle of universal jurisprudence, this time it was Israel's Foreign Ministry that cautioned Israeli officials to take care in traveling abroad because some countries might be prepared to charge them with violating Palestinians' human rights. The warning followed a legal case brought in Belgium by survivors of the 1982 massacre of Palestinians at the Sabra and Shatila refugee camps against Israel's then prime minister, Ariel Sharon. The massacre was carried out by Israel's Lebanese Christian allies, but an official Israeli investigation attributed "indirect responsibility" to Sharon, then the defense minister, for failing to stop the killing.[19] Although nothing came of the case against Sharon (who in 2006 fell into a coma that lasted until his death in 2014), in 2009 Israel's fears were shown to have some substance when a British magistrate's court issued a warrant for the arrest of Israel's foreign minister, Tzipi Livni, who was due to attend a conference in London. The warrant was granted after an application by lawyers acting on behalf of Palestinian victims of Israel's military operation in Gaza earlier that year. Livni canceled her planned visit, and the warrant was withdrawn, amid apologies from Gordon Brown, the British prime minister. Subsequently, the British parliament passed legislation giving the director of public prosecutions power to veto arrest warrants. The legislation did not affect the principle of universal jurisdiction but gave the government control over the issue of warrants. In 2011, after the legislation was passed, Livni, by then the leader of the Israeli opposition, visited Britain.[20]

To reduce the risk of a proliferation of charges brought by individual states invoking universal jurisdiction, both Lord Browne-Wilkinson and his colleague Lord Phillips prefer the use of international courts, unless the country whose citizen has been charged has signed a treaty accepting universal jurisdiction for the relevant offenses, as in the case of Chile, which had signed the Convention against Torture. Even those who support universal jurisdiction agree that an international court is a valuable additional option. If it works well enough, it should make universal jurisdiction unnecessary. Like the Nuremberg Tribunal, more recent international tribunals have arisen in the wake of tragic events: the wars that followed the breakup of the former Yugoslavia, the massacre of Hutus in Rwanda, the Serbian attacks on the Albanian inhabitants of Kosovo, and the killings in East Timor by militia supported by the Indonesian armed forces. By strengthening the resolve of all decent people not to allow such tragedies to continue, these tribunals are pushing us toward a global system of criminal justice for such crimes. In contrast to the Nuremberg Tribunal, trials such as that of Habré and Slobodan Milosevic, the former president of Yugoslavia, who was sent to the international tribunal in The Hague by the government he once led, are not instances of justice exacted by the occupying forces against the leaders of a state that has been forced into unconditional surrender. They are a sign of the recognition that state sovereignty is no defense against a charge of crimes against humanity.

These international tribunals have been one-off arrangements, specially set up to try particular crimes. (The long-standing International Court of Justice deals only with states, not with individuals.) To make the prosecution of crimes against humanity a permanent feature of international law, representatives of 160 states met in Rome in 1998 and agreed, by an overwhelming majority, to set up an International Criminal Court, or ICC. In 2002, when 60 countries had ratified the legal basis for establishing the court, known as the Rome Statute, the world had, for the first time, a permanent global criminal law, although one that deals only with the gravest crimes, such as genocide, crimes against humanity, and war crimes, and acts only when national courts are unable or unwilling to prosecute. By 2016, 124 states had ratified the treaty.

The ICC has a prosecutor who can bring charges of genocide, crimes against humanity, and war crimes against individuals as long as they are a national of a state that has ratified the treaty or the crime was committed on the territory of such a state. The only other way in which a case can come before the ICC is if the United Nations Security Council refers a specific case to it.

The United States has played a less than distinguished role in this process. Initially, it sought amendments to the Rome Statute that would have exempted U.S. soldiers and government officials from prosecution. (Why the United States should expect its nationals to be treated differently from the nationals of all other states has never been made clear.) When these amendments were rejected, the United States was one of seven states to vote against the treaty to set up the ICC (joining Saddam Hussein's Iraq, Muammar Gaddafi's Libya, Qatar, Yemen, China, and Israel). President Clinton nevertheless signed the treaty in 2000 but did not submit it to the Senate for ratification. Under President George W. Bush, the United States announced that it no longer intended to ratify the treaty.[21] The steps taken by the United States during the Bush years to undermine the court were many and varied and not without their amusing side. In 2002 Bush signed legislation that authorized the president to use military force to free any American held by the ICC. The act became known as The Hague Invasion Act, after the Dutch city in which the ICC is based and has its detention center. The law also provided for the withdrawal of U.S. military assistance to any country ratifying the ICC treaty and restricted U.S. participation in United Nations peacekeeping forces unless the United States obtained immunity from prosecution.[22] Subsequently, Condoleezza Rice, Bush's own secretary of state, conceded that cutting off military aid to states that were fighting terrorism was "sort of the same as shooting ourselves in the foot," but that is exactly what happened, for example, in Mali, where an Islamist extremist group established a base.[23] The law was weakened in 2006 and repealed in 2008.

Ironically, while the United States was refusing to contemplate its citizens being tried by an open international court operating in accordance with international rules of due process and eschewing the death penalty, it was itself setting up military tribunals with the power to impose the death sentence to try suspected terrorists who were not U.S. citizens, using evidence that was not produced in open court.[24] The United States was demanding one standard for its own citizens while applying a very different one for citizens of other countries.

Under President Obama the U.S. stance toward the ICC shifted. Although there was no move to become a member of the ICC, the United States sent delegations with observer status to some ICC meetings and participated in discussions. Speaking after one of these meetings, held in Kampala, Uganda, in 2010, Harold Koh, the legal advisor to the U.S. delegation, said that after 12 years the default on the U.S. relationship with the court had been "reset . . . from hostility to positive engagement." Stephen Rapp, the U.S. ambassador-at-large for war crimes issues, referred to past American concerns that the ICC prosecutor might engage in politically motivated prosecutions, and he acknowledged that this had not happened. Instead, the court had been focused on the crimes against humanity committed in northern Uganda by Joseph Kony, by the Lord's Resistance Army in the Democratic Republic of the Congo, and on other crimes against humanity committed by militia groups in Darfur and in the Central African Republic.[25]

In 2006 Thomas Lubanga became the first person to be arrested under a warrant issued by the ICC. Lubanga had been the founder and leader of a rebel group in the Democratic Republic of the Congo that had been accused of widespread violations of human rights. In 2004 the Congolese government authorized the ICC to investigate and prosecute crimes committed in the Democratic Republic of the Congo subsequent to the passing of the Rome Statute. After an investigation, Lubanga was charged with the war crime of "conscripting and enlisting child soldiers under the age of fifteen years and using them to participate actively in hostilities." He was convicted in 2012 and sentenced to 14 years' imprisonment.[26] Two years later another Congolese, Germain Katanga, became the second person to be convicted by the ICC. He received a 12-year prison sentence for his role in the massacre of hundreds of villagers in 2003.[27]

From "Humanitarian Intervention" to "the Responsibility to Protect"

Punishing the criminals after they commit an atrocity is something most people would support because of their belief that this is what justice requires. From a utilitarian perspective, punishing those guilty of past crimes will, one hopes, put others who might do something similar on notice that they will have no refuge from justice and so deter them from committing new crimes. Since the fear of punishment will not always be sufficient to prevent the crimes taking place, however, the question of intervention to stop ongoing genocide or crimes against humanity will still arise. If punishment can be justified, so can intervention to stop a crime that is about to occur or is already in progress. Perhaps, though, we should go further: not merely accepting that there is a right to intervene when atrocities are being committed but affirming that those with the ability to stop such crimes have a positive responsibility to protect the victims or potential victims even if the only way to do so is to invade another country. If that responsibility exists, under what circumstances should countries act on it?

For philosophers to take up these questions is not a new idea. Kant wrote a "philosophical sketch" entitled *Perpetual Peace* in which he argued that no state should, by force, interfere with the constitution or government of another state. He also thought that states preparing for war should seek the opinions of philosophers on the possibility of peace.[28] John Stuart Mill said that few questions are more in need of attention from philosophers than the issue of when a state that is not itself under attack may go to war. He thought that philosophers should seek to establish "some rule or criterion whereby the justifiableness of intervening in the affairs of other countries, and (what is sometimes fully as questionable) the justifiableness of refraining from intervention, may be brought to a definite and rational test."[29]

What rule or criterion would satisfy Mill's "definite and rational test" of when intervention is justified, and even obligatory, and when it is not? One phrase often heard in this context is that used by Lassa Oppenheim in the following passage from his influential treatise on international law:

> There is general agreement that, by virtue of its personal and territorial supremacy, a State can treat its own nationals according to discretion. But there is a substantial body of opinion and practice in support of the view that there are limits to that discretion; when a state renders itself guilty of cruelties against and persecution of its nationals in such a way as to deny their fundamental rights and to shock the conscience of mankind, intervention in the interests of humanity is legally permissible.[30]

Michael Walzer has adopted this criterion. In *Just and Unjust Wars* he wrote,

> Humanitarian intervention is justified when it is a response (with reasonable expectations of success) to acts "that shock the moral conscience of mankind." The old-fashioned language seems to me exactly right. . . . The reference is to the moral convictions of ordinary men and women, acquired in the course of their everyday activities. And given that one can make a persuasive argument in terms of those convictions, I don't think that there is any moral reason to adopt that posture of passivity that might

be called waiting for the UN (waiting for the universal
state, waiting for the messiah . . .).[31]

Those words date from 1977. Though there has been no sign in
the intervening years of the arrival of the messiah, the UN has
shown, as we shall see later in this chapter, that there are occasions on which it does authorize intervention.

Walzer has continued to support the "shock the moral conscience" criterion and has pointed out that in an age in which
"the camera crews arrive faster than rigor mortis," the acts that
do shock the conscience of humankind are more shocking than
they used to be because we are so intimately linked to them.[32]
Nevertheless, Walzer insists on retaining a strong presumption
against intervention. He specifically rejects the idea that the violation of human rights is in itself a sufficient justification for
intervention or that it is legitimate to intervene for the sake of
democracy.[33] Sometimes he argues for the strong presumption
against intervention in terms of the importance of protecting the
sovereignty of states in which people can live a communal life
and struggle for freedom in their own way within their own communal structures.[34] At other times his argument is more pragmatic: ever since Roman times, he reminds us, imperial powers
have sought to expand their empires by intervening in civil wars.
Intervention can too easily become an excuse for annexation,
in one form or another. Walzer does mention some examples of
intervention that he thinks were justified: by India in what was
then East Pakistan and is now Bangladesh, in 1971; by Tanzania
in 1979 against the regime of Idi Amin in Uganda; and by the
Vietnamese against the Khmer Rouge regime in Cambodia in
the same year. On the whole, though, he thinks people "should
be allowed to work out their difficulties without imperial assistance, among themselves."[35]

The problem with Walzer's appeal to the "conscience of mankind" criterion is that this conscience has, at various times and places, been shocked by such things as interracial sex, atheism, and mixed bathing. Ironically, the Nazis themselves elevated "the healthy sensibility of the people" to the status of a legal norm and used it as a ground for suppressing homosexuality.[36] We know that when international lawyers talk of acts that shock the conscience of humankind, they don't mean things like *that*, but how can we specify precisely what they do mean?

Kofi Annan, when he was United Nations secretary-general, suggested that intervention is justified "when death and suffering are being inflicted on large numbers of people, and when the state nominally in charge is unable or unwilling to stop it." He defended this view by saying that the aim of the United Nations Charter is "to protect individual human beings, not to protect those who abuse them."[37] Annan's criterion has the advantage of being more specific than "shocking the conscience of mankind." In order to make it more precise still, however, the reference to "suffering" should be replaced by an enumeration of more specific harms. This is done in various international legal documents, including the 1948 Convention on the Prevention and Punishment of the Crime of Genocide, which is followed in the 1998 Rome Statute of the International Criminal Court. Article 2 of the convention defines the crime of genocide as follows:

> Genocide means any of the following acts committed
> with intent to destroy, in whole or in part, a national,
> ethnic, racial or religious group, as such:
> (a) Killing members of the group;
> (b) Causing serious bodily or mental harm to members
> of the group;

(c) Deliberately inflicting on the group conditions of life
calculated to bring about its physical destruction in whole
or in part;

(d) Imposing measures intended to prevent births within
the group;

(e) Forcibly transferring children of the group to another
group.[38]

Although all of these acts should count as crimes, and those who
carry them out should be prosecuted and charged whenever possible, it is possible to draw distinctions between them. Because
military intervention runs the risk of causing widespread casualties, the imposition of measures intended to prevent births within
a group and the forcible transfer of children from one group to
another are arguably insufficient in themselves to justify military
intervention. Of course, such measures will often be accompa-
nied by physical violence and can cause serious mental harm to
members of the group, thus bringing the situation under one of
the other clauses of the definition of genocide and opening the
way for the possible justification of intervention. In addition,
whether the acts are carried out against a specific national, racial,
ethnic, or religious group serves only to identify these crimes as
genocide. Random acts of violence against an equivalent number of innocent people would be crimes against humanity and
could also serve as a trigger for justifiable intervention.

The definition of a crime against humanity is less well settled
than the definition of genocide, but the Rome Statute of the
International Criminal Court uses the following definition:

"Crime against humanity" means any of the following
acts when committed as part of a widespread or
systematic attack directed against any civilian population,
with knowledge of the attack:

(a) Murder;

(b) Extermination;

(c) Enslavement;

(d) Deportation or forcible transfer of population;

(e) Imprisonment or other severe deprivation of physical liberty in violation of fundamental rules of international law;

(f) Torture;

(g) Rape, sexual slavery, enforced prostitution, forced pregnancy, enforced sterilization, or any other form of sexual violence of comparable gravity;

(h) Persecution against any identifiable group or collectivity on political, racial, national, ethnic, cultural, religious, gender as defined in paragraph 3, or other grounds that are universally recognized as impermissible under international law, in connection with any act referred to in this paragraph or any crime within the jurisdiction of the Court;

(i) Enforced disappearance of persons;

(j) The crime of apartheid;

(k) Other inhumane acts of a similar character intentionally causing great suffering, or serious injury to body or to mental or physical health.[39]

Again, if we are seeking a trigger for military intervention, we need to focus on widespread, flagrant examples of these crimes.

We can now draw on the definitions of genocide and crimes against humanity as well as Walzer's and Annan's criteria to say,

Intervention is justified when it is a response (with reasonable expectations of success) to acts that kill or inflict serious bodily or mental harm on large numbers of people, or deliberately inflict on them conditions of life calculated to bring about their physical destruction, and when the state nominally in charge is unable or unwilling to stop it.

Admittedly, this definition gives rise to more questions than it answers. How many people is a "large number"? How serious does the bodily or mental harm have to be? Who will decide when conditions of life that bring about the physical destruction of large numbers of people have been deliberately inflicted upon them? If intervention is justified when this criterion is met, is there also an obligation on the part of other states to intervene? Could knowingly causing or being unwilling to stop environmental pollution that will kill large numbers of people be regarded as meeting the definition? Is it only things done to human beings that count? Might we one day see the wiping out of tens of thousands of chimpanzees or the destruction of a unique ecosystem, bringing with it the extinction of many species, as grounds for intervention?

There is, however, a more fundamental difference between Annan's approach and those that came before. Oppenheim asked when humanitarian intervention is legally permissible. Walzer asked when it is ethically justifiable. Annan, thinking from the perspective of the head of the United Nations in the post-Rwanda era, asks, What are our responsibilities? The world, he says, "cannot stand aside" when atrocities are being committed. We need, he says, to adapt our international system to a world in which we have "new responsibilities."

This line of thought was taken up by the International Commission on Intervention and State Sovereignty (ICISS), a body of 12 distinguished experts from as many countries set up by the Canadian government in 2000 under the chairmanship of Gareth Evans, a former foreign minister of Australia, and Mohamed

Sahnoun, an experienced Algerian diplomat. Many such bodies meet, talk, and issue a long, dull report that has few readers and little influence. In sharp contrast to this familiar outcome, *The Responsibility to Protect,* the ninety-page report issued by ICISS in 2001, has reframed the global debate about humanitarian intervention.[40] Instead of focusing on the rights of those who may be considering intervening, the report argues, we should look at the issues from the perspective of those in need of protection. Moreover, emphasizing the responsibility to protect is compatible with acknowledging that this duty falls primarily on the state concerned and thus is less confrontational and more respectful of the idea of state sovereignty than the idea of a right to intervene. On the other hand, the notion of a responsibility to protect does imply that sovereignty is not absolute: if the state is unable or unwilling to carry out its responsibility to protect its people, the responsibility then falls to the international community, either to aid the state if it is willing but unable to fulfill its responsibility or to protect those in need directly if the state is unwilling to do so.[41]

Within just four years of ICISS making this argument, the idea of a responsibility to protect was discussed and unanimously accepted at the United Nations 2005 World Summit, a follow-up to the United Nations Millennium Summit meeting of representatives of the 191 UN member states and one of the largest gatherings of world leaders ever to have taken place.[42] The World Summit Outcome Document recognizes that the responsibility to protect falls primarily on states but goes on to express readiness to take collective action when peaceful means have failed and where national authorities are "manifestly failing" to protect their people from "genocide, war crimes, ethnic cleansing, crimes against humanity."[43]

In 2009 UN Secretary-General Ban Ki-moon began making annual reports to the General Assembly on the responsibility to protect. The initial report was especially noteworthy for setting out three pillars on which the responsibility rests. The first pillar is the responsibility of the state to protect its populations (whether or not they are its own nationals) from the four specified crimes and violations, that is, genocide, war crimes, ethnic cleansing, and crimes against humanity. The second pillar is the commitment of the international community to assist states in meeting these obligations by helping them to build the capacity to do so. The third pillar is "the responsibility of Member States to respond collectively in a timely and decisive manner when a State is manifestly failing to provide such protection." This response should not, Ban emphasized, be thought of narrowly as involving only military force, and he referred to the example of the UN's successful role in Kenya in 2008, when a disputed election led to widespread violence. Mediation by Annan, then the secretary-general, brought the disputing parties to the negotiating table, and a compromise was reached that prevented further bloodshed. Where force is to be used, however, Ban states, it must, in accordance with the United Nations Charter, be authorized by the Security Council.[44]

Since 2009 the secretary-general's reports have focused on specific issues relating to the responsibility to protect and how it should operate. After each report the General Assembly has a dialogue on the issues raised and the recommendations made in the report. In the view of the International Coalition for the Responsibility to Protect, a group of nongovernmental organizations from all over the world that seeks to increase understanding of and support for the responsibility to protect, this dialogue has been evolving in a positive direction. The discussion has ceased to question whether there is a responsibility to protect and instead has moved on, with increasingly wide participation, to how best to implement it.[45]

The United Nations has not merely accepted the responsibility to protect in theory but also put it into practice. In 2010 the West African state of Côte d'Ivoire held elections which, it was hoped, would restore peace in a country that had suffered greatly through a civil war and had remained divided after the fighting stopped. When Laurent Gbagbo, the incumbent leader, refused to accept the outcome of UN-certified presidential elections and step down, however, a second civil war broke out, and both sides were reported to have killed civilians. In March 2011 the Security Council invoked the responsibility to protect and authorized United Nations forces to use all necessary means to protect civilians "under imminent threat of physical violence."[46] Further fighting, in which UN forces were involved, resulted in the defeat and arrest of Gbagbo.

In the same month that the Security Council acted on the responsibility to protect civilians in Côte d'Ivoire, it also had to deal with an extremely threatening situation in Libya. Muammar Gaddafi, the longtime Libyan dictator, had threatened to show "no mercy, no pity" toward the dissident population of Benghazi.[47] The Security Council first reminded the Libyan government of its responsibility to protect its civilians and condemned the violence against civilians that had already occurred. The Council also stressed that those complicit in attacks on civilians should be held to account and referred the situation to the prosecutor of the International Criminal Court. As Gaddafi's forces advanced on Benghazi, the Security Council passed a second resolution authorizing the enforcement of a no-fly zone as well as "all necessary measures"—but specifically excluding a "foreign occupation force"—to protect civilians in Libya.[48] The operation, as Evans wrote at the time, "[was] not about bombing for democracy, or Muammar Gaddafi's head." Its only justification, in his view, was to protect Libya's people from the harm

Gaddafi had already inflicted on unarmed protestors and was threatening to inflict on people in rebel-held areas. Evans concluded by saying that in Libya "a hugely important precedent has been set" and that "the Security Council has written exactly the right script—it is just a matter now of following it."[49]

The NATO forces did not stick to the script. Russia and China had had reservations about the resolution to authorize the no-fly zone in Libya and the use of all necessary means to protect civilians. They did not vote in favor of it but abstained, refraining from using their veto power and thus allowing the resolution to pass. Soon, however, they were protesting that the NATO forces had exceeded their mandate and were using the resolution as a pretext for bringing about regime change. Those protests were not without justification. The NATO forces reversed the tide of battle, not merely protecting civilians but inflicting enough damage on Gaddafi's forces to pave the way for the rebel victory that ended with Gaddafi being shot by rebel fighters. NATO was still attacking Gaddafi's forces even as his palace in Tripoli was overrun, and he himself was fleeing. What happened in Libya then rebounded on the responsibility to protect when Russia and China vetoed a much milder resolution calling for nonmilitary sanctions against Syria, the Russian Foreign Ministry referring to what had happened in Libya as a ground for Russia's veto.[50] Whether UN action in Syria in 2011 could have made a difference to the tragic course of the civil war in that country, which by 2016 had claimed at least 250,000 lives, is something we will never know.

On the other hand, the distrust caused by the "mission creep" in Libya proved not to be, as had been suggested, "the end of the responsibility to protect."[51] In the annual debates on the subject in the General Assembly, states from all regions have shown overwhelming support for basic principles of the responsibility to protect. In the debate on the secretary-general's 2014 report, for example, representatives of 81 countries spoke. In the Security Council itself, in the three years that followed the fierce divisions engendered by events in Libya, 22 resolutions passed by the Council explicitly used the language of the "responsibility to protect," in the context of threatened atrocities in Yemen, Mali, South Sudan, and the Central African Republic.[52]

State Sovereignty, the United Nations, and the Responsibility to Protect

As we have seen, Secretary-General Ban asserted, in his 2009 report to the General Assembly, that where military intervention is required in order to meet the responsibility, it must be authorized by the Security Council. Ten years earlier, then Secretary-General Annan had posed the dilemma that advocates of such a requirement must face. He referred to the genocide in Rwanda as indicative of the consequences of inaction and to the intervention in Kosovo as an example of action taken by "a regional organization [NATO] without a United Nations mandate." He continued,

> To those for whom the greatest threat to the future of international order is the use of force in the absence of a Security Council mandate, one might ask—not in the context of Kosovo but in the context of Rwanda: If, in those dark days and hours leading up to the genocide, a coalition of States had been prepared to act in defense of the Tutsi population, but did not receive prompt Council authorization, should such a coalition have stood aside and allowed the horror to unfold?
>
> To those for whom the Kosovo action heralded a new era when States and groups of States can take military action outside the established mechanisms for

enforcing international law, one might ask: Is there
not a danger of such interventions undermining the
imperfect, yet resilient, security system created after the
Second World War, and of setting dangerous precedents
for future interventions without a clear criterion to
decide who might invoke these precedents, and in
what circumstances?[53]

Annan made his own position clear, saying that state sovereignty
is being redefined by the forces of globalization and international cooperation: "The State is now widely understood to be
the servant of its people, and not vice versa." The acceptance of
the responsibility to protect as a ground for intervention in what
had previously been considered the domestic affairs of a sovereign state confirms Annan's view that a change in our conception of state sovereignty was under way. As we saw in chapter 1,
the British historian Martin Gilbert, writing two years after the
World Summit, called the adoption of this doctrine "the most
significant adjustment to sovereignty in 360 years."[54]

Although the responsibility to protect is now firmly embed-
ded in United Nations institutions and resolutions, questions
can still be raised about its justification and its compatibility
with the United Nations Charter which states, in article 2(7):

Nothing contained in the present Charter shall authorize
the United Nations to intervene in matters which are
essentially within the domestic jurisdiction of any state
or shall require the Members to submit such matters to
settlement under the present Charter; but this principle
shall not prejudice the application of enforcement measures under Chapter VII.

Chapter VII does not refer to human rights but only to "threats
to the peace, breaches of the peace, and acts of aggression." If we

take this at face value, it would seem that the United Nations cannot set up procedures to authorize intervention because in doing so it would be violating its own Charter.

How can this section of the Charter be reconciled with the responsibility to protect? The Charter places two sets of obligations on its members, to respect human rights and not to interfere in the internal matters of another state. As Brad Roth puts it: "The Organization and its Members are pledged to observe and promote, but bound not to impose, wholesome internal practices."[55] The "Declaration on Principles of International Law Concerning Friendly Relations and Co-Operation among States in Accordance with the Charter of the United Nations," adopted by the General Assembly in 1970 on the 25th anniversary of the United Nations, gives some support to this view. This declaration elaborates on Article 2(7) of the Charter as follows:

> Armed intervention and all other forms of interference or attempted threats against the personality of the State or against its political, economic and cultural elements, are in violation of international law. . . . Every state has an inalienable right to choose its political, economic, social and cultural systems, without interference in any form by another state.[56]

So, does intervention to prevent atrocities violate the UN Charter's acceptance of the principle of nonintervention in the domestic affairs of another sovereign state? We could reconcile the Charter with the responsibility to protect if we could defend at least one of the following claims:

1. The violation of human rights, even in one country, is itself a threat to international peace.
2. The existence of tyranny itself constitutes a threat to international peace.

3. The rights of domestic jurisdiction retained by the states in Article 2(7) do not extend to committing crimes against humanity or to allowing them to be committed within one's domestic jurisdiction.

1. The Violation of Human Rights Is Itself a Threat to International Peace

The first of these arguments is one that Annan himself has put forward. In referring to the United Nations Charter in his September 1999 speech, he said,

> The sovereign States who drafted the Charter over half a century ago were dedicated to peace, but experienced in war.
>
> They knew the terror of conflict, but knew equally that there are times when the use of force may be legitimate in the pursuit of peace. That is why the Charter's own words declare that "armed force shall not be used, save in the common interest". But what is that common interest? Who shall define it? Who will defend it? Under whose authority? And with what means of intervention? These are the monumental questions facing us as we enter the new century.

Taking these remarks in context, we can read Annan as suggesting that the common interest should be defined so as to include an interest in preventing tyrants from violating the rights of the citizens of the countries over which they rule, even if the tyrant poses no threat to other states. Though this may seem far-fetched, several decisions of the Security Council carry the same implication. In regard to Iraq the Security Council resolved in 1991 that the repression of the civilian population, including that in Kurdish-populated areas, had consequences that were a threat to international peace and security. Since the Council mentioned the flow of refugees to other countries, it is arguable that this repression did have some consequences outside the borders of Iraq.[57] In authorizing intervention during the civil war in Somalia in the early 1990s, however, the Council simply determined that "the magnitude of the human tragedy caused by the conflict in Somalia, further exacerbated by the obstacles being created to the distribution of humanitarian assistance, constitutes a threat to international peace and security."[58] No further explanation was offered, and since the conflict was purely a civil one, it is not easy to guess how international peace would have been threatened if the Somalians had simply been left to starve, terrible as that would have been. Similarly, in Haiti the overthrow of the democratically elected president Jean-Bertrand Aristide in 2004 was seen as a threat to "international peace and security in the region" and thus as justifying the use of Chapter VII powers.[59] The resolution authorizing intervention in Libya in 2011 also included a determination that the situation there "continues to constitute a threat to international peace and security."[60]

Given the human tragedies in Iraq, Somalia, Haiti, and Libya that the Security Council was trying to overcome, it is understandable that it should have been willing to stretch the language of its Charter to the breaking point. It might seem that an ethic that looks to the consequences of our actions as determining what is right or wrong would lead us to support whatever stratagems offer the best prospect of preventing such tragedies. Taking a long-term view, however, a utilitarian ethic may point to desirable changes in international law but will nevertheless give strong support to international law because it offers the best chance of avoiding or reducing the horrors of war. Hence we should reject such blatant fictions as the idea that the overthrow of the president of Haiti is a threat to international peace. Once that is accepted, anything goes, and effectively the Security Council has an unconstrained mandate to interfere wherever it sees fit. In practice, at least as long as each of the permanent members of the Security Council has a veto on any resolution, there is little danger of the Security Council intervening without sufficient justification for doing so. Nevertheless, there is no basis in international law for attributing such powers to the Security Council.

2. Tyranny Is a Threat to International Peace

A second strategy would be to invoke the argument that, because no war has ever occurred between two democratic states, tyranny is itself a threat to international peace.[61] That thesis is controversial, and much depends on the definitions of "war" and of "democracy." For example, the Russian military intervention in Ukraine in 2014–16 is a possible counterexample to the thesis that no wars occur between democracies, but one might question whether the intervention amounts to a war and whether Russia and Ukraine were, at the time, democracies. In any case, the existence of a few counterexamples would not refute a more cautiously stated version of the thesis, namely, that democratic states are less likely to go to war with each other than states that are not democracies. If this is the case, then it could be argued that Article 2(7) no longer stands in the way of intervention for the sake of establishing or restoring democracy, since such interventions do reduce the general "threat to the peace" posed by nondemocratic regimes. But should so vague and indefinite a threat to peace be sufficient reason for military intervention? Again, it seems that accepting it as such is to use a pretext to cover intervention that is really motivated by another purpose altogether.

3. The Rights of Domestic Jurisdiction Retained by the States in Article 2(7) Do Not Extend to Committing Genocide or Other Crimes Against Humanity or to Allowing Them to Be Committed

The third strategy points out that it is question-begging to assume that the reference in Article 2(7) to "matters which are essentially within the domestic jurisdiction of any state" excludes intervention to prevent genocide or other crimes against humanity. In granting domestic jurisdiction to the states, this argument runs, the United Nations Charter cannot have intended to set aside the prohibition of such crimes by customary international law.

One problem with interpreting the United Nations Charter as limiting domestic sovereignty in this manner is that the International Law Commission did not recommend that there should be international criminal responsibility for crimes against humanity until 1954, long after the Charter had been written and accepted by the original member states of the United Nations. Thus the Charter could well have been formulated and signed in the absence of any such belief.

Nevertheless, taking the view that domestic jurisdiction, as accepted in the United Nations Charter, does not extend to committing or allowing to be committed acts of genocide or crimes against humanity is the most plausible and promising of the three strategies so far considered. As we have seen, the International Commission on Intervention and State Sovereignty reached a similar conclusion, arguing that state sovereignty implies that the state has a responsibility for the protection of its people, but when a state is unwilling or unable to fulfill that responsibility, the responsibility falls upon the international community, and more specifically, on the Security Council. The UN Charter's strong bias against military intervention is, therefore, "not to be regarded as absolute."[62]

Unlike the first strategy, which asserts that the violation of human rights is itself a threat to international peace, this third approach does not rely on a fiction, and, unlike the second strategy, it does not rest on an unproven theory about the link between democracy and peace. Moreover, it has built-in limits to the grounds on which intervention may take place. This does, therefore, provide a sound basis for the remarkably rapid acceptance of the responsibility to protect that occurred in the first decade after the International Commission on Intervention and State Sovereignty published its report.

Could the Spread of Democracy Provide Protection Against Genocide?

In the previous section we found that the acceptance of the responsibility to protect implies that state sovereignty is not absolute. I will now consider a much more speculative, far-reaching strategy limiting the sovereignty of some states. This strategy builds on the discussion in the previous chapter questioning the standard view of what it takes for a government to be legitimate. As we saw there, although governments are generally accepted as legitimate if they have effective control over the territory they claim to rule, there is an alternative democratic view of legitimacy, according to which a regime that seizes power by force is not legitimate unless the people over whom it rules give a freely expressed indication of support. As we have seen, this democratic view can be defended both in terms of an argument from the right to self-government and in consequentialist terms. If the democratic view of legitimate government were accepted, then the proposals made in the previous chapter in the context of trading restrictions might have a more far-reaching application. For if a government that comes to power by force of arms and remains in power through the repression of all opposition is, in virtue of that fact, not to be considered a legitimate government, it could not take its place at the United Nations. Hence if it were engaging in widespread violence against its own population, the provisions of the UN Charter restraining member states against intervening in the internal affairs of other members would not apply. Though this doctrine could lead to an increase in war, this risk must be weighed against the positives of supporting democracy and reducing the number of governments that are little more than gangs of brigands pillaging a country over which they hold sway. Of course, the usual consequentialist argument against going to war will still apply. War causes immense suffering and loss of life and should always be a last resort, entered into when there is no other way of preventing still greater suffering, and the prospects of success at low cost, in terms of loss of life or other great harms, are good.

In the first section of this chapter I argued that there might be a genetic basis for the willingness of some human beings to massacre those who are not part of their group. Now I have suggested that where a regime rules by force, rather than in a democratic way, there is no legitimate sovereign to stand in the way of an intervention that can reasonably be expected to have good consequences—and presumably will, if possible, set up a democratic form of government. But, it may be objected, how can we have any faith in democracy as a means of preventing, rather than promoting, genocide? If the genes of violence are in many of us, why are they less likely to be in democratically elected rulers than in dictators?[63]

The worst genocides of this century have been carried out by governments that were very far from being democracies: Ottoman Turkey at the time of the Armenian massacres, Nazi Germany, the Soviet Union under Stalin, Cambodia under the

Khmer Rouge. But Rwanda was moving toward a multiparty democracy at the time of the massacres, and since 85 percent of the population was Hutu, it is possible that more democracy would not have stopped the massacres of the Tutsis. An even more difficult counterexample is the government of Milosevic, which bore substantial responsibility for the massacres in Bosnia and Kosovo. Milosevic was twice elected president of Serbia by large majorities and, later, of Yugoslavia as well. While neither Serbia nor Yugoslavia during this period was an entirely free and open society, to raise the bar for acceptance of a state as being democratic so high as to exclude them would imply that very many other putatively democratic states should also be excluded.[64]

Democracy, in the sense of the rule of the majority, does not guarantee that human rights will be respected. But a democratic process requires that the policies of the government must be publicly defended and justified. They cannot simply be implemented from above. Although some of us may have the capacity to commit terrible crimes, many of us also have a moral sense, that is, a capacity to reflect on the rights and wrongs of what we are doing and what our rulers are doing. That capacity emerges in the public arena. A small group may plot genocide and inspire or terrify their followers to carry it out, but if genocide has to be defended on primetime television, it will become rare indeed. Even when the Nazis had been in power for eight years, ruling without opposition and making use of all the means of propaganda that Joseph Goebbels, their minister of propaganda, could devise, they did not dare to be open about what they were doing to the Jews. Heinrich Himmler, the SS leader, told a group of senior SS officers that their work in exterminating the Jews was "an unwritten, never-to-be written, glorious page of our history."[65] If it had been possible to ensure that every page of Nazi history was written as it took place and offered for discussion to the German people, it is hard to believe that the Holocaust would have taken place. When the prosecutors at the Nuremberg Tribunal screened a film of Nazi concentration camps made by Allied military photographers, some of the defendants appeared to be visibly shocked. Even they may not have grasped exactly what the results of their policies looked like, close-up. Open procedures and public scrutiny may not be a perfect bulwark against genocide, but they do help.

Does Military Intervention Do More Good Than Harm?

To make the notion of legitimate government dependent on some degree of democracy implies that when government rests on force alone, state sovereignty carries no weight. It would seem that intervention in countries with such governments would then be readily justified. But if intervention is so easy to justify, will it not be used so often that it will be abused?

This objection rests on a failure to distinguish between legal and ethical justification. Even if intervention against a tyrannical regime that commits crimes against humanity violates neither international law nor the UN Charter, it might still be wrong to intervene. As Michael Doyle puts it, "It makes no moral sense to rescue a village and start World War Three, or destroy a village in order to save it."[66] We need to have rules and procedures that make intervention difficult to justify, so that states will not deceive themselves into believing that their desire to expand their influence in the world is really an altruistic concern to defend democracy and human rights. But even when those rules and procedures have been satisfied, the key question must always be, Will intervention do more good than harm?

Thomas Hobbes, who lived through the English Civil War, argued in *Leviathan* that a sovereign, even a tyrannical one, should be obeyed because the alternative is a reversion to a state of nature in which life is "solitary, poor, nasty, brutish and short."[67] A similar argument that anarchy is a greater evil than tyranny has been used by Tzvetan Todorov against military intervention for humanitarian purposes. Pointing to the downfall of the former communist regimes of Eastern Europe, Todorov wrote that in some cases the collapse of the nation-state led to a situation in which power is wielded by armed criminals. Intervention, even from humanitarian motives, can lead to the same outcome because it too destroys the nation-state.[68] Todorov was writing in 2001. Fifteen years later he could have reinforced his argument with examples that make his point more forcefully still: the U.S.-led invasion of Iraq that overthrew Saddam Hussein in 2003 and the UN-sanctioned NATO military operations in Libya in 2011 that brought down the Gaddafi regime.

The invasion of Iraq was not sanctioned by the United Nations, and its primary justification, at least as put forward by the Bush administration, was not humanitarian but to eliminate the threat posed by the weapons of mass destruction that Saddam was supposed to have possessed. Nevertheless, Bush did say, speaking to the United Nations, "Liberty for the Iraqi people is a great moral cause." He also referred to atrocities that Saddam had committed against his people.[69] Those atrocities had taken place some years earlier, however, and although Saddam continued to torture and execute people suspected of opposing his rule, the killings were on a small scale. In contrast, as I noted in chapter 1, the U.S.-led invasion of Iraq in 2003 is estimated to have caused 654,000 more Iraqi deaths than would have been expected under prewar conditions.[70] At the time of writing, the extremist organization Islamic State occupies part of Iraq, where it has executed people it regards as apostates or heretics and forced thousands of captive Yazidi women and girls into sex slavery. Bad as Saddam's rule was, the present situation seems still worse.

We have already examined the circumstances that led the Security Council to invoke the responsibility to protect as the basis for military intervention in Libya that eventually led to the downfall of Gaddafi's regime. The result has not, however, been a democratic government or indeed any kind of stable government at all. Instead, it has been a chaotic situation in which, as the *New York Times* put it in February 2015, "the broader Libya bedlam has now degenerated into a stalemated battle between two coalitions of armed groups, each of which claims its own competing national government."[71] Civilians are again bearing much of the brunt of the fighting. As in the case of Iraq, it is not clear that the overthrow of a dictator has improved the lives of most people. Hobbes could have said, "I told you so," and indeed there were experts who warned that Iraq and Libya could descend into chaos.[72] To the extent that such outcomes are predictable, military intervention should not take place, and the responsibility to protect does not imply that it should. If the regime in a country is unable or unwilling to protect its people from genocide or crimes against humanity, and the international community will be able to get rid of that regime but is not likely to be able to ensure that a new regime can be put in place that will protect the population from similar or even worse crimes at a later date, then the international community may have to accept that its powers are limited and that it is unable to meet its responsibility to protect.

That it is absolutely essential to consider the consequences of intervention is often forgotten when people argue about when it is right to intervene in the domestic affairs of another state. At the time of the NATO intervention against Serbia in Kosovo, some argued that if it was justifiable to intervene to protect the Kosovars from Serbia, NATO should also have intervened to protect the Chechens against Russia. Later the argument was made that if it was justifiable to intervene against Gaddafi in Libya, it must also have been justifiable to intervene against Assad in Syria. What this objection overlooks is that it is one thing for there to be a legal basis, and even a just cause, for intervening and a totally different thing for intervention to be justified, all things considered. The reason NATO would have been wrong to intervene against Russia in Chechnya is not that (at least on one account of what Russia was doing in Chechnya) there was no legal basis or just cause to intervene, but that the predictable human costs of the resulting war made it wrong to intervene. This should not be thought of as a case of double standards. The responsibility to protect implies that it is right to do what will prevent atrocities like genocide and crimes against humanity. That principle also tells us not to intervene when the costs of doing so are likely to be greater than the benefits achieved. In Chechnya the problem was the size of the Russian army and the danger of becoming involved in a war with a nuclear power. In Syria it was the lack of a unified opposition to Assad. President Obama later told Thomas Friedman of the *New York Times* that in Libya he had underestimated the chaos that would occur after the overthrow of Gaddafi, and, after seeing that happen, every time he considered military intervention he asked himself, "Do we have an answer for the day after?"[73] That is a critically important question. If military intervention is not likely to succeed in protecting civilians over the long term, then, although there may be a legal basis and a just cause for intervention, we ought not to intervene. That does, however, raise a further question: Do we need to increase our capacity to meet our responsibility to protect people threatened with violence and death?

Cultural Imperialism, Moral Relativism, and a Global Ethic

It is sometimes said that to intervene in other countries to protect human rights is a form of cultural imperialism. By what right, those who take this view ask, do we impose on other people our view of the kind of society they should have? Are we not repeating the errors of the Western missionaries who sailed out to Africa and to the South Sea Islands and told the supposed primitive people they found there to cover their nakedness and to have sex only when prone, with the man on top? Have we not learned from this experience that morality is relative to one's own society and that our morals are no better than theirs?

This objection is confused. Moral relativists imagine they are defending the rights of peoples of non-Western cultures to preserve their own values, but when moral relativism is taken seriously, it undermines all ethical arguments, including those against cultural imperialism. For if morality is always relative to one's own society, then you, coming from your society, have your moral standards and I, coming from my society, have mine. It follows that when I criticize your moral standards I am simply expressing the morality of my society, but it also follows that when you condemn me for criticizing the moral standards of your society you are simply expressing the morality of your society. There is, on this view, no way of moving outside the morality of one's own society and expressing a transcultural or objective moral judgment about anything, including respect for the cultures of different peoples. Hence if we happen to live in a culture that honors those who subdue other societies and suppress their cultures—and the very same people who defend moral relativism often tell us that this *is* the Western tradition—then that is our morality, and the relativist can offer no cogent reason why we should not simply get on with it. The point was neatly made by General Sir Charles Napier, the British army's commander in chief in India in the mid-nineteenth century, with regard to the practice of sati, in which widows were burned alive on the funeral pyres of their husband. When Napier ordered that the practice stop, Hindu priests complained to him that it was their custom, and customs should be respected. "This burning of widows is your custom," Napier replied. "Prepare the funeral pile. But my nation has also a custom. When men burn women alive, we hang them. . . . Let us all act according to national customs."[74]

We should reject moral relativism. A much better case against cultural imperialism can be made from the standpoint of a view of ethics that allows for the possibility of moral argument beyond the boundaries of one's own culture. Then we can argue that distinctive cultures embody ways of living that have been developed over countless generations, that when they are destroyed the accumulated wisdom they represent is lost, and that we are all enriched by being able to observe and appreciate a diversity of cultures. We can recognize that Western culture has no monopoly on wisdom, has often learned from other cultures, and still has much to learn. We can urge sensitivity to the values of other people and understanding of what gives them self-respect and a sense of identity. On that basis we can criticize the nineteenth-century missionaries for their insensitivity and for their obsession with sexual behavior, an area in which human relationships take a wide variety of forms, without any one pattern being clearly superior to others. We can also argue that we should be doing much more to preserve diverse cultures, especially indigenous cultures that are in danger of disappearing. But once we accept that there is scope for rational argument in ethics, independent of any particular culture, we can also ask whether the values we are upholding are sound, defensible, or justifiable. Although reasonable people can disagree about many areas of ethics, and culture plays a role in these differences, sometimes what people claim to be a distinctive cultural practice really serves the interests of only a small minority of the population rather than all of them. Or perhaps it harms the interests of some without being beneficial to any and has survived because it is associated with a religious doctrine or practice that is resistant to change. Acts of the kind carried out by Nazi Germany against Jews, Gypsies, and homosexuals, by the Khmer Rouge against Cambodians they considered to be their class enemies, by Hutus against Tutsis in Rwanda, and by cultures that practice female genital mutilation or forbid the education of women are not elements of a distinctive culture that are worth preserving, and it is not imperialist to say that they lack the element of consideration for others that is required of any justifiable ethic.[75]

Some aspects of ethics can fairly be claimed to be universal, or very nearly so. Reciprocity, at least, seems to be common to ethical systems everywhere.[76] The notion of reciprocity may have served as the basis for the Golden Rule—treat others as you would like them to treat you—which elevates the idea of reciprocity into a distinct principle not necessarily related to how someone actually has treated you in the past. The Golden Rule can be found, in differing formulations, in a wide variety of cultures and religious teachings, including, in roughly chronological order, those of Zoroaster, Confucius, Mahavira (the founder of Jainism), the Buddha, the Hindu epic *Mahabharata,* the book of Leviticus, Hillel, Jesus, Mohammed, Kant, and many others.[77]

The terrorist attacks of September 2001 and subsequent acts by other Islamic extremist organizations appear to constitute a breach in the idea of common cross-cultural ethical standards, for they suggest that it is consistent with Islamic teachings, and perhaps even a duty, to kill "infidel" civilians of countries that are seen as a threat to Islam, or "apostates" who are members of other Muslim sects (for example, the Islamic State has justified killing Shiites on this ground).[78] The overwhelming majority of Islamic clerics and scholars, however, repudiate this view. Though the killings and the support they evoke among some radical Muslims suggest that agreement even on the prohibition of intentionally killing civilians is not entirely universal, it is very nearly so. So the search for an ethic that is global in the sense of drawing on aspects of ethics common to all or virtually all human societies could still meet with success. It would be easier to agree on common ethical principles if we could first agree on questions that are not ethical but factual, such as whether there is a god, or gods, and if there is, or are, whether he, she, or they has or have expressed his, her, or their will or wills in any of the various texts claimed by the adherents of different religions to be divinely inspired. Unfortunately, on these matters we seem to be even further from agreement than we are on basic ethical principles. If we are to achieve consensus on a common ethic, we are unlikely to be able to go beyond a few very broad principles. Hence, it may be said, these universally accepted ethical standards, if they exist at all, will not be the kind of thing that political leaders can draw on to show that they are justified in intervening in the affairs of another state.

Consider, for example, a country with a conservative, devoutly religious population that supports a hereditary monarch ruling in accordance with the laws of the dominant religion. Suppose that the citizens support the Golden Rule, since their religion endorses it, but are opposed to the idea of democracy. On what grounds can others tell them that their country should become a democracy?

The first point to make here is one that has already been mentioned. That a regime is not democratic does not mean that any form of intervention should take place. If the regime is not engaging in genocide, crimes against humanity, or similar atrocities, the question of intervention does not arise. It is reasonable to distinguish between rulers exercising traditional authority and those that gain and hold power by military supremacy and repressive measures. Second, however, if the people living under hereditary monarchies prefer their form of government to a democracy, that preference ought to be testable. Hence it is possible to envisage a country choosing, at free and open referenda held at regular intervals, not to have elections for political office. This could then itself be seen as giving legitimacy to the nondemocratic regime.

Nevertheless, the ultimate question of the relationship between democracy and sovereignty remains. What if the monarchy, though expressing confidence that its people support it, does not wish to hold a referendum on its existence? How can we give reasons, independent of our culture, for the view that legitimacy requires popular support rather than resting on, say, religious law? Attempts to argue for the separation of church and state will not work since that begs the question against the defenders of the religion that rejects such a separation. In the end the challenge cannot be met without confronting the basis for belief in the religion. But one cannot argue that the religious faith of people of a different culture is false while upholding a religious faith of one's own that rests on no firmer ground. That really would be cultural imperialism. In the end, at least as far as we are concerned with practices based on propositions about the existence of a god or gods and the authenticity of what are claimed to be divinely inspired scriptures, it is our capacity to reason that is the universal solvent. But this is not a question into which I can go further here.

Reforming the United Nations

As we have seen, the states that make up the United Nations have accepted that they have a responsibility to protect people against genocide, war crimes, ethnic cleansing, and crimes against humanity. When a government is manifestly failing to fulfill this responsibility to protect its own people, the responsibility falls to the international community, subject to there being reasonable grounds for believing it can meet that responsibility without doing greater harm than it prevents. There is, therefore, not only a right to intervene but also, in appropriate circumstances, a duty to intervene. To be able to meet this obligation the United Nations needs to be able to draw on sufficient military force to make intervention effective. Ideally, the United Nations would have sufficient revenue to have its own military forces available for that purpose to defend civilians anywhere in the world threatened with genocide or crimes against humanity.

I have also suggested, more tentatively, that there are reasons for moving toward a democratic idea of sovereignty which would make it easier to justify intervention against a government that was not even minimally democratic. The combination of these two suggestions is not without its irony, for the United Nations is scarcely a model of democracy. It was set up after the Second World War, and the Allies made sure they retained firm control of it. This is most evident in the Security Council, which is the body that decides on matters of security, including whether to intervene in a dispute, either militarily or by means of sanctions. The Security Council has five permanent members—the United States, the United Kingdom, France, China, and Russia—corresponding to the major powers that were victorious in 1945. The General Assembly elects ten additional states to the Security Council for two-year terms, but no substantive decision can be taken against the overt opposition of any of the five permanent members. The veto power of the permanent members, which was frequently used by both the Soviet Union and the United States during the cold war era, explains why during the 1960s and 1970s the Security Council effectively ignored the dominant conflict of the era, the Vietnam War.

There can be no justification today for giving special status to states that were great powers in 1945 but are no longer so today. Why should France and the United Kingdom have veto rights, and not Germany or Japan? Why should China be a permanent member, and not India or Brazil or Indonesia? Why should four of the five permanent members be European states or states of European origin when there is no permanent member from Africa or Latin America or southern or southeastern Asia, or from anywhere in the southern hemisphere? Is it desirable that four of the five permanent members are states with roots in Christianity, and none of them has Islamic roots?

What, then, should be done? Expanding the number of permanent members with veto rights runs the risk of making the Security Council unworkable. A better idea would be to replace the veto with a requirement that substantive decisions be made by a special majority, perhaps two-thirds or three-quarters, of a reconstituted Security Council. To this it may be objected that the existing Security Council works reasonably well, and it is not clear that we would get a Council that worked better if we changed it to make it fairer. But if it is important and desirable to move toward greater global governance in a variety of areas—trade and the environment, for example, as well as peace and the protection of human rights—then the present structure of the Security Council will make this difficult because it is a constant reminder that the institutions of global governance are dominated by the wealthiest, most powerful states. In the long run it is hard to see that giving special privileges to a small group of states will be the best way to maintain either the authority of the United Nations or world peace.

A second objection to reform of the Security Council is simply that it is unthinkable and would be perilous for the Council to take military action against the implacable opposition of the United States or whatever other military superpower may in time emerge. Hence political realism requires allowing such superpowers a veto. This claim may be true; but if it is, the veto rights of the superpowers should be seen for what they are: the exercise of might, not right. Moreover, the veto is not restricted to decisions involving military action. It is not unthinkable for a reformed Security Council to impose sanctions against one of the states that currently has a veto.

Compared to the Security Council, the General Assembly of the United Nations, which includes all 193 member states, seems more democratic. It is certainly not dominated by the same small circle of states that dominates the Security Council. The General Assembly, however, can take action only in very limited circumstances. Moreover, its appearance of egalitarianism is misleading. It is an assembly of the world's states, not of the world's people. Some of the states are not themselves democratic, but even if we overlook this, there is the problem—as in the case of the WTO—that the government of India has the same voting power as the government of Iceland. In fact, if the 97 states with the smallest populations were to line up against the 96 states with the largest populations, it is possible that a General Assembly resolution could be supported by a majority of states that represented a combined total of approximately 250 million people, while on the other side, the outvoted 96 largest states would represent 6.96 billion. States representing less than 4 percent of the total UN member-state population could carry the day in the General Assembly.[79]

There is an obvious solution to this problem, and it is not a new idea. At the end of the Second World War, when Britain's House of Commons debated the plan for a new United Nations, Ernest Bevin, the British foreign secretary, called for the "completion" of the UN design with "a world assembly elected directly from the people (to) whom the governments who form the United Nations are responsible."[80] In this respect the European Union, with its parliament directly elected by the people, could provide a model for a future, more democratic United Nations. The European Parliament has, at present, only very limited powers. Prior to the United Kingdom's vote to leave the European Union, the long-term plan was for these powers to expand as the people and governments of Europe become comfortable with the parliament playing a larger role. That expansion is now unlikely to take place anytime soon. There are major differences between the European Union and the United Nations. Most important to our present concerns is that, as we have seen, the European Union is in a position to set minimum standards for admission, including a democratic form of government and basic human rights guarantees. If the United Nations took a similar view and ceased to recognize undemocratic governments as eligible for United Nations membership, it could then turn its General Assembly into a democratically elected World Assembly, as Bevin envisaged. But arguably a United Nations that denied a voice to China, Saudi Arabia, and many other states would be less effective at maintaining world peace than one that was more inclusive.

A position halfway between the present system and one that excludes undemocratic governments is worth considering. The United Nations could remain open to all governments, irrespective of their form of government or observance of human rights, but it could replace the present General Assembly with a World Assembly consisting of delegates allocated to its member states in proportion to their population. The United Nations would then supervise democratic elections, in every member country, to elect this delegation. A country that refused to allow the United Nations to supervise the election of its delegation would have only one delegate, irrespective of its population. That system would provide experience in democracy for the citizens of most countries but would retain the inclusiveness that is an important feature of the United Nations.

Summing Up: State Sovereignty and a Global Ethic

A truly global ethic would not stop at or give great significance to state boundaries. State sovereignty has no *intrinsic* moral weight. What weight state sovereignty does have comes from the role that an international principle requiring respect for state sovereignty plays, in normal circumstances, in promoting peaceful relationships between states. It is a secondary principle, a rule of thumb that sums up the hard-won experience of many generations in avoiding war. This is not to deny that in the world in which we live, it carries great weight.

In this chapter I have argued that although we continue to live in a world of sovereign states and are still a long way from a truly global ethic, state sovereignty is no longer absolute. In addition to the world of sovereign states, we have a global community that is willing, where practicable and without too heavy a cost, to take up the burden of protecting people anywhere in the world from genocide, war crimes, ethnic cleansing, and crimes against humanity if the government that has the primary responsibility to protect them is manifestly failing to do so. The world has seen the horrific consequences of the failures of states to protect their citizens, and there is now a broad consensus that, if it is at all possible to prevent such atrocities, they should be prevented. To that extent, as Evans has put it, the "crude notion of Westphalian sovereignty that a state should be immune from international scrutiny and possible intervention, whatever the scale of the horrors perpetrated within its borders," has gone and is beyond redemption.[81]

What we still need is a United Nations that has both the authority to make the judgment that a state is so manifestly failing to meet its responsibility to protect its people that military intervention is required and the capacity to act on that judgment. If the world's most powerful states can accept the authority of the United Nations to be the "protector of last resort," and if those states will also provide the United Nations with the means to fulfill this responsibility, the world will have taken a crucial step toward becoming a global ethical community.

5 one community

Human Equality: Theory and Practice

An avalanche, a flood—these were the terms used to describe the response to public appeals for the victims of the terrorist attacks on the World Trade Center and the Pentagon of September 11, 2001. Three months after the disaster the total stood at $1.3 billion. Of this, according to a *New York Times* survey, $353 million was exclusively for the families of about 400 police officers, firefighters, and other uniformed personnel who died trying to save others. That came to $880,000 for each family. The families of the firefighters killed would have been adequately provided for even if there had been no donations at all. Their spouses received New York state pensions equal to the lost salaries, and their children are entitled to full scholarships to state universities. The federal government gave an additional $250,000 to families of police officers and firefighters killed on duty.[1] That families received close to a million dollars in cash on top of these considerable benefits may well leave us thinking that something has gone awry. But there was more to come. The American Red Cross received more than $564 million in donations and had trouble finding needy recipients for so much money. It therefore set aside nearly half the funds for future needs, including possible future victims of terrorist attacks. When that fact became public, a wave of criticism forced the organization to spend all the money on victims of the 9/11 attacks. To do so it abandoned any attempt to examine whether potential recipients needed help. Instead it drew a line across lower Manhattan and offered anyone living below that line the equivalent of three months' rent (or, if they owned their own apartment, three months' mortgage and maintenance payments) plus money for utilities and groceries, if they claimed they had been affected by the destruction of the World Trade Center. Most of the residents of the area below the line were not displaced or evacuated, but they were offered mortgage and rent assistance nevertheless. One woman was told she could have the cost of her psychiatric treatment reimbursed, even though she said she had been seeing her psychiatrist before September 11. Red Cross volunteers set up card tables in the lobbies of expensive apartment buildings in Tribeca, where financial analysts, lawyers, and rock stars live, to inform residents of the offer. The higher your rent, the more money you got. The Red Cross acknowledged that money was going to people who did not need it. According to a spokesperson, "In a program of this sort, we're not going to make judgments on people's needs."[2]

As the terrorists were planning the attack, the United Nations Children's Fund was getting ready to issue its 2002 report, *The State of the World's Children.*[3] According to the report, released to the media on September 13, 2001, more than ten million children under the age of five died each year from such preventable causes as malnutrition, unsafe water, and the lack of even the most basic health care. September 11, 2001, was just another day for most of the world's desperately poor people, so presumably close to 30,000 children under five died from these causes on that day—about ten times the number of victims of the terrorist attacks. The publication of these figures did not lead to an avalanche of money for UNICEF or other aid agencies helping to reduce infant mortality. In the year 2000 Americans made private donations for foreign aid of all kinds totaling about $4 per person in extreme poverty, or roughly $20 per family. New Yorkers who were living in lower Manhattan on September 11, 2001, whether wealthy or not, were able to receive an average of $5,300 per family.[4] The distance between these amounts encapsulates the way in which, for many people, the circle of concern for others stops at the boundaries of their own country—if it extends even that far. "Charity begins at home," people say, and, more explicitly, "We should take care of poverty in our own country before we tackle poverty abroad." They take it for granted that national boundaries carry moral weight and that it is worse to leave one of our fellow citizens in need than to leave someone from another country in that state. This is another aspect of the attitudes I described in the introduction. We put the interests of our fellow citizens far above those of citizens of other countries, whether the reason for doing so is to avoid damaging the economic interests of Americans at the cost of bringing floods to the people of Bangladesh or to help those in need at home rather than those in need abroad.

While we do all these things, most of us unquestioningly support declarations proclaiming that all humans have certain rights and that all human life is of equal worth. We condemn those who say that the life of a person of a different race or nationality is of less account than the life of a person of our own race or nation. Can we reconcile these attitudes? If those "at home" to whom we might give are already able to provide for their basic needs and seem poor only relative to our high standard of living, is the fact that they are our compatriots sufficient to give them priority over others with greater needs? Asking these questions leads us to consider to what extent we really can or should make one world a moral standard that transcends the nation-state.

A Preference for Our Own

The popular view that we may or even should favor those of "our own kind" conceals a deep disagreement about who our own kind are. In the late nineteenth century Henry Sidgwick, a professor of moral philosophy at Cambridge University, described the common moral outlook of his own times as follows:

> We should all agree that each of us is bound to show kindness to his parents and spouse and children, and to other kinsmen in a less degree: and to those who have rendered services to him, and any others whom he may have admitted to his intimacy and called friends: and to neighbors and to fellow-countrymen more than others: and perhaps we may say to those of our own race more than to black or yellow men, and generally to human beings in proportion to their affinity to ourselves.[5]

When I discuss this passage with my students, they have no problem with the various circles of moral concern Sidgwick mentions, until they get to the suggestion that we should give preference to our own race more than to "black or yellow men." At that point they disagree, often vehemently.

Coming a little closer to our own time, we can find defenders of a much more extreme form of partiality:

> We must be honest, decent, loyal and friendly to members of our blood and to no one else. What happens to the Russians, what happens to the Czechs, is a matter of

utter indifference to me. Such good blood of our own kind as there may be among the nations we shall acquire for ourselves, if necessary by taking away the children and bringing them up among us. Whether the other races live in comfort or perish of hunger interests me only in so far as we need them as slaves for our culture; apart from that it does not interest me. Whether or not 10,000 Russian women collapse from exhaustion while digging a tank ditch interests me only in so far as the tank ditch is completed for Germany.[6]

That quotation is from a speech by Heinrich Himmler to SS leaders in Poland in 1943. Why do I quote such dreadful sentiments? Because there are many who think it self-evident that we have special obligations to those nearer to us, including our children, our spouses, lovers and friends, and our compatriots. Reflecting on Sidgwick's description of the attitudes of Victorian England and on Himmler's much more stark preference for his own kind should subvert the belief that this kind of self-evidence is a sufficient ground for accepting a view as right. What is self-evident to some is not at all self-evident to others. Instead, we need another test of whether we have special obligations to those closer to us, such as our compatriots.

Ethics and Impartiality

How can we decide whether we have special obligations to our own kind, and if we do, who is our own kind in the relevant sense? Let us return for a moment to the countervailing ideal that there is some fundamental sense in which neither race nor nationality determines the value of a human being's life and experiences. This ideal rests on an understanding of impartiality that underlies the nature of the moral enterprise as its most significant thinkers have come to understand it. The twentieth-century Oxford philosopher R. M. Hare argued that for judgments to count as moral judgments they must be universalizable, that is, the speaker must be prepared to prescribe that they be carried out in all real and hypothetical situations, not only those in which she benefits from them but also those in which she is among those who lose.[7] Consistently with Hare's approach, one way of deciding whether there are special duties to our own kind is to ask whether accepting the idea of having these special duties can itself be justified from an impartial perspective.

In 1971, at a time when several million Bengalis were on the edge of starvation, living in refugee camps in India to escape from the massacres the Pakistani army was carrying out in what was then East Pakistan, I used a simple example to argue that we have an obligation to help strangers in distant lands. I asked the reader to imagine that on my way to give a lecture I pass a shallow pond. As I do so I see a small child fall into it and realize that she is in danger of drowning. I could easily wade in and pull her out, but I am wearing a new, expensive pair of shoes that would be ruined. Nevertheless, it would be grotesque to allow such a minor consideration to outweigh the good of saving a child's life. Saving the child is what I ought to do, and if I walk on I have done something seriously wrong.

Generalizing from this situation, I then argued that we are all, with respect to the Bengali refugees, in the same situation as the person who, at small cost, can save a child's life. The vast majority of us living in the developed countries of the world have disposable income that we spend on frivolities and luxuries, things of no more importance to us than avoiding getting our shoes and trousers muddy. If we do this when people are in danger of dying of starvation and when there are agencies that can, with reasonable efficiency, turn our modest donations into lifesaving food and basic medicines, how can we consider ourselves any better than the person who sees the child fall in the pond and walks on? Yet this was the situation at the time: the amount that had been given by the rich countries was less than a sixth of what was needed to sustain the refugees. Britain had given rather more than most countries, but it had still given only one-thirtieth as much as it was prepared to spend on the nonrecoverable costs of building the Concorde supersonic jetliner (which proved to be a short-lived experiment).

I examined various possible differences that people might find between the two situations and argued that they were not sufficiently significant, in moral terms, to shield us from the judgment that in failing to give to the Bengali refugees, we were doing something that was seriously wrong. In particular, I wrote,

> it makes no moral difference whether the person I help is a neighbor's child ten yards from me or a Bengali whose name I shall never know, ten thousand miles away.[8]

As far as I am aware, no one has disputed this claim in respect of distance per se—that is, the difference between ten yards and ten thousand miles. Of course, the degree of certainty that we can have that our assistance will get to the right person and will really help that person may be affected by distance, and that can make a difference to what we ought to do, but that is a different matter and will depend on the particular circumstances in which we find ourselves. What people *have* disputed, however, is that our obligation to help a stranger in another country is as great as the obligation to help one of our own neighbors or compatriots. Surely, they say, we have special obligations to our neighbors and fellow citizens and to our family and friends that we do not have to strangers in another country.[9]

These objections are reminiscent of the response William Godwin received to his book *Political Justice,* which shocked and electrified British society at the time of the French Revolution. In the book's most famous passage Godwin imagined a situation in which a palace is on fire and two people are trapped inside it. One of them is a great benefactor of humanity—Godwin chose as his example Archbishop Fénelon, "at the moment when he was conceiving the project of his immortal *Telemachus.*" The other person trapped is the archbishop's chambermaid. The choice of Fénelon seems odd today since few people know his "immortal" work, but let's suppose we share Godwin's high opinion of Fénelon. Whom should we save? Godwin answers that we should save Fénelon because by doing so we would be helping thousands who have been cured of "error, vice and consequent unhappiness" by reading *Telemachus.* Then he goes on to make his most controversial claim:

Supposing I had been myself the chambermaid, I ought to have chosen to die rather than that Fénelon should have died. The life of Fénelon was really preferable to that of the chambermaid. But understanding is the faculty that perceives the truth of this and similar propositions; and justice is the principle that regulates my conduct accordingly. It would have been just in the chambermaid to have preferred the archbishop to herself. To have done otherwise would have been a breach of justice.

Supposing the chambermaid had been my wife, my mother or my benefactor. That would not alter the truth of the proposition. The life of Fénelon would still be more valuable than that of the chambermaid; and justice— pure, unadulterated justice—would still have preferred that which was most valuable. Justice would have taught

me to save the life of Fénelon at the expense of the other.
What magic is there in the pronoun "my" to overturn the
decisions of everlasting truth? My wife or my mother may
be a fool or a prostitute, malicious, lying or dishonest. If
they be, of what consequence is it that they are mine?[10]

In comparison to Godwin's claims, my argument was quite
timid. I am not suggesting that one must allow one's wife or
mother or, for that matter, children to die in order to save a
stranger or even several strangers; but, like Godwin, I am urging
that we take a universal perspective and recognize that when it
comes to saving the life of a stranger at a quite modest cost to
ourselves, the far greater interest of the stranger should prevail
over our own much more minor interest.

One of Godwin's critics was Samuel Parr, a well-known liberal clergyman of the time. He preached and subsequently published a sermon that was a sustained critique of "universal phi-
lanthropy."[11] As the text for his sermon, Parr takes an injunction
from Paul's epistle to the Galatians, in which Paul offers yet another variant on who is of our own kind: "As we have, therefore,
opportunity, let us do good unto all men, especially unto them
who are of the household of faith."[12] In Paul's words Parr finds a
Christian text that rejects equal concern for all and instead urges
greater concern for those to whom we have a special connection.
Parr defends Paul by arguing that to urge us to show impartial
concern for all is to demand something that human beings cannot, in general and most of the time, give. "The moral obligations of men," he writes, "cannot be stretched beyond their
physical powers."[13] Our real desires, our lasting and strongest
passions, are not for the good of our species as a whole but, at
best, for the good of those who are close to us.

Modern critics of what is variously called impartialism, universalism, or cosmopolitanism hold that an advocate of an impartial ethic would make a poor parent, lover, spouse, or friend because the very idea of such personal relationships involves being partial toward the other person with whom one is in the relationship. This means giving more consideration to the interests of your child, lover, spouse, or friend than to those of a stranger, and from the standpoint of an impartial ethic this seems wrong. Feminist philosophers in particular tend to stress the importance of personal relationships, which they accuse male moral philosophers of neglecting. Nel Noddings, the author of *Caring*, limits our obligation to care to those with whom we can be in some kind of relationship. Hence, she states, we are "not obliged to care for starving children in Africa."[14]

Those who favor an impartial ethic have responded to these objections by denying that they are required to hold that we should be impartial in every aspect of our lives. Godwin himself wrote (in a memoir of Mary Wollstonecraft after her death following the birth of her and Godwin's first child),

A sound morality requires that *nothing human should be regarded by us as indifferent;* but it is impossible we should not feel the strongest interest for those persons whom we know most intimately, and whose welfare and sympathies are united to our own. True wisdom will recommend to us individual attachments; for with them our minds are more thoroughly maintained in activity and life than they can be under the privation of them, and it is better that man should be a living being, than a stock or a stone. True virtue will sanction this recommendation; since it is the object of virtue to produce happiness; and since the

man who lives in the midst of domestic relations will have
many opportunities of conferring pleasure, minute in
the detail, yet not trivial in the amount, without inter-
fering with the purposes of general benevolence. Nay, by
kindling his sensibility, and harmonising his soul, they
may be expected, if he is endowed with a liberal and
manly spirit, to render him more prompt in the service
of strangers and the public.[15]

In the wake of his own grieving feelings for his beloved wife
from whom he had been so tragically parted, Godwin found an
impartial justification for partial affections. In our own times,
Hare's two-level version of utilitarianism leads to the same conclusion. Hare argues that in everyday life it will often be too difficult to work out the consequences of every decision we make,
and if we were to try to do so we would risk getting it wrong
because of our personal involvement and the pressures of the
situation. To guide our everyday conduct we need a set of principles of which we are aware without a lot of reflection. These
principles form the intuitive, or everyday, level of morality. In a
calmer or more philosophical moment, on the other hand, we
can reflect on the nature of our moral intuitions and ask whether
we have developed the right ones, that is, the ones that will lead
to the greatest good, impartially considered. When we engage
in this reflection, we are moving to the critical level of morality,
which informs our thinking about what principles we should
follow at the everyday level. Thus the critical level serves as a
testing ground for moral intuitions.[16] We can use it to test the list
of special obligations suggested by the common moral sense of
Victorian England as described by Sidgwick: to parents, spouse,
children, other kin, those who have rendered services to you,
friends, neighbors, fellow countrymen, to "those of our own race

. . . and generally to human beings in proportion to their affinity to ourselves." Do any of these survive the demand for impartial justification, and if so, which ones?

Assessing Partial Preferences

The first set of preferences mentioned by Sidgwick—family, friends, and those who have rendered services to us—stands up quite well. The love of parents for their children and the desire of parents to give preference to their children over the children of strangers go very deep. It may be rooted in our nature as social mammals with offspring who need our help during a long period of dependence when they are not capable of fending for themselves. We can speculate that the children of parents who did not care for them would have been less likely to survive, and thus uncaring parents did not pass their genes on to future generations as frequently as caring parents did. Bonds between parents and children (and especially between mothers and children, for in earlier periods a baby not breast-fed by its mother was very unlikely to survive) are therefore found in all human cultures.

To say that a certain kind of behavior is universal and has its roots in our evolutionary history does not necessarily mean that it cannot be changed, nor does it mean that it should not be changed. Nevertheless, in this particular case the experience of utopian social experiments has shown that the desire of parents to care for their children is highly resistant to change. In the early days of the Israeli kibbutzim, the more radical of these socialist agricultural collectives sought to equalize the upbringing of children by having all children born to members of the kibbutz brought up communally in a special children's house. For parents to show particular love and affection for their own child was frowned upon. Nevertheless, mothers used to sneak into the communal nursery at night to kiss and hold their sleeping children. Presumably, if they shared the ideals of the kibbutz, they felt guilty for doing so.[17]

So even if, like the founders of these collective settlements, we were to decide that it is undesirable for parents to favor their own children, we would find such favoritism very difficult to eradicate. Any attempt to do so would have high costs and would require constant supervision or coercion. Unless we are so intent on suppressing parental bias that we are willing to engage in an all-out campaign of intense moral pressure backed up with coercive measures and draconian sanctions, we are bound to find that most parents constantly favor their children in ways that cannot be directly justified on the basis of equal consideration of interests. If we were to engage in such a campaign, we might well bring about guilt and anxiety in parents who want to do things for their children that society now regards as wrong. Such guilt will itself be a source of much unhappiness. Will the gains arising from diminished partiality for one's children outweigh this? That seems unlikely because for the children themselves the care of loving and partial parents is likely to be better than the care of impartial parents or impartial community-employed caretakers. There is evidence, too, that children are more likely to be abused when brought up by people who are not their biological parents.[18] Given the unavoidable constraints of human nature and the importance of bringing children up in loving homes, there is an impartial justification for approving of social practices that presuppose that parents will show some degree of partiality toward their children.

It is even easier to find an impartial reason for accepting love and friendship. If loving relationships and relationships of friendship are necessarily partial, they are also, for most people, at the core of anything that can approximate to a good life. Very few human beings can live happy, fulfilled lives without being attached to particular other human beings. To suppress these partial affections would destroy something of great value and therefore cannot be justified from an impartial perspective.

Bernard Williams claimed that this defense of love and friendship demands "one thought too many."[19] We should, he says, visit our sick friend in hospital because he is our friend and is in hospital, not because we have calculated that visiting sick friends is a more efficient way of maximizing utility than anything else we could do with our time. This objection may have some force if pressed against those who claim we should be thinking about the impartial justification of love or friendship at the time when we are deciding whether to visit our sick friend; but it is precisely the point of two-level utilitarianism to explain why we *should* have an extra thought when we are thinking at the critical level rather than at the level of everyday moral decision making.

Consider the idea, supported to various degrees in the passages I have quoted from Sidgwick and Himmler, to the effect that whites should care more for and give priority to the interests of other whites, or that Aryans should give priority to the interests of others of their blood. These ideas have had, in their time, an intuitive appeal very similar to the intuitive appeal of the idea that we have obligations to favor family and friends. But racist attitudes have contributed to many of the worst crimes of our era, and it is not easy to see that they have done any good, certainly not good that can compensate for the misery to which they have led. Moreover, although the suppression of racism is difficult, the hope that it will not prove impossible can be supported by the existence of genuinely multiracial societies and, to some extent, by the progress made since desegregation in the American South. Racism still exists in the South—and in the North—but most white southerners are not at all troubled by sharing a bus seat with an African American, and even those who fought to defend segregation have, by and large, come to accept that they were wrong. Racism is a form of partialism that we can and should oppose because our opposition can be effective in preventing great harm being done to innocent people.

Thus we can turn Williams's aphorism against him: philosophers who take his view have one thought too few. To be sure, to think *always* as a philosopher would mean that, in our roles as parents, spouse, lover, or friend, we would indeed have one thought too many. But if we *are* philosophers, or students of philosophy, there should be times when we reflect critically on our intuitions—indeed not only philosophers but all thoughtful people should do this. If we were all simply to accept our feelings without the kind of extra reflection we have just been engaged in, we would not be able to decide which of our intuitive inclinations to endorse and support and which to oppose. The fact that some intuitive responses are widely held is not evidence that they are justified. Some of them—roughly, those we share with others of our species, irrespective of their cultural background— are responses that, for most of our evolutionary history, have been well suited to the survival and reproduction of beings like us. Others—roughly, those we do not share with people from different cultures—may be the product of our particular cultural history. Neither the biological nor the cultural basis of our intuitive responses provides us with a sound reason for taking them as a guide to how we ought to live.

To return to the issue of partiality for family, lovers, and friends, we have seen that there are impartial reasons for accepting some degree of partiality here; but how much? In broad terms we should accept as much partiality as is necessary to promote the goods mentioned above, but no more. Thus the partiality of parents for their children must extend to providing them with the necessities of life and also to satisfying their more important wants, and it must allow them to feel loved and protected; but there is no requirement to satisfy every desire a child expresses, and there are many reasons we should not do so. If we live in affluent countries like the United States, most European countries, Canada, and Australia, we should bring up our children to know that others are in much greater need than we are and to be aware of the possibility of helping them by, for example, reducing our unnecessary spending. Our children should also learn to think critically about the forces that lead to high levels of consumption and to be aware of the environmental costs of this way of living. With lovers and friends, something similar applies: the relationships require partiality, but they are stronger where there are shared values or at least respect for the values that each holds. Where the values shared include concern for the welfare of others, irrespective of whether they are friends or strangers, then the partiality demanded by friendship or love will not be so great as to interfere in a serious way with the capacity for helping those in great need.

What of the other categories on Sidgwick's list of those to whom we are under a special obligation to show kindness: parents, kin, "those who have rendered services," neighbors, and fellow countrymen? Can all of these categories be justified from an impartial perspective? The inclusion of "those who have rendered services" is seen by ethicists who rely on intuition to be a straightforward case of the obligation of gratitude.[20] From a two-level perspective, however, the intuition that we have a duty of gratitude is not an insight into some independent moral truth but something desirable because it helps to encourage reciprocity, which makes cooperation and all its benefits possible. Again, evolutionary theory can help us to see why reciprocity and with it the sense of gratitude should have evolved and why it is, in some form or other, a universal norm in all human societies. (To give such an evolutionary explanation, however, says nothing about the motives people have when they engage in cooperative behavior, any more than explaining sexual behavior in terms of reproduction suggests that people are motivated to have sex because they wish to have children.)

Once a duty of gratitude is recognized, it is impossible to exclude parents from the circle of those to whom a special duty of kindness is owed. Parents have generally rendered countless services to their children, so we can hardly subscribe to a general principle of gratitude without recognizing a duty of children toward their parents. The exception here would be children who have been maltreated or abandoned by their parents—and it is the exception that proves the rule, in the sense that it shows that the obligation is one of gratitude, not one based on blood relationships.

Another of Sidgwick's categories, our neighbors, can be handled in the same way. Geographical proximity is not in itself of any moral significance, but it may give us more opportunities to enter into relationships of friendship and mutually beneficial reciprocity. Increasing mobility and communication have, over the course of the past century, eroded the extent to which neighbors are important to us. We walk past our neighbors, barely nodding at them as we talk on our cell phones to distant friends. When we run out of sugar, we don't go next door to borrow some, as our parents or grandparents used to do, because we will soon be passing the supermarket anyway. In these circumstances it becomes doubtful if we have special duties of kindness to our neighbors at all, apart from, perhaps, a duty to do the things that neighbors can most easily do, such as feeding the cat when you are on vacation.

Kin, the next on Sidgwick's list, is an expression that ranges from the sibling with whom you played as a child and with whom you may later share the task of caring for your parents to the distant cousin you have not heard from in decades. The extent to which we have a special obligation to our kin should vary accordingly. Kin networks can be important sources of love, friendship, and mutual support, and then they will generate impartially justifiable reasons for promoting these goods. But if that cousin you have not heard from in decades suddenly asks for a loan because she wants to buy a new house, is there an impartially defensible ground for believing you are under a greater obligation to help her than you would be to help an unrelated, equally distant acquaintance? At first glance, no, but perhaps a better answer is that it depends on whether there is a recognized system of cooperation among relatives. In rural areas of India, for example, such relationships between relatives can play an important role in providing assistance when needed and thus in reducing harm when something goes awry.[21] Under these circumstances there is an impartial reason for recognizing and supporting this practice. In the absence of any such system, there is not. (In different cultures, the more impersonal insurance policy plays the same harm-reduction role and thus reduces the need for a system of special obligations to kin, no doubt with both good and bad effects.)

The Ethical Significance of the Nation-State

What impartial reasons can there be for favoring one's compatriots over foreigners? On some views of nationality, to be a member of the same nation is like an extended version of being kin. Michael Walzer expresses this view when, in discussing immigration policy, he writes,

> Clearly, citizens often believe themselves morally bound to open the doors of their country—not to anyone who

wants to come in, perhaps, but to a particular group of outsiders, recognized as national or ethnic "relatives." In this sense, states are like families rather than clubs, for it is a feature of families that their members are morally connected to people they have not chosen, who live outside the household.[22]

Germany's former citizenship law embodied the sense of nationality that Walzer has in mind. Descendants of German farmers and craft workers who settled in eastern Europe in the eighteenth century are recognized in the German constitution as having the right to return to Germany and become citizens, although most of them do not speak German and come from families who have not set foot in the country for generations. On the other hand, before new citizenship laws came into effect in 2000 foreign guest workers could live in Germany for decades without becoming eligible for citizenship, and the same was true of their children, even though they were born in Germany, educated in German schools, and had never lived anywhere else. While Germany's pre-2000 laws were an extreme case of racial or ethnic preference, most other countries have, for much of their history, used racist criteria to select immigrants and thus citizens. As late as 1970, when immigrants of European descent were being actively encouraged to become Australian citizens, the White Australia policy prevented non-European immigrants from settling in Australia.

We should reject racist immigration policies, for the same reason that we should reject racism. Neither race nor ethnicity should be a requirement for citizenship. It is therefore impossible to defend the intuition that we ought to favor our fellow citizens because they are a kind of extended kin. Citizenship and kinship are distinct.

Sandel on Solidarity and Loyalty

Michael Sandel, in his widely read book *Justice,* argues that we have an obligation of solidarity to others in groups that we identify with, such as our compatriots. He denies that solidarity is merely "a prejudice for our own kind," pointing out that it can even impose obligations on us to do things for others, for example, to make reparation for wrongs our country has done to others. This is true, and it shows that when we identify ourselves as a member of a group, we do not do so only in order to benefit ourselves or those like us. It might still be the case, however, that this kind of identification and the feelings that flow from it are aspects of our psychology about which we should, on reflection, have considerable reservations. That thought is reinforced by the appeal Sandel makes to the case of Robert E. Lee. As Sandel tells the story, at the outbreak of the U.S. Civil War, Lee was serving in the Union army and was opposed to the secession of the southern states. Lincoln offered him the leadership of the Union army, but Lee, who was from Virginia, a slaveholding state that had joined the Confederacy, replied that he could not fight against "my relatives, my children, my home." Instead, as events unfolded he became the leader of the army of the Confederacy. Sandel concedes that, since the cause Lee sided with included slavery as well as secession, Lee's decision is "hard to defend"; yet he also argues that loyalty is a virtue and should carry some moral weight, even if not enough to justify Lee's choice:

> Unless we take loyalty seriously, as a claim with moral
> import, we can't make sense of Lee's dilemma as a moral
> dilemma at all. If loyalty is a sentiment with no genuine
> moral weight, then Lee's predicament is simply a conflict
> between morality on the one hand and mere feeling or

prejudice on the other. But by conceiving it that way, we misunderstand the moral stakes.

The merely psychological reading of Lee's predicament misses the fact that we not only sympathize with people like him but also admire them, not necessarily for the choices they make, but for the quality of character their deliberation reflects. What we admire is the disposition to see and bear one's life circumstance as a reflectively situated being—claimed by the history that implicates me in a particular life, but self-conscious of its particularity, and so alive to competing claims and wider horizons. To have character is to live in recognition of one's (sometime conflicting) encumbrances.[23]

This is an eloquent statement of the case for loyalty; but it also enables us to see clearly what is wrong with the idea of loyalty as a virtue, independently of the value of the cause or group to which we are being loyal. Once again, an understanding of the circumstances in which our species evolved makes it easy enough to understand why we should have positive feelings about people who are loyal. Groups, large or small, will benefit from the loyalty of their members, and those groups that fail to cultivate loyalty are likely to be at a disadvantage in competing with other groups. But that is no reason why a "reflectively situated being" ought to feel "claimed by the history that implicates me in a particular life." If Lee had really reflected adequately on what was right he would have recognized that he should set aside, as a factor likely to distort proper reflection, his feelings of loyalty to his native Virginia. Then he would have shown more (and better) character—and the Civil War would have reached the same outcome but most likely with far fewer casualties. Lee's loyalty was tragic, and not only for him.

A Community of Reciprocity

Eamonn Callan has suggested that to be a citizen in a state is to be engaged in a community of reciprocity:

So far as citizens come to think of justice as integral to a particular political community they care about, in which their own fulfillment and that of their fellow citizens are entwined in a common fate, the sacrifices and compromises that justice requires cannot be sheer loss in the pursuit of one's own good.[24]

Walter Feinberg takes a similar view:

The source of national identity is . . . connected to a web of mutual aid that extends back in time and creates future obligations and expectations.[25]

The outpouring of help from Americans for the families of the victims of September 11 was a striking instance of this web of mutual aid, based on the sense that Americans will help each other in times of crisis. In more normal times, Americans can still feel that by their taxes they are contributing to the provision of services that benefit their fellow Americans by providing social security and medical care when they retire or become disabled, fight crime, defend the country from attack, protect the environment, maintain national parks, educate their children, and come to the rescue in case of floods, earthquakes, and other natural disasters. If they are old enough, they may have served in the armed forces in wartime, and if they are younger they might have to do so in the future.

It is therefore possible to see the obligation to assist one's fellow citizens ahead of citizens of other countries as an obligation of reciprocity. It is reasonable to hold that there is a limited obligation of this kind, though one that is attenuated by the size of the community and the lack of direct contact between or even bare knowledge of other members of the community. But it can be important to build and maintain a sense of community, and this is sufficient reason for giving some priority to aiding one's fellow citizens ahead of citizens of other countries. This priority should, however, be balanced against the amount of good that our aid will do.

The Imagined Community

If reciprocity alone is not enough to show why we have a significantly stronger obligation to our fellow citizens than to anyone else, one might try to supplement this idea by recourse to Benedict Anderson's account of a nation as an "imagined political community," one that lives only in the minds of those who see themselves as citizens of the same nation.[26] Though citizens never encounter most of the other members of the nation, they think of themselves as sharing an allegiance to common institutions and values, such as a constitution, democratic procedures, principles of toleration, the separation of church and state, and the rule of law. The imagined community makes up for the lack of a real, face-to-face community in which there would be personal ties and more concrete obligations of reciprocity. Acknowledging special obligations to other members of the nation can then be seen as part of what it takes to form and maintain this imagined community.

Anderson's conception of nationalism is an account of how the idea of belonging to a nation took hold in the modern world. Because it is a description and not a prescription, it cannot ground a moral argument for the importance of maintaining the imagined communities that he describes. It is nevertheless an illuminating account, precisely because it shows that the modern idea that we owe special loyalty to our national community is not based on a community that exists independently of the way we think about ourselves. If Anderson is right, and the modern idea of the nation rests on a community we imagine ourselves to be part of rather than one that we really are part of, then it is also possible for us to imagine ourselves to be part of a different community. That fits well with the view I have defended in each chapter of this book: the complex set of developments we refer to as globalization should lead us to reconsider the moral significance we currently place on national boundaries. We need to ask whether it will, in the long run, be better if we continue to live in the imagined communities we know as nation-states or if we become more open to the idea that we are members of an imagined community of the world. I have already offered several arguments for the latter view. Our problems are now too intertwined to be well resolved in a system consisting of nation-states, in which citizens give their primary, near-exclusive loyalty to their own nation-state rather than to the larger global community. Moreover, such a system has not led to a morally adequate response to the pressing needs of those living in extreme poverty. Imagining ourselves to be part of a national community seems fine when we think of it as broadening our concerns beyond more limited tribal loyalties, but it is less appealing when we think of it as erecting fences against the rest of the world.

An Argument from Efficiency

Robert Goodin defends a system of special obligations to our compatriots "as an administrative device for discharging our general duties more efficiently."[27] If you are sick and in hospital, Goodin argues, it is best to have a particular doctor made responsible for your care rather than leaving it up to all the hospital doctors in general; so too, he says, it is best to have one state that is clearly responsible for protecting and promoting the interests of every individual within its territory. There is no doubt something in this, but it is an argument with very limited application in the real world. In any case, efficiency in administration within units is one thing, and the distribution of resources between units is another. Goodin recognizes this:

> If there has been a misallocation of some sort, so that some states have been assigned care of many more people than they have been assigned resources to care for them, then a reallocation is called for.[28]

While it may, other things being equal, be more efficient for states to look after their own citizens, this is not so if wealth is so unequally distributed that an affluent couple spends more on going to the theater than many others have to live on for a full year. In these circumstances the argument from efficiency, understood in terms of gaining the maximum utility for each available dollar, far from being a defense of special duties toward our compatriots, provides grounds for holding that any such duties are overwhelmed by the much greater good that we can do abroad. That is the conclusion we should draw from our scrutiny of several arguments for the ethical significance of the nation-state.

Justice Within States and Between States

Christopher Wellman has suggested three further impartial reasons for thinking it may be particularly important to prevent economic inequality from becoming too great *within* a society rather than *between* societies. The first is that political equality within a society may be adversely affected by economic inequality within a society but is not adversely affected by economic inequality between societies; the second is that inequality is not something that is bad in itself but something that is bad insofar as it leads to oppressive relationships, and hence we are right to be more concerned about inequality among people living in the same country than we are about inequality between people living in different countries who are not in a meaningful relationship with each other; and the third is a point about the comparative nature of wealth and poverty.[29]

Wellman's first two points are at least partly answered by the phenomenon that underlies so much of the argument of this book: increasingly, we are facing issues that affect the entire planet. Whatever it is we value about political equality, including the opportunity to participate in the decisions that affect us, globalization means that we should value equality between societies and, at the global level, at least as much as we value political equality within one society. Globalization also means that there can be oppressive relationships at the global scale as well as within a society, and we have already seen, especially in chapters 2 and 3 of this book, that that is the case.

Marx provided the classic formulation of Wellman's third point:

> A house may be large or small; as long as the surrounding houses are equally small it satisfies all social demands for a dwelling. But let a palace arise beside the little house, and it shrinks from a little house to a hut . . . however high it may shoot up in the course of civilization, if the neighboring palace grows to an equal or even greater extent, the occupant of the relatively small house will feel more and more uncomfortable, dissatisfied and cramped with its four walls.[30]

But today it is a mistake to think that people compare themselves only with their fellow citizens (or with all their fellow citizens). Inhabitants of rural Mississippi, for example, may not often compare themselves with New Yorkers, or at least not in regard to income. Their lifestyle is so different that income is merely one element in a whole package. On the other hand, many Mexicans obviously do look longingly north of the border and think how much better off they would be financially if they could live in the United States. They reveal their thoughts by trying to get across the border. And the same can be true of people who are not in close geographical proximity, as we can see from the desperate attempts of Africans to cross the Mediterranean to enter Europe and of Chinese to travel illegally to the United States, not because they are being politically persecuted but because they already have enough of an idea about life in those far-away countries to want to live there.

Despite the different picture that globalization offers, let us grant that there are some reasons for thinking we should place a higher priority on avoiding marked economic inequality within a given society than across the entire range of the planet's inhabitants. Wellman's three points can be granted some weight when they are brought against the strong claim that it is, other things being equal, *no less* desirable to eliminate marked economic inequality between any of the world's inhabitants than it is to eliminate it within a single society. But the weight we should give them is limited and subject to particular circumstances. In particular, the question of whether to seek greater equality within societies or between societies arises only if we cannot do both. Sometimes we can. We can increase taxes on people in rich countries who have higher incomes or leave large sums to their heirs and use the revenue to increase aid to those people in the world's poorest countries who have incomes well below average even for the country in which they are living. That would reduce inequality both in the poor countries and in the rich countries as well as, slightly, between countries.

Granted, if we live in a rich country we could reduce inequality within our own society even further if we used the revenue generated by taxes on the wealthiest people to help the worst-off within our own society. But even if we accept Wellman's arguments, that would be the wrong choice. For then we would be choosing to reduce inequality within our own country rather than reducing inequality both within poor countries and between countries. Wellman has offered reasons why it may be more important to focus on inequality within a country than on inequality between countries, but that is not the same as finding reasons for giving greater priority to overcoming inequality within one's own society than in any other society. If I, living in America, can do more to reduce inequality in, say, Kenya by helping those at the bottom of Kenyan society than I can do to reduce inequality in my own country, then Wellman has not given me any grounds for preferring to reduce inequality in America—and if giving money to those near the bottom of the economic ladder in Kenya will both reduce inequality there and reduce inequality between countries, that seems the best thing to do. Wellman has failed to find any magic in the pronoun "my."

In any case, in the present situation we have duties to foreigners that override duties to our fellow citizens. For even if inequality is often relative, the state of extreme poverty I described in chapter 3 is a state of poverty that is not relative to someone else's wealth. Reducing the number of human beings living in extreme poverty is surely a more urgent priority than reducing the relative poverty caused by some people living in palaces while others live in modest but adequate houses. Here Sidgwick's account of the common moral consciousness of his time is in agreement.

After giving the list of special obligations I quoted above, he continues as follows:

> And to all men with whom we may be brought into relation we are held to owe slight services, and such as may be rendered without inconvenience: but those who are in distress or urgent need have a claim on us for special kindness.

Rawls and *The Law of Peoples*

I have already referred to the remarkable fact that the most influential work on justice written in twentieth-century America, John Rawls's *A Theory of Justice*, does not address the issue of justice between societies. Rawls did write about the issue of justice beyond the borders of our own society in a later, much shorter work, *The Law of Peoples* (1999). There he argued that well-off societies have significant obligations toward struggling societies, but he does not focus on obligations toward individuals who are currently destitute in other countries. The book is, after all, called *The Law of Peoples*, not, for example, *A Theory of Global Justice*.

Here is one example of how the book Rawls has written differs from the book he might have written. Rawls asks us to consider a world in which there are two societies, each of which satisfies internally the two principles of justice in *A Theory of Justice* and in which the worst-off representative person in the first society is worse off than the worst-off representative person in the second. He then supposes that it is possible to arrange a global redistribution that would improve the lot of the worst-off representative person in the first society while allowing both societies to continue to satisfy his two principles of justice internally. We are, in other words, being asked to consider two societies, each of which is just if we confine our gaze to its own boundaries, but one of which has people in it who are worse off than anyone in the other society. Should we prefer a redistribution that would lessen the gap between the worst-off people in the two societies? No, Rawls says: "The Law of Peoples is indifferent between the two distributions."[31]

In *A Theory of Justice* Rawls argued for a system of justice in which "no one is advantaged or disadvantaged in the choice of principles by the outcome of natural chance or the contingency of social circumstances."[32] Now, however, he declares his theory to be indifferent to the consequences of something as contingent as which side of a state border one happens to live on. These two positions cannot be reconciled. In *The Law of Peoples* Rawls uses an approach quite different from that of *A Theory of Justice.* Though both books refer to an "original position," in the earlier work the deliberating parties in the original position weigh up alternative principles of justice, such as classical utilitarianism and moral perfectionism, and choose between them. In the original position of *The Law of Peoples,* on the other hand, the deliberating parties—whose task now is to decide on a framework for international relationships—do not even consider classical utilitarianism as a possible principle by which they might regulate the way in which peoples behave toward each other. This is because, Rawls tells us,

> a classical, or average, utilitarian principle would not be accepted by peoples, since no people organized by its government is prepared to count, *as a first principle,* the benefits for another people as outweighing the hardships imposed on itself.[33]

This claim, which looks like an odd anticipation of President George W. Bush's assertion that "first things first are the people who live in America," is no doubt true, at the level of sociological description of peoples organized as governments in existing societies. But how does that justify Rawls in using it as a conclusive ground for ruling out of consideration any possibility that peoples *would* choose to accept this principle, if they were choosing in the original position, in which they did not know which society they would be living in? Why should we regard what governments are *now* prepared to accept as decisive about what they *would* accept, if they were choosing impartially?

Another strange aspect of *The Law of Peoples* is Rawls's readiness to invoke, against the idea of economic redistribution between countries, arguments that could easily be brought—indeed have been brought—against economic redistribution between individuals or families *within* the same state. Thus he invites us to consider an example of two countries that are at the same level of wealth and have the same size population. The first decides to industrialize while the second prefers a more pastoral, leisurely society and does not. Decades later, the first is twice as wealthy as the second. Assuming that both societies freely made their own decisions, Rawls asks whether the industrializing society should be taxed to give funds to the pastoral one. That, he says, "seems unacceptable."[34] But if Rawls finds this unacceptable, how does he answer the critics of his position in *A Theory of Justice* who find it unacceptable for a person who has worked hard and achieved wealth to be taxed in order to support someone who has led a more relaxed life and so is now, in terms of resources held, among the worst-off members of society? Both cases raise a problem for anyone who supports the redistribution of wealth, and if the problem can be answered in the case of redistribution within a society, it should be possible to answer it in the case of redistribution between societies.

Rawls does urge, in *The Law of Peoples,* that "well-ordered peoples have a *duty* to assist burdened societies," that is, those societies that "lack the political and cultural traditions, the human capital and know-how, and, often, the material and technological resources needed to be well-ordered."[35] The duty extends only to the requirement of assistance to help the societies to become "well-ordered," by which Rawls means a society that is designed to advance the good of its members and is effectively regulated by a public conception of justice.[36] In considering what can help a society to become well-ordered, Rawls emphasizes the need for societies to develop a suitable culture, for he conjectures that "there is no society anywhere in the world—except for marginal cases—with resources so scarce that it could not, were it reasonably and rationally organized and governed, become well-ordered."[37] This conjecture may or may not be correct, but the emphasis on the need for a change of culture leaves untouched the plight of individuals who are dying from starvation, malnutrition, or easily preventable diseases *right now,* in countries that presently lack the capacity to provide for the needs of all their citizens.

Rawls says, in the course of discussing contrary views of international justice advanced by Charles Beitz and Thomas Pogge, that he shares their goals "of attaining liberal or decent institutions, securing human rights and meeting basic needs." These goals are, he believes, "covered by the duty of assistance."[38] But if this means that wealthy societies have a duty of assistance to help individuals who are starving or otherwise unable to satisfy their basic needs, it fails to receive the emphasis it deserves. Instead, Rawls writes of the duty of assistance always as part of a much broader project of helping *peoples* to attain liberal or decent institutions. As Leif Wenar has said of *The Law of Peoples,* "Rawls in this work is concerned more with the legitimacy of global coercion than he is with the arbitrariness of the fates of citizens of different countries."[39] As a result, the economic concerns of individuals play no role in Rawls's laws for regulating international relations. In the absence of mass starvation or abuse of human rights, Rawls's principles of international justice do not extend to aiding individuals. Tragically, in the years that have passed since the publication of *The Law of Peoples,* tens of millions of people have died from poverty-related illnesses in countries that have yet to gain liberal or decent institutions and become "well-ordered." The issue of how the rich countries and their citizens are to respond to the needs of the hundreds of millions of people in extreme poverty has an urgency that overrides the longer-term goal of changing the culture of societies that are not effectively regulated by a public conception of justice. But that issue is not one to which the author of *A Theory of Justice* ever gave serious attention.

The Reality

There are few strong grounds for giving preference to the interests of one's fellow citizens, at least when subjected to the test of impartial assessment, and none that can override the obligation that arises whenever we can, at little cost to ourselves, make an absolutely crucial difference to the well-being of another person in real need. Hence the issue of foreign aid is a matter with which citizens of any country of the developed world ought to be concerned.

Many years ago the United Nations set a target for development aid of 0.7 percent of gross national product. Only a handful of countries—Denmark, Luxembourg, Norway, and Sweden—have, for at least the past decade, met or surpassed this very modest target of giving $0.70 in every $100 that their economy produces to the developing countries. The Netherlands reached it in every year from 1974 to 2012 but fell just below it in 2013, and its aid continued to fall, to 0.64 percent, in 2014, the most recent year for which figures are available at the time of writing. The United Kingdom reached the 0.7 percent target for the first time in 2013, boosting its aid by 27 percent as compared to 2012, and since then has maintained its aid at that level. The United Arab Emirates leapt to the top of the table in 2013, giving $1.34 from every $100 the country earned, dropping back slightly to $1.17 in 2014. All other developed countries were, in 2014, below the UN's recommended level. Switzerland was at 0.50 percent, Germany at 0.42 percent, France at 0.37 percent, Australia at 0.31 percent, and Canada's aid had fallen well below previous levels to 0.24 percent. Citizens of the United States should feel particularly troubled about their country's contribution of 0.19 percent, below that of most affluent countries although the same as Japan's and Italy's. For affluent countries overall, the total amount of aid contributed was only 0.30 percent of their combined gross national income. In fact, to say that the assistance the United States gives to help people in extreme poverty amounts to $0.19 in every $100 the country earns overlooks the fact that a big slice of U.S. aid is strategically targeted for political purposes. During the period when the United States had troops fighting in Iraq, that country was the largest single recipient of U.S. official development assistance. In 2014 the United States no longer had troops in Iraq but still had them in Afghanistan, which had moved to the top of the list of U.S. aid recipients, receiving $1.8 billion. The next country on the list was Jordan, not one of the world's poorest countries but a strategic ally in the Middle East. Only after those two beneficiaries of U.S. strategic largesse do we get to a country that may be receiving its allocation independently of strategic considerations, namely, Kenya, which received $854 million. (One can't help wondering, though, whether Kenya's high position was affected by President Obama's personal connection with that country.) After that the list goes back to places of strategic significance: West Bank and Gaza Strip (the largest recipient of U.S. aid on a per capita basis), Pakistan, and Syrian Arab Republic. Then we get to countries to which it is reasonable to donate on the basis of greatest need, with Ethiopia in seventh position, followed by Tanzania, South Sudan, and Nigeria.[40]

When I make these points to audiences in the United States, some object that to focus on official aid is misleading. The United States, they say, is a country that does not believe in leaving everything to the government, as some other countries do. If private aid sources were also included, the United States would turn out to be exceptionally generous in its aid to other countries. It is true that Americans give more "private development assistance"—defined as "finance from private sources given voluntarily through formal channels, such as non-profit organisations, and transferred across borders for international development and to reduce poverty"—than the citizens of any other country, although on a per capita basis they do not give more than the citizens of the United Kingdom, which is the second largest donor of private development assistance. In the United States the total amount given annually is around $30 billion, which is slightly less than U.S. official aid. Adding U.S. private and official aid together, we find total U.S. aid to be at a level similar to that of the official aid given by France, but French people do give about $1 billion in private development assistance, and their total aid, official and private, therefore remains at a higher percentage of their gross national income than that of the United States. Similarly, U.S. development aid from all sources remains well below the total aid given by such countries as Switzerland, the Netherlands, United Kingdom, Sweden, Denmark, Luxembourg, Norway, and United Arab Emirates. The U.S. total, official and private, is approximately half the UN-recommended target—for official aid alone—of 0.7 percent and, as a percentage of gross national income, only about a third of what the most generous countries are giving.[41]

These facts are consistent with the claim made at the start of this chapter: despite the lip service most people pay to human equality, their circle of concern barely extends beyond the boundary of their country. The same attitude is shown by the answer Americans give when asked where the federal government should spend less. Foreign aid usually tops the list: often more than 70 percent of respondents say it should be cut.[42] This figure may, however, be an indication not of the American public's lack of concern for people in other countries but of their abysmal ignorance of their government's foreign aid program. In a series of polls dating back to 1995, Americans have been asked to estimate how much of the federal budget (that is, of government spending, not of gross national income) was devoted to foreign aid. In the first of these polls, carried out by the University of Maryland's Program on International Policy Attitudes, the median estimate—that is, the one in the middle of all the responses—was 15 percent. The correct answer is less than 1 percent. And when asked what an appropriate percentage would be, the median response was 5 percent, an increase on the amount actually spent that is beyond the wildest hopes of any foreign aid advocates on Capitol Hill. The *Washington Post,* working with the Kaiser Foundation, decided to run its own survey to see if these results could really be accurate. It got an even higher median estimate, that 20 percent of the federal budget was spent on foreign aid, and the median view about what the "right amount" of foreign aid would be was 10 percent. Some skeptics thought the figures might be explained by the fact that people were including military expenditure in defense of other countries, but further research showed that this was not the case. A survey in 1997 by the *Washington Post,* the Kaiser Family Foundation, and Harvard University listed five programs and asked on which ones the federal government spent the most. Foreign aid ranked first, followed by Defense and Social Security. In fact, Defense and Social Security between them make up more than a third of the federal budget. Foreign aid is insignificant by comparison. In the same year a Pew survey showed that 63 percent of Americans thought the federal government spends more on foreign aid than it spends on Medicare, when Medicare spending is ten times foreign aid spending.[43] In 2000 the University of Maryland's Program on International Policy Attitudes asked a different sample the same questions it had asked five years earlier and received a median estimate of 20 percent for the percentage of federal spending that went to foreign aid, the same as in the 1995 *Washington Post* survey. Only one respondent in twenty gave an estimate of 1 percent or less. Even among those with postgraduate education, the median estimate was 8 percent. Asked what would be an appropriate percentage, the median answer was again the same as that found by the earlier *Washington Post* survey, 10 percent. Such ignorance is not showing any signs of being dispelled. Ten years later World Public Opinion asked the same questions and got an even higher median estimate of how much of the federal budget is spent on foreign aid—25 percent—with, once again, a median response of 10 percent for what percentage of the federal budget should go to foreign aid.[44] In 2013 the Kaiser Foundation tried again, with similar results.[45]

Americans, it seems, are incorrigibly ignorant about their country's dismal foreign aid record, and for the past twenty years the best efforts of aid organizations have been unable to change that fact. It is, nevertheless, worth trying harder to do so because when people are told that only 1 percent of federal government spending goes to foreign aid, they are less likely to think that foreign aid should be reduced. Respondents to the 2013 Kaiser Foundation poll were given this information, and the percentage saying that the United States spends too little on foreign aid more than doubled, from 13 percent to 28 percent, while the number saying that it spends too much halved, from 61 percent to 30 percent.[46] Unfortunately, no U.S. political leader in recent times has attempted to educate the public about how little the country spends on foreign aid, let alone to campaign for an increase.

An Ethical Challenge

If America's leaders continue to give only the most trifling attention to the needs of people in extreme poverty (and the leaders of most other rich countries do only a little better), what should the citizens of those rich countries do? We are not powerless to act on our own. We can take practical steps to expand our concern across state boundaries by supporting organizations working to aid those in need, wherever they may be. But how much should we give?

More than 700 years ago Thomas Aquinas, later canonized by the Catholic Church, faced up to this question without flinching. Material goods are, he wrote, provided for the satisfaction of human needs and should not be divided in a way that hinders that goal. From this he drew the logical conclusion that "whatever a man has in super-abundance is owed, of natural right, to the poor for their sustenance." He was even willing to say, "It is not theft, properly speaking, to take secretly and use another's property in a case of extreme need: because that which he takes for the support of his life becomes his own property by reason of that need."[47] We tend to think of the Roman Catholic Church as a conservative institution, yet this is a very radical doctrine. And it is not just a relic of medieval thinking that the contemporary church would rather forget about. On the contrary, recent Catholic leaders have made similarly strong statements. Pope Paul VI said, in his encyclical *Populorum Progressio*, "We must repeat once more that the superfluous wealth of rich countries should be placed at the service of poor countries. The rule which up to now held good for the benefit of those nearest to us, must today be applied to all the needy of this world."[48] Pope John Paul II reiterated this doctrine in his encyclical *Sollicitudo Rei Socialis*, and Pope Francis has voiced the same view.[49] Unfortunately, at least until Francis became pope, the church gave much more emphasis to condemning homosexuality and abortion than it did to condemning a failure to give one's surplus wealth to the poor. But even for non-Catholics, how exactly we are to justify keeping what we have in "super-abundance" when others are starving is not so easy to say.

In his book *Living High and Letting Die* (1996) the philosopher Peter Unger of New York University presents an ingenious series of imaginary examples designed to probe our intuitions about whether it is wrong to live well without giving substantial amounts of money to help people who are hungry, malnourished, or dying from easily treatable illnesses like diarrhea. Here is my paraphrase of one of these examples.

Bob is close to retirement. He has invested most of his savings in a very rare and valuable old car, a Bugatti, which he has not been able to insure. The Bugatti is his pride and joy. In addition to the pleasure he gets from driving and caring for his car, Bob knows that its rising market value means that he will always be able to sell it and live comfortably after retirement. One day when Bob is out for a drive, he parks the Bugatti near the end of a disused railway siding and goes for a walk up the track. As he does so, he sees that a runaway train, with no one aboard, is running down the railway track. Looking further down the track he sees the small figure of a child playing in a tunnel and very likely to be killed by the runaway train. He can't stop the train and the child is too far away to warn of the danger, but he can throw a switch that will divert the train down the siding where his Bugatti is parked. Then nobody will be killed—but since the barrier at the end of the siding is in disrepair, the train will destroy his Bugatti. Thinking of his joy in owning the car, and the financial security it represents, Bob decides not to throw the switch. The child is killed. But for many years to come Bob enjoys owning his Bugatti and the financial security it represents.[50]

Bob's conduct, most of us will immediately respond, was gravely wrong. Unger agrees. But then he reminds us that we too have opportunities to save the lives of children. We can give to organizations that will use our donations to save the lives of children living in extreme poverty. In his book Unger does a "back of the envelope" calculation that comes to the conclusion that you can save a life for $200. Twenty years on, we have much better ways of evaluating which charities are the most effective and what they can achieve with your donation. It is easy to say how much a bednet costs and even how much it costs to deliver it to a family in a malaria-prone region, but to calculate the cost of saving a life, one needs to know how often the delivery of a net saves a life. According to an estimate by GiveWell, a pioneer rigorous charity evaluator, although it costs the Against Malaria

Foundation no more than $7.50 to provide and deliver a bednet to a family in a malaria-prone region of Africa, the cost of a life saved as a result of this distribution is $3,340. (This figure does not take into account the value of preventing many nonfatal but nevertheless debilitating cases of malaria as well as other mosquito-borne diseases.) GiveWell regards a charity as being highly cost-effective if it can save a life for less than $5,000.[51] That sum is significantly more than Unger's earlier estimate and more than I had expected it to be when I first wrote about saving the drowning child at the cost of ruining an expensive pair of shoes. Nevertheless, if you think it was very wrong of Bob not to throw the switch that would have diverted the train and saved the child's life, it is hard to see how you could deny that it is also very wrong not to send at least $5,000 to an effective charity, if you have that sum and are not spending it on necessities for yourself or your family.

Is there, perhaps, some morally important difference between the two situations? A commonly suggested difference is that we cannot be sure that the assistance we give will reach the people who need it. It is true that not all aid achieves what it is intended to achieve, but such uncertainties are taken into account in GiveWell's estimates and are part of the reason their estimate of the cost of saving a life is already considerably higher than previous estimates.

One genuine difference between Bob and those who could donate to overseas aid organizations but do not do so is that only Bob can save the child in the tunnel, whereas there are perhaps a billion affluent people in the world who could give to an effective aid organization. The problem is that most of them aren't doing it. This may lead us to think that it can't be wrong not to do it.

Suppose that in addition to Bob there were more owners of valuable vintage cars—Carol, Dave, Emma, Fred, and so on, down to Ziggy—all in exactly the same situation as Bob, with their own siding and their own switch, all sacrificing the child in order to preserve their own cherished car. Would that make it all right for Bob to do the same? To answer this question affirmatively is to endorse follow-the-crowd ethics—the kind of ethics that led many Germans to look away when the Nazi atrocities were being committed. We do not excuse them because others were behaving no better.

We seem to lack a sound basis for drawing a clear moral line between Bob's situation and that of anyone with $5,000 to spare who does not donate it to an effective aid agency. These people seem to be acting at least as badly as Bob was acting when he chose to let the runaway train hurtle toward the unsuspecting child. Indeed, their behavior seems to be far worse because for most Americans parting with $5,000 is less of a sacrifice than Bob would have to make to save the child. So it seems we must be doing something seriously wrong if we are not prepared to give $5,000 to an effective charity to save a life. Since there are a lot of very needy children in the world, however, this is not the end of the moral claims on us. There will always be another child whose life you could save for another $5,000. Are we therefore obliged to keep giving until we have nothing left? At what point can we stop?

Consider Bob once again. Think of how much his beloved Bugatti means to him and of its importance to his future financial security. Now think about how much money you would have to give away in order to make a sacrifice that is roughly equal to that. It's almost certainly much more than $5,000. For most middle-class Americans it could easily be more like

$250,000. When Bob first grasped the dilemma that faced him as he stood by that railway switch, he must have thought how extraordinarily unlucky he was to be placed in a situation in which he must choose between the life of an innocent child and the sacrifice of most of his savings. But he was not unlucky at all. We are all in that situation.

Against the argument I have been advancing, it may be objected that to advocate a morality that most people will not follow is poor policy. If we tell people that unless they make extremely demanding sacrifices for strangers they are doing something wrong, their response may be not to give more but to become indifferent to morality altogether. To attempt to make people feel guilty when they buy an ice cream instead of donating the money to help the global poor is to risk making the whole of morality something that few people take seriously as a guide to how to live.

This objection effectively concedes that we ought to do a great deal more than we are now doing but denies that advocating this will really lead to the poor getting more assistance. The question then becomes, What policy will produce the best consequences? If it is true that advocating a highly demanding morality will lead to worse consequences than advocating a less demanding morality, then indeed we ought to advocate a less demanding morality. We could do this while still knowing that, at the level of critical thinking, we ought to be impartial. Here, another point made by Sidgwick holds good: there is a distinction between "what it may be right to do, and privately recommend" and "what it would not be right to advocate openly."[52] We might, among ourselves, feel that we should forego all "super-abundance" in order to help those who are unable to provide for their bare subsistence, whereas in public we might decide to advocate whatever level of giving we believe will yield the greatest amount of assistance while not making people feel that morality is so demanding that they will disregard it. If, say, by advocating that people give 1 percent of their income we will raise more money than would be raised by advocating that people give 10 percent, then 1 percent is what we should advocate. The point is to nominate as a target the figure that will lead to the greatest amount of money being raised. For that to happen, it needs to be a target that makes sense to people.

In *The Life You Can Save* I tried a different approach. On the one hand, instead of proposing a flat rate irrespective of income I urged that those who earn more could afford to give a higher percentage of their income (as is assumed by a progressive tax scale). At the same time, working from the other direction, I calculated what it would take for the world's affluent people to give enough to make a dramatic reduction in the extent of extreme poverty. I found that it was possible for the world's affluent people to donate $1.5 trillion annually without making unreasonable sacrifices. This huge amount of aid could be achieved without asking the bottom 90 percent of taxpayers in affluent countries to give, on average, more than 1 percent of their income and without asking even the superrich—the top 0.01 percent of all taxpayers—to give more than a third of their income, which, since they all have annual incomes of more than $11 million a year, still leaves them more than $7 million a year to live on. The suggested percentage then drops through various levels for the top 1 percent, the top 5 percent, and the top 10 percent before getting to the level of 1 percent for those not in the top 10 percent.[53] These levels do not impose a harsh burden on anyone, yet they would yield more than ten times the official development assistance given by *all* the affluent countries, which in 2013 came to $136 billion.[54]

A factual assumption lies behind this argument: aid works. William Easterly, in *The White Man's Burden,* and Dambisa

Moyo, in *Dead Aid,* have offered scathing critiques of aid.[55] There is, they insist, an empirical question to be answered: "How much will each additional dollar of aid, given by me or by my government, contribute to the long-term well-being of people in areas receiving that aid?" They claim that trillions of dollars have been spent on aid, but there is little to show for it. In fact, we can only get to trillions of dollars—Easterly refers to a total of $2.3 trillion—if we add up all the aid that has been given over the past five decades. If we assume that there have been, on average, one billion people living in extreme poverty during this period, then $2.3 trillion amounts to roughly $60 per person per year. It's no wonder that this modest sum has not eliminated extreme poverty, especially given that, as we have seen, much of this aid has been given to further the strategic interests of the donor states and is not aimed at helping the world's poorest people. Looking at the total amount of aid from the perspective of the wealthy, it amounts to 0.3 percent of the gross national income of the affluent countries—in other words, $0.30 for every $100 that was earned. That amount isn't all that generous.

Angus Deaton also takes a critical look at aid in *The Great Escape,* arguing that aid often does harm by allowing governments to avoid their responsibilities to their citizens. Deaton accepts, however, that there is a strong case for aid to fight disease, such as HIV/AIDS or smallpox.[56] Smallpox is a particularly interesting example because it was the first disease to be completely eradicated by a deliberate campaign, and that eradication was undoubtedly the outcome of aid. Indeed, William MacAskill argues, in *Doing Good Better,* that even if the only thing foreign aid had ever done was to eliminate smallpox, it would still have been excellent value. This claim is so striking that it is worth repeating the figures MacAskill puts forth. He accepts Easterly's figure of $2.3 trillion as the total amount spent on aid, one small part of which was the program to eradicate smallpox. The last naturally occurring case of smallpox was in 1977, and in 1980 smallpox was officially declared eradicated. Prior to the eradication campaign, smallpox used to kill, in very distressing ways, between 1.5 million and 3 million people per year. Take the lower figure and multiply it by 38, the number of years that have passed since smallpox was eradicated, and we reach a total of 57 million lives saved. Divide that into $2.3 trillion, and we find that the cost per life saved was just over $40,000. By the standards of what affluent countries typically spend to save a human life, that is a tiny amount. Keeping an extremely premature infant alive in an intensive care unit in a modern hospital can churn through that amount in less than two weeks, and such babies often spend several months under intensive care, with total costs of over $1 million.[57] U.S. government departments try to establish estimates of how much should be spent on saving lives by, for example, building safer roads and requiring higher standards of safety for consumer products and workplaces. The figures are currently in the region of $6 to $9 million, or about 150 times the cost of saving a life through foreign aid, *even if foreign aid had done nothing but eliminate smallpox.*[58]

In reality, we know that foreign aid has done many other good things. As we saw in chapter 3, child mortality has declined dramatically since 1990, from 90 per 1,000 births to only 43. Between 1960 and 2014 the world's population increased from 2.5 billion to more than 7 billion. If child mortality had remained at the same level it was in 1960, then in 2014, 56 million children under the age of five would have died. Instead, 5.9 million died. The reduction of child mortality therefore saved 50 million lives in 2014 alone and presumably saved a similar or greater number in 2015, and hopefully will save at least as many each year thereafter. That is a huge number of lives saved and a vast reduction in the amount of suffering endured by children as a result of preventable diseases (far more children suffer from the diseases than the number of children who die from them) as well as an equally great reduction in the grief experienced by parents who lose a child. Just for comparison, the number of people who died in all wars since 1973—including the killings in Cambodia, the genocide in Rwanda, the two wars in the Congo, and the wars in Afghanistan and Iraq—is 12 million.[59]

Now, it is true that aid is not responsible for the entire reduction in child deaths just mentioned. Economic growth has made it possible for hundreds of millions of people to have safe drinking water, to feed their children better, and to get medical help for them when they fall ill. But there can also be no doubt that aid initiatives like the Global Alliance for Vaccines and Immunization have saved millions of lives by immunizing children against measles, that charities distributing bednets have saved millions of lives by protecting children against malaria, that aid programs providing safe drinking water in rural areas have reduced the incidence of diarrhea, and that other programs making oral rehydration therapy available for children who get diarrhea have reduced the death toll of that disease. When compared with domestic expenditures, therefore, foreign aid has offered extraordinary value for money.

One final comment: when I point to the reduction in child mortality that has been achieved in recent decades, some people say that more surviving children will mean that the world's population keeps growing and in the end this will lead to more people starving. It's a view that reminds me of Garrett Hardin's suggestion, back in 1974, that countries like India and Bangladesh were so hopelessly overpopulated that aid should be cut off and they should be left alone until famine had reduced their populations to more sustainable levels.[60] Both of those countries now have much larger populations than they had in 1974, but they also have a smaller proportion of their population in extreme poverty, and their rate of population growth has slowed markedly. Keeping people in poverty has never been shown to reduce fertility. What does reduce fertility is an improving standard of living, education (particularly for girls), and providing women with the means to control their fertility.[61] The idea that we have no other option but to cut off aid so that famine can bring expanding populations back to sustainable levels is neither factually accurate nor ethically defensible.

6 a better world?

In the fifth century before the Christian era the Chinese philosopher Mozi, appalled at the damage caused by war, asked, "What is the way of universal love and mutual benefit? It is to regard other people's countries as one's own."[1] When asked what country he came from, the ancient Greek iconoclast Diogenes is said to have replied, "I am a citizen of the world."[2] In the late twentieth century John Lennon sang that it is easy to "imagine there's no countries . . . Imagine all the people/Sharing all the world."[3] Until recently such thoughts have been the dreams of idealists, devoid of practical impact on the hard realities of a world of nation-states. But now we are beginning to live in a global community. Most of the world's leaders recognize the need for global action on greenhouse gas emissions. The global economy has given rise to the World Trade Organization, the World Bank, and the International Monetary Fund, institutions that take on, if imperfectly, some functions of global economic governance. We now have a functioning International Criminal Court. Acceptance of the idea of a responsibility to protect people from genocide and crimes against humanity indicates that we are living in a global community that is willing to exercise, if only in extreme emergencies, coercive power over sovereign states whose rulers do not or cannot protect their people from such crimes. In ringing declarations and resolutions the world's leaders have recognized that relieving the plight of the world's poorest countries is a global responsibility. One of these, the United Nations Millennium Declaration, approved at the United Nations Millennium Summit in 2000, set the framework for the subsequent adoption of the Millennium Development Goals. Although the actions that followed did not enable the goals to be met completely, they nevertheless made an important difference in the lives of hundreds of millions of the world's poorest people.

When people in different regions led more separate lives it was more understandable that people in one country might think of themselves as owing no obligations, beyond that of noninterference, to people in another state. But those times are long gone. Today, our greenhouse gas emissions alter the climate in which everyone in the world lives. Our purchases of oil, diamonds, and timber make it possible for dictators to buy weapons and strengthen their hold on the countries they tyrannize. Our agricultural subsidies make it harder for peasant farmers in developing countries to sell their crops at prices from which they can earn enough income to feed themselves and their families.

Then there is the question of migration. Instant communication shows us how others live, and they in turn learn about us and aspire to our way of life. Modern transport can move people, even relatively poor people, thousands of miles, and when people are desperate to improve their situation, national boundaries prove porous. In 2001 Branko Milanovic warned, "It is unrealistic to hold that large income differences between the Northern and Southern shore of the Mediterranean, or between Mexico and the United States, or between Indonesia and Malaysia, can continue without adding further pressure to migrate."[4] Income differences between rich and poor nations were certainly one factor, along with the crisis in Syria, in the fact that more than a million would-be immigrants entered Europe from Africa, the Middle East, and South Asia in 2015, causing a surge in the popularity of right-wing nationalist political parties.[5] The security of the United States border with Mexico has become a volatile political issue. Climate change will dramatically increase the number of people seeking to migrate and make it apparent that the refugee issue needs a global solution.

The era that followed the Treaty of Westphalia was the highwater mark of the independent sovereign state. Behind the supposed inviolability of state borders, liberal democratic institutions took hold in some countries, while in others, rulers carried out genocide against their own citizens or permitted their more favored citizens to do it to less favored ones. At intervals, bloody wars broke out between the independent states. Though we may look back on that era with some nostalgia, we should not regret its passing. Instead, we should be developing the ethical foundations of the coming era of a single world community.

I have argued that as more and more issues increasingly demand global solutions, the extent to which any state can independently determine its future diminishes. We therefore need to strengthen institutions for global decision making and make them more responsible to the people they affect. This leads in the direction of a world community with its own directly elected legislature.

There is little political support for such ideas at present, and the United Kingdom's decision to leave the European Union after being a member for 43 years indicates the resilience of ideas of national independence. Apart from the threat that the idea world federalism poses to the self-interest of the citizens of the rich countries, many would say it puts too much at risk for gains that are too uncertain. It is widely believed that a world government will be, at best, an unchecked bureaucratic behemoth that makes the bureaucracy of the European Union look lean and efficient. At worst, it will become a global tyranny, unchecked and unchallengeable.

These thoughts have to be taken seriously. How to prevent global bodies from becoming either dangerous tyrannies or self-aggrandizing bureaucracies and instead make them effective and responsive to the people whose lives they affect is something we still need to learn from the experience, good and bad, of other multinational organizations.[6]

To rush into world federalism would be foolhardy, but we do not have to do that. We could accept the diminishing significance of state boundaries and take a pragmatic, step-by-step approach to greater global governance. The preceding chapters have argued that there is a good case for global environmental and labor standards and for adopting international standards of "clean trade" in order to cease buying resources from regimes that have stolen the goods from their people. These and other specific proposals for stronger global institutions to accomplish a particular task should be considered on their merits. In time, we will see how well they work and whether they point toward opportunities for more comprehensive global governance.

The fifteenth and sixteenth centuries are celebrated for the voyages of discovery that proved that the world is round. The eighteenth century saw the first proclamations of universal human rights. The twentieth century's conquest of space made it possible for a human being to look at our planet from a point not on it and so to see it, literally, as one world. Now, the twenty-first century faces the task of developing a suitable form of governance for our world. It is a daunting moral and intellectual challenge but one we cannot refuse to take up, for the future of the world surely depends on how well we meet it.

notes

1 a changing world

1. *New York Times*, March 30, 2001, A11.
2. Philip Elmer-Dewitt, "Summit to Save the Earth: Rich vs. Poor," *Time*, 139:2 (June 1992), 42–8, http://www.cddc.vt.edu/tim/tims/Tim599.htm.
3. Bill Keller, "The World According to Colin Powell," *New York Times Sunday Magazine*, November 25, 2001, 67.
4. Ivan Eland, quoted in Alessandria Masi, "Does the US Need Ground Forces to Fight ISIS in Iraq, Syria? The Impact of Airstrikes vs. Combat Troops," *International Business Times*, September 17, 2014, http://www.ibtimes.com/does-us-need-ground-forces-fight-isis-iraq-syria-impact-airstrikes-vs-combat-troops-1690915.
5. Timothy Garton Ash, "War over Kosovo," in *History of the Present: Essays, Sketches, and Dispatches from Europe in the 1990s*, Vintage, New York, 2001, 390. Center for Refugee and Disaster Response, Bloomberg School of Public Health, Johns Hopkins University, "Updated Iraq Study Confirms Earlier Mortality Estimates," http://www.jhsph.edu/research/centers-and-institutes/center-for-refugee-and-disaster-response/publications_tools/iraq/index.html.

6. *Report of the Independent Inquiry into the Actions of the United Nations During the 1994 Genocide in Rwanda,* United Nations, Office of the Spokesman for the Secretary-General, New York, 15 December 1999, http://www.un.org/News/ossg/rwanda_report.htm.

7. Kofi Annan, "Two Concepts of Sovereignty," *The Economist,* 18 September 1999, http://www.un.org/Overview/SG/kaecon.htm.

8. Martin Gilbert, "The Terrible Twentieth Century," *Globe and Mail* (Canada), January 31, 2007.

9. John Langdon, *July 1914: The Long Debate, 1918–1990,* Berg, New York, 1991, 175.

10. G. Gooch and H. Temperley, eds., *British Documents on the Origins of the War, 1898–1914,* London, 1926–38, vol. XI, no. 91; cited in Zara Steiner, *Britain and the Origins of the First World War,* St. Martin's Press, New York, 1977, 221–22.

11. Charles Horne, ed., *Source Records of the Great War,* vol. 1, The American Legion, Indianapolis, 1931, 285.

12. Security Council Resolution 1373 (2001), http://www.un.org/Docs/scres/2001/res1373e.pdf.

13. Report of the High-Level Panel on Financing for Development appointed by the United Nations Secretary-General, United Nations General Assembly, Fifty-fifth Session, Agenda item 101, June 26, 2001, A/55/1000, 3, http://www.un.org/esa/ffd/a55-1000.pdf.

14. Juliet Eilperin, "House Approves U.N. Payment Legislation Would Provide $582 Million for Back Dues," *Washington Post,* September 25, 2001, A01.

15. See John Rawls, *A Theory of Justice,* Oxford University Press, Oxford, 1971. The objection to Rawls that I have put here was made by Brian Barry in *The Liberal Theory of Justice,* Oxford University Press, Oxford, 1973, 129–30. See also the same author's *Theories of Justice,* University of California Press, Berkeley, 1989. Other arguments to the same end have been pressed by Charles Beitz, *Political Theory and International Relations,* Princeton University Press, Princeton, 1979, and "Social and cosmopolitan liberalism," *International Affairs* 75:3 (1999): 515–29; by Thomas Pogge, *Realizing Rawls,* Cornell University Press, Ithaca, NY, 1990, and "An Egalitarian Law of Peoples," *Philosophy and Public Affairs* 23:3 (1994); and by Andrew Kuper, "Rawlsian Global Justice: Beyond *The Law of Peoples* to a Cosmopolitan Law of Persons," *Political Theory* 28:5 (2000): 640–74.

16. Yael Tamir, "Who's Afraid of a Global State?," in Kjell Goldmann, Ulf Hannerz, and Charles Westin, eds., *Nationalism and Internationalism in the Post-Cold War Era,* Routledge, New York, 2000, 244–67.

17. David Held and Pietro Maffettone, *Global Political Theory,* Polity, Cambridge, 2016; for other work taking a global perspective, see also David Held, *Democracy and the Global Order,* Stanford University Press, Stanford, 1995; Carol Gould, *Globalizing Democracy and Human Rights,* Cambridge University Press, Cambridge, 2004; Gillian Brock, *Global Justice,* Oxford University Press, Oxford, 2009; and the essays included in Thomas Pogge and Keith Horton, eds., *Global Ethics,* Paragon House, St. Paul, 2008, and in Thomas Pogge and Darrel Moellendorf, eds., *Global Justice,* Paragon House, St. Paul, 2008.

18. *The Poverty of Philosophy,* in David McLellan, ed., *Karl Marx: Selected Writings,* Oxford University Press, Oxford, 1977, 202.

19. Thomas Friedman, *The Lexus and the Olive Tree,* Anchor Books, New York 2000, 104–6.

20. Ibid., 112.

21. Ibid., 104.

22. On the evolution of ethics, see Peter Singer, *The Expanding Circle,* 2d ed., Princeton University Press, Princeton, 2011, and Joshua Greene, *Moral Tribes,* Penguin, New York, 2013.

23. For more detailed discussion of the role of reason in ethics, see Katarzyna de Lazari-Radek and Peter Singer, *The Point of View of the Universe,* Oxford University Press, Oxford, 2014.

2 one atmosphere

1. IPCC, "Summary for Policymakers" in T. F. Stocker et al., eds., *Climate Change 2013: The Physical Science Basis. Contribution of Working Group I to the Fifth Assessment Report of the Intergovernmental Panel on Climate Change,* http://www.ipcc.ch/report/ar5/wg1. Statements on the following pages about the physical science of climate change are drawn from this document, which summarizes the work of Working Group I, presented in full in *Climate Change 2013: The Physical Science Basis.*

2. Justin Gillis, "2014 Was the Warmest Year Ever Recorded on Earth," *New York Times,* January 16, 2015; Justin Gillis, "Climate Accord Is a Healing Step, If Not a Cure," *New York Times,* December 12, 2015; Justin Gillis, "2015 Was Hottest Year in Historical Record, Scientists Say," *New York Times,* January 20, 2016.

3. On the organized movement to deny the scientific consensus on climate change, see Naomi Oreskes and Erik Conway, *Merchants of Doubt: How a Handful of Scientists Obscured the Truth on Issues from Tobacco Smoke to Global Warming*, Bloomsbury, New York, 2010.

4. The precise temperatures required to trigger tipping points for abrupt and irreversible climate change are uncertain, but the risks increase as temperatures rise. See IPCC, "Summary for policymakers" in C. B. Field et al., eds., *Climate Change 2014: Impacts, Adaptation, and Vulnerability, Part A: Global and Sectoral Aspects. Contribution of Working Group II to the Fifth Assessment Report of the Intergovernmental Panel on Climate Change.* 20: http://www.ipcc.ch/report/ar5/wg2.

5. Sophie Lewis and David Karoly, "Anthropogenic contributions to Australia's record summer temperatures of 2013," *Geophysical Research Letters* 40 (2013): 3705–9.

6. Fraser Lott, Nikolaos Christidis, and Peter Stott, "Can the East African Drought Be Attributed to Human-Induced Climate Change?," *Geophysical Research Letters* 40 (2013): 1177–81.

7. World Health Organization, *Quantitative Risk Assessment of the Effects of Climate Change on Selective Causes of Death, 2030s and 2050s*, World Health Organization, Geneva, 2014, 1–2; http://www.who.int/globalchange/publications/quantitative-risk-assessment/en/.

8. James Hansen et al., "Ice melt, sea level rise and superstorms: evidence from paleoclimate data, climate modeling, and modern observations that 2°C global warming is highly dangerous," *Atmospheric Chemistry and Physics, Discussions* 15 (2015): 20059–20179, www.atmos-chem-phys-discuss.net/15/20059/2015/.

9. This summary of the meaning and use of the term "Anthropocene" draws on Dale Jamieson and Marcello Di Paola, "Political Theory for the Anthropocene," in David Held and Pietro Maffettone, eds., *Global Political Theory*, Polity, Cambridge, 2016; for a more popular account, see Dale Jamieson's and Bonnie Nadzam's introduction to their engaging work of fiction, *Love in the Anthropocene*, OR Books, New York, 2015.

10. *United Nations Framework Convention on Climate Change*, Article 4, section 2, subsections (a) and (b), available at http://www.unfccc.int/resource/conv/conv.html; *Guide to the Climate Change Negotiation Process*, http://www.unfccc.int/resource/process/components/response/respconv.html.

11. "U.S. Carbon Emissions Jump in 2000," *Los Angeles Times,* November 11, 2001, citing figures released by the U.S. Department of Energy's Energy Information Administration on November 9, 2001.

12. Eileen Claussen and Lisa McNeilly, *The Complex Elements of Global Fairness,* Pew Center on Global Climate Change, Washington, DC, October 29, 1998, http://www.pewclimate.org/projects/pol_equity.cfm.

13. Associated Press, "Obama Commends Climate Change Accord," *New York Times,* December 12, 2015.

14. Ibid.

15. United Nations, Framework Convention on Climate Change, Conference of the Parties, 21st Session, *Adoption of the Paris Agreement,* 12 December 2015, http://unfccc.int/resource/docs/2015/cop21/eng/l09.pdf.

16. Jennifer Jacquet and Dale Jamieson, "Here's What to Hope For from the Paris Climate Talks," *Grist,* October 13, 2015, http://grist.org/climate-energy/heres-what-to-hope-for-from-the-paris-climate-talks/.

17. Rodney Boyd, Joe Cranston Turner, and Bob Ward, *Intended nationally determined contributions: what are the implications for greenhouse gas emissions in 2030?,* ESRC Centre for Climate Change Economics and Policy and Grantham Research Institute on Climate Change and the Environment, 30 October 2015, http://www.lse.ac.uk/GranthamInstitute/wp-content/uploads/2015/10/Boyd_Turner_and_Ward_policy_paper_October_2015.pdf.

18. Robert Nozick, *Anarchy, State and Utopia,* Basic Books, New York, 1974, 153.

19. John Locke, *Second Treatise on Civil Government,* ed. C. B. Macpherson, Hacket, Indianapolis, 1980, sec 27, 19.

20. See Garrett Hardin, "The Tragedy of the Commons," *Science* 162 (1968): 1243–48.

21. *Second Treatise on Civil Government,* sec 41.

22. Adam Smith, *A Theory of the Moral Sentiments,* IV i. 10.

23. World Bank Data, CO2 emissions, available at http://data.worldbank.org/indicator/EN.ATM.CO2E.PC.

24. D. Archer et al., "Atmospheric lifetime of fossil fuel carbon dioxide," *Annual Review of Earth and Planetary Sciences* 37 (2009): 117–34.

25. See Intergovernmental Panel on Climate Change, *First Assessment Report,* especially J. T. Houghton, G. J. Jenkins, and J. J. Ephraums, eds., *Scientific Assessment of Climate Change—Report of Working Group I,*

Cambridge University Press, Cambridge, 1990. For a discussion of U.S. policy on climate change at the time of the Earth Summit, see Henrik Selin and Stacy Vandeveer, "U.S. Climate Change Politics: Federalism and Complexity," in Sheldon Kamieniecki and Michael Kraft, eds., *The Oxford Handbook of Environmental Policy,* Oxford University Press, Oxford, 2012.

26. See Teng Fei et al., "Metric of Carbon Equity: Carbon Gini Index Based on Historical Cumulative Emissions per Capita, *Advances in Climate Change Research* 2 (2011): 134–40. See also Peter Singer and Teng Fei, "Fairness and Climate Change," *Project Syndicate,* April 11, 2013, http://www.project-syndicate.org/commentary/fair-distribution-of-rights-to-carbon-emissions-by-peter-singer-and-teng-fei.

27. John Vidal, "Vulnerable Nations Reject 2C Target," *The Guardian,* December 11, 2009, http://www.theguardian.com/environment/2009/dec/10/copenhagen-climate-change. The current level is updated monthly at http://co2now.org.

28. IPCC, "Summary for Policymakers," in T. F. Stocker et al., eds., *Climate Change 2013: The Physical Science Basis. Contribution of Working Group I to the Fifth Assessment Report of the Intergovernmental Panel on Climate Change,* 27. http://www.ipcc.ch/report/ar5/wg1.

29. Food and Agriculture Organization, *Livestock's Long Shadow,* FAO, Rome, 2006, http://www.fao.org/docrep/010/a0701e/a0701e00.HTM.

30. These figures are derived from World Resources Institute Climate Data, available through CAIT 2.0 Equity Explorer (Beta version). The data are for 2010 and include emissions from land use changes and forestry—which slightly reduces the figure for the United States.

31. Paul Baer et al., "Equity and Greenhouse Gas Responsibility," *Science* 289 (29 September 2000), 2287; Dale Jamieson, "Climate Change and Global Environmental Justice," in Edwards and C. Miller, eds., *Changing the Atmosphere: Expert Knowledge and Global Environmental Governance,* MIT Press, Cambridge, 2001.

32. John Rawls, *Political Liberalism,* Columbia University Press, New York, 1993, 5–6, and also *A Theory of Justice,* esp. 65–83. For a different way of giving priority to the worst-off, see Derek Parfit, "Equality or Priority?," The Lindley Lecture, University of Kansas, 21 November 1991, reprinted in Matthew Clayton and Andrew Williams, eds., *The Ideal of Equality,* Macmillan, London, 2000.

33. This is Rawls's "difference principle," applied without the restriction to national boundaries that are difficult to defend in terms of his own argument. See chapter 5 for further discussion of this point.
34. "President Announces Clear Skies and Global Climate Change Initiative," Office of the Press Secretary, White House, February 14, 2002. For amplification of the basis of the administration's policy, see Executive Office of the President, Council of Economic Advisers, *2002 Economic Report of the President,* U.S. Government Printing Office, Washington, DC, 2002, chapter 6, 244–49.
35. World Bank data indicate that in 2013 exports amount to only 13.5 percent of U.S. GDP. http://data.worldbank.org/indicator/NE.EXP.GNFS .ZS. Figures for previous years are similar.
36. International Energy Agency, *Key World Energy Statistics 2014,* 48–57, available at http://www.iea.org/publications/freepublications/ publication/key-world-energy-statistics-2014.html. The figures quoted are for 2012 and are adjusted for purchasing power parity. For the figures at the time Bush made his claim, see Andrew Revkin, "Sliced Another Way: Per Capita Emissions," *New York Times,* June 17, 2001.
37. Bjorn Lomborg, *The Skeptical Environmentalist,* Cambridge University Press, Cambridge, 2001.
38. See Richard Newell and William Pizer, *Discounting the Benefits of Future Climate Change Mitigation: How Much Do Uncertain Rates Increase Valuations?,* Pew Center on Global Climate Change, Washington, DC, December 2001. Available at http://www.pewclimate.org/projects/ econ_discounting.cfm.
39. For discussion of equal votes as a compromise, see my *Democracy and Disobedience,* Clarendon Press, Oxford, 1973, 30–41.
40. For a range of reports on emission trading schemes, see ICAP (International Carbon Action Partnership), *Emissions Trading Worldwide: Status Report 2014,* https://icapcarbonaction.com/component/attach/ ?task=download&id=152; on China's plans, see International Center for Trade and Sustainable Development, "China unveils plans for national carbon market by 2016," *Bridges,* 18 September, 2014, http://www. ictsd.org/bridges-news/bridges/news/china-unveils-plans-for-national -carbon-market-by-2016.
41. *Laudato Si, Encyclical Letter of the Holy Father Francis on Care for Our Common Home,* The Holy See, Vatican, 2015, paragraph 171.

42. Joseph Heath, "Pope Francis' Climate Error," *New York Times,* June 19, 2015.

43. For details, see United States Environmental Protection Agency, "EPA Collaboration with Canada," http://www2.epa.gov/international -cooperation/epa-collaboration-canada.

44. David Victor and Charles Kennel argue that keeping climate change below 2°C is unachievable in "Climate Policy: Ditch the 2°C Warming Goal," *Nature* 514 (October 2, 2014), 30–31; http://www.nature.com/polopoly_fs/1.16018!/menu/main/topColumns/topLeftColumn/pdf/514030a.pdf. James Hansen et al. give reasons for believing that we are already committed to sufficient climate change to cause the melting of sufficient Antarctic ice to cause sea levels to rise by several meters in a matter of decades, whether temperature rise is kept to 2°C or not. See James Hansen et al., "Ice melt, sea level rise and superstorms: evidence from paleoclimate data, climate modeling, and modern observations that 2°C global warming is highly dangerous," *Atmospheric Chemistry and Physics, Discussions* 15 (2015): 20059–20179, www.atmos-chem-phys -discuss.net/15/20059/2015/.

45. World Bank *Economics of Adaptation to Climate Change Synthesis Report,* World Bank, Washington, DC, 2010, xix. Available at: https:// openknowledge.worldbank.org/bitstream/handle/10986/12750/702670 ESW0P10800EACCSynthesisReport.pdf.

46. Smita Nakhooda et al., *Climate Finance: Is it Making a Difference?,* Overseas Development Institute, London, 2014, 3. This report also indicates that climate finance money is, on the whole, being used for its intended purposes.

47. "What Does a Climate Deal Mean for the World?" *New York Times,* December 12, 2015.

48. Paul Baer, "Adaptation: Who Pays Whom," in J. Adger et al., eds., *Fairness in Adaptation to Climate Change,* MIT Press, Cambridge, 2006, reprinted in Stephen Gardner et al., eds., *Climate Ethics: Essential Readings,* New York: Oxford University Press, 250.

49. John Shepherd et al., *Geoengineering the Climate: Science, Governance and Uncertainty,* Policy Document 10/09, Royal Society, London, 2009.

50. Dale Jamieson, *Reason in a Dark Time,* Oxford University Press, New York, 2014, 219; the "Plan B" label comes from Jeff Goodell, *How to Cool the Planet,* Boston: Houghton Mifflin Harcourt. 2010, 110.

51. Jamieson, *Reason in a Dark Time,* 207.
52. For the importance of the monsoon to India, see Soutek Biswas, "Why is India obsessed with monsoon rains?," BBC News, June 4, 2013, http://www.bbc.com/news/world-asia-india-22750169. The suggestion that geoengineering could disrupt the monsoon comes from Jamieson, *Reason in a Dark Time,* 220, citing studies by A. Robock, L. Oman, and G. L. Stenchikov, "Regional climate responses to geoengineering with tropical and Arctic SO2 injections," *Journal of Geophysical Research* 113 (2008): D16101; G. Bala, B. Duffy, and K. E. Taylor, "Impact of Geoengineering Schemes on the Global Hydrological Cycle," *Proceedings of the National Academy of Sciences* 105 (2008): 7664–69; and Victor Brovkin, Vladimir Petoukhov, Martin Claussen, Eva Bauer, David Archer, Carlo Jaeger, "Geoengineering Climate by Stratospheric Sulfur Injections: Earth System Vulnerability to Technological Failure," *Climatic Change* 92 (2009): 243–59.
53. K. E. Trenberth and A. Dai, "Effects of Mount Pinatubo Volcanic Eruption on the Hydrological Cycle as an Analog of Geoengineering," *Geophysical Research Letters* 34 (2007): L15702; I owe this reference to Jamieson, *Reason in a Dark Time.*
54. On "the other carbon dioxide problem," see http://www.pmel.noaa.gov/co2/story/Ocean+Acidification/. I owe this reference to Jamieson, *Reason in a Dark Time.* On the effect on shell development and the oyster industry, see http://www.noaa.gov/features/01_economic/pacificoysters .html. (Both sites viewed July 29, 2015.)
55. U.S. Geological Survey, "Volcanic Gases and Climate Change Overview," http://volcanoes.usgs.gov/hazards/gas/climate.php.
56. Planet Editor, "Two Years After Russ George Illegally Dumped Iron in the Pacific, Salmon Catches Are Up 400%," September 2, 2014, http://www.planetexperts.com/two-years-russ-george-illegally-dumped-iron -pacific-salmon-catches-400/.
57. Jamieson, *Reason in a Dark Time,* 224.
58. Here I draw on Ian Lloyd and Michael Oppenheimer, "On the Design of an International Governance Framework for Geoengineering," *Global Environmental Politics* 14 (2014): 45–63. See this article for further discussion of the possible structure of such a body and the political feasibility of realizing it.

3 one economy

1. Thomas Friedman, "Senseless in Seattle," *New York Times,* December 1, 1999, A23.

2. Victor Menotti, *Free Trade, Free Logging: How the World Trade Organization Undermines Global Forest Conservation,* International Forum on Globalization, San Francisco, 1999, ii.

3. *Agscene,* Autumn 1999, 20.

4. "How the South is getting a raw deal at the WTO," in Sarah Anderson, ed., *Views from the South: The Effects of Globalization and the WTO on Third World Countries,* International Forum on Globalization, San Francisco, n.d. (1999), 11.

5. Vandana Shiva, "War against nature and the people of the South," in Sarah Anderson, ed., *Views from the South: The Effects of Globalization and the WTO on Third World Countries,* International Forum on Globalization, San Francisco, n.d. (1999), 92, 93, 123.

6. Thomas Friedman, *The Lexus and the Olive Tree,* Anchor Books, New York, 2000, 190.

7. See World Economic Forum, *Summaries of the Annual Meeting 2000,* Geneva, 2000, summary of session 56.

8. World Trade Organization, *WTO in Brief,* Part II, https://www.wto.org/english/thewto_e/whatis_e/inbrief_e/inbr02_e.htm, viewed December 28, 2015.

9. World Trade Organization, *WTO in Brief* http://www.wto.org/english/thewto_e/whatis_e/inbrief_e/inbr00_e.htm.

10. "The WTO in Brief, Part 3: The WTO Agreements," available at http://www.wto.org/english/thewto_e/whatis_e/inbrief_e/inbr03_e.htm.

11. *10 Things the WTO Can Do,* 41, available at: http://www.wto.org/english/thewto_e/whatis_e/10thi_e/10thi00_e.htm (downloaded February 17, 2015). This document has replaced an earlier document, *10 Common Misunderstandings about the WTO,* which was criticized in the first edition of this book. The newer version is more conciliatory in that it acknowledges that different perspectives are possible on some issues.

12. *10 Things the WTO Can Do,* 42.

13. World Trade Organization, *Agreement on Technical Barriers to Trade,* http://www.wto.org/english/docs_e/legal_e/17-tbt.pdf.

14. http://www.wto.org/english/thewto_e/whatis_e/tif_e/bey5_e.htm.

15. World Trade Organization, *Trading into the Future* (2d revised edition, March 2001), http://www.wto.org/english/res_e/doload_e/tif.pdf.
16. http://www.wto.org/english/thewto_e/whatis_e/tif_e/bey5_e.htm.
17. World Trade Organization, *United States: Import Prohibition of Certain Shrimp and Shrimp Products,* AB-1998–4, 12 October 1998, http://www.wto.org/english/tratop_e/dispu_e/58abr.pdf.
18. "DSB Adopts Two Appellate Body Reports on Shrimp and Corn Syrup," *WTO News,* 21 November 2001, http://www.wto.org/english/news_e/news01_c/dsb_21nov01_e.htm; *Bridges Weekly Trade News Digest,* vol. 5, no. 40, 28 November, 2001; http://www.wto.org/english/news_e/news01_c/dsb_21nov01_e.htm.
19. As quoted in the Appellate Body judgment, *European Communities: Measures Prohibiting the Importation and Marketing of Seal Products, (AB 2014–1, AB 2014–2),* 22 May 2014, par. 5.179, 142.
20. *European Communities,* par. 5.198–5.199, 148.
21. *10 Things the WTO Can Do,* 28.
22. See, for example, the *New York Times* editorial "The Urgency of Cheaper Drugs," October 31, 2001, and Nicolo Itano, "Double Standards," *Christian Science Monitor,* November 9, 2001.
23. World Trade Organization, "Declaration on the TRIPS Agreement and Public Health," November 14, 2001, WT/MIN(01)/DEC/2, pars 4, 5; http://www-chil.wto-ministerial.org/english/thewto_e/minist_e/min01_e/mindecl_trips_e.htm.
24. Martin Khor, "How the South is getting a raw deal at the WTO," in Sarah Anderson, ed., *Views from the South: The Effects of Globalization and the WTO on Third World Countries,* International Forum on Globalization, San Francisco, n.d. (1999), 14; Walden Bello, "Building an Iron Cage: The Bretton Woods Institutions, the WTO and the South," in Anderson, ed., *Views from the South,* 85–86. The point is conceded, for the period up until the mid-1990s, in *10 Things the WTO Can Do,* 38.
25. John Weekes, "The WTO at Sixteen," in *The ACWL at Ten: Looking Back, Looking Forwards,* Conference held at the WTO, 4 October 2011, http://www.acwl.ch/e/documents/reports/ACWL%20AT%20TEN.pdf.
26. Pascal Lamy, "Introductory Remarks," in ibid.
27. Frank Bruni and David Sanger, "Bush urges shift to direct grants for poor nations," *New York Times,* July 18, 2001.

28. Vandana Shiva, "War against nature and the people of the South," in Anderson, ed., *Views from the South,* 98, 99.

29. Figures in this paragraph come from World Bank, "Poverty Overview," http://www.worldbank.org/en/topic/poverty/overview; the exception is the inflation adjustment, which was calculated using www.dollartimes .com.

30. World Bank, "World Bank Forecasts Global Poverty to Fall Below 10% for First Time; Major Hurdles Remain in Goal to End Poverty by 2030," Press release, October 4, 2015, http://www.worldbank.org/en/ news/press-release/2015/10/04/world-bank-forecasts-global-poverty -to-fall-below-10-for-first-time-major-hurdles-remain-in-goal-to-end -poverty-by-2030.

31. United Nations, *The Millennium Development Goals Report, 2015.* United Nations, New York, 2015, 4. The 2015 figure is a projection of trends, as the report was issued before the end of the year.

32. United Nations Development Programme, *Human Development Report, 2014,* United Nations Development Programme, New York, 2014, 41, 71. http://hdr.undp.org

33. The sources for the figures in this paragraph are as follows: undernutrition: United Nations, *The Millennium Development Goals Report, 2015.* United Nations, New York, 2015, 20; sanitation: World Health Organization, "Water Supply, Sanitation and Hygiene Development," http://www.who.int/water_sanitation_health/ hygiene/en/ (accessed February 20, 2015); child mortality: United Nations Development Programme, *Human Development Report, 2014,* United Nations Development Programme, New York, 2014, Table 7, and United Nations Children's Fund (UNICEF), *Committing to Child Survival: A Promise Renewed (Progress Report, 2014)* UNICEF, New York, 2014, 5; child stunting: United Nations Development Programme, *Human Development Report, 2014,* United Nations Development Programme, New York, 2014, Table 7; physicians per 10,000 people and life expectancy: United Nations Development Programme, *Human Development Report, 2014,* United Nations Development Programme, New York, 2014, Table 8.

34. Robert McNamara in World Bank, *World Development Report, 1978,* World Bank, New York, 1978, iii.

35. Oxfam, *Even It Up: Time to End Extreme Inequality,* Oxfam GB for Oxfam International, Oxford, 2014, http://www.oxfam.org/sites/www .oxfam.org/files/file_attachments/cr-even-it-up-extreme-inequality -291014-en.pdf. The report has been criticized (and defended) on methodological grounds; for discussion, see Vauhina Vara, "Critics of Oxfam's Poverty Statistics Are Missing the Point," *New Yorker,* January 28, 2015, http://www.newyorker.com/business/currency/critics -oxfams-poverty-statistics-missing-point.

36. World Bank, Overview, http://www.worldbank.org/en/topic/poverty/ overview (viewed December 37, 2015).

37. Branko Milanovic, "Global Income Inequality by the Numbers: in History and Now," Policy Research Working Paper 6259, World Bank Development Research Group, Poverty and Inequality Team, November 2012, 12, 17.

38. World Health Organization, *World Health Statistics 2014,* http://www. who.int/mediacentre/news/releases/2014/world-health-statistics-2014/n/.

39. United Nations, *The Millennium Development Goals Report, 2015,* United Nations, New York, 2015, 32; see also United Nations Children's Fund, (UNICEF), *Committing to Child Survival: A Promise Renewed (Progress Report, 2014),* UNICEF, New York, 2014, 5.

40. United Nations, *We Can End Poverty: Millennium Development Goals and Beyond 2015,* http://www.un.org/millenniumgoals/poverty.shtml.

41. United Nations, *The Millennium Development Goals Report, 2015,* United Nations, New York, 2015, 24.

42. Francisco Ferreira and Martin Ravallion, "Global Poverty and Inequal- ity: A Review of the Evidence," World Bank Development Research Group, Poverty Team, Policy Research Working Paper 4623, May 2008, 25, http://elibrary.worldbank.org/doi/pdf/10.1596/1813-9450-4623.

43. Jonathan Ostry, Andrew Berg, and Charalambos Tsangardies, "Redistribution, Inequality and Growth," International Monetary Fund Research Department, IMF staff discussion note, February 2014, revised April 2014, http://www.imf.org/external/pubs/ft/sdn/2014/sdn1402.pdf. See also Alberto Alesina and Roberto Perotti, "The Political Economy of Growth: A Critical Survey of the Recent Literature," *World Bank Economic Review* 8:3 (1994): 350–71, and Roberto Perotti, "Growth, Income Distribution and Democracy: What the Data Say," *Journal of Economic Growth* 1 (1996): 149–87.

44. Did Brandeis ever say this? See Peter Campbell, "Democracy v. Concentrated Wealth: In Search of a Louis B. Brandeis Quote," University of Louisville, School of Law, Legal Studies Research Paper Series, Paper No. 2014–11, http://papers.ssrn.com/sol3/papers.cfm?abstract_id=2434225.

45. Karl Marx and Friedrich Engels, *The Communist Manifesto,* Penguin, Harmondsworth, 1967, 82.

46. Herman E. Daly, "Globalization and Its Discontents," *Philosophy and Public Policy Quarterly* 21, 2/3 (2001): 19.

47. Vandana Shiva, "Social environment clauses—a 'political diversion,' " in *Third World Economics* 118 (1996): 8–9, as quoted in Michelle Swenarchuk, "The International Confederation of Free Trade Unions Labour Clause Proposal: A Legal and Political Critique," in Stephen McBride and John Wiseman, eds., *Globalization and Its Discontents,* St. Martin's Press, New York, 2000, 167.

48. Jim Yardley, "Report on Deadly Factory Collapse in Bangladesh Finds Widespread Blame," *New York Times,* May 22, 2013; Editorial, "One Year After Rana Plaza," *New York Times,* April 27, 2014; International Labour Organization, "Bangladesh: Improving Working Conditions in the Ready-Made Garment Industry: Progress and Achievements," Press Release, February 5, 2015, http://www.ilo.org/global/about-the-ilo/activities/all/safer-garment-industry-in-bangladesh/WCMS_240343/lang—en.

49. For the Singapore declaration, see World Trade Organization, Ministerial Declaration, December 13, 1996, WT/MIN(96)/DEC, par 4; http://www.wto.org/english/thewto_e/minist_e/min96_e/wtodec_e.htm. For Doha, see World Trade Organization, Ministerial Declaration, 14 November 2001, WT/MIN(01)/DEC/1, par 8; http://www-chil.wto-ministerial.org/english/thewto_e/minist_e/min01_e/mindecl_e.htm.

50. World Trade Organization, "Labour Standards: Consensus, Coherence, Controversy," *Understanding the WTO,* http://www.wto.org/english/thewto_e/whatis_e/tif_e/bey5_e.htm (accessed February 22, 2015).

51. Joseph Kahn, "U.S. Sees Trade Talks as a Test of Leadership," *New York Times,* November 9, 2001, C6.

52. World Trade Organization, "Background Paper: The WTO's 2-year strategy comes to fruition," January 2002, paragraph 17.

53. Quoted from Raymond Zhong, "How Can India Be Breaking WTO Rules When Rich Countries Spend So Much More on Their Farm-

ers?," *Wall Street Journal,* August 13, 2014, http://blogs.wsj.com/
indiarealtime/2014/08/13/how-can-india-be-breaking-wto-rules
-when-rich-countries-spend. See also Timothy Wise and Jeronim
Capaldo, "Will the WTO fast-track trade at the expense of food
security?," *Al Jazeera,* July 24, 2014, http://www.aljazeera.com/indepth/
opinion/2014/07/wto-negotiations-food-security-20147237431402983
.html.

54. BBC News, "India and US reach WTO breakthrough over food,"
November 13, 2014, http://www.bbc.com/news/business-30033130.

55. See www.behindthebrands.org.

56. Michael Ross, *Extractive Sectors and the Poor,* Oxfam America, Boston,
2001; available at http://www.sscnet.ucla.edu/polisci/faculty/ross/oxfam
.pdf; Jeffrey Sachs and Andrew Warner, "Natural Resource Abundance
and Economic Growth," National Bureau of Economic Research
Working Paper 5398, 1995, http://www.nber.org/papers/w5398. Some
of this research is helpfully summarized in the opening pages of Leif
Wenar, "Property Rights and the Resource Curse," *Philosophy and
Public Affairs* 36 (2008), and, for a fuller account, see the same author's
Blood Oil, Oxford University Press, New York, 2015. To appreciate the
complexities of the research and some problems with it, see Graham
Davis, "Extractive Economies, Growth, and the Poor," in J. Richards,
ed., *Mining, Society and a Sustainable World,* Springer-Verlag, Berlin
2009, 37–60.

57. Nicholas Kristof, "Deadliest Country for Kids," *New York Times,*
March 19, 2015; Nicholas Kristof, "Two Women, Opposite Fortunes,"
New York Times, March 21, 2015; Kerry Dolan and Rafael Marques de
Morais, "Daddy's Girl: How an African 'Princess' Banked $3 Billion in
a Country Living on $2 a Day," *Forbes,* August 14, 2013.

58. African Economic Outlook, "Equitorial Guinea," http://www.african
economicoutlook.org/en/countries/central-africa/equatorial-guinea;
Borko Handjiski and Alexander Huurdeman, "Lucky Countries or
Lucky People?: Will East Africans Benefit from Their Natural Resources
Discoveries?," World Bank, *Africa Can End Poverty,* February 5, 2015,
http://blogs.worldbank.org/africacan/lucky-countries-or-lucky-people
-will-east-africans-benefit-their-natural-resource-discoveries.

59. Reuters, "Insight-Equatorial Guinea Tries to Shake Off 'Oil Curse'
Image," *New York Times,* March 10, 2014, http://www.nytimes.com/
reuters/2014/03/10/business/10reuters-equatorial-image-insight.html.

60. Justin Blum, "U.S. Oil Firms Entwined in Equatorial Guinea Deals," *Washington Post*, September 7, 2014, http://www.washingtonpost .com/wp-dyn/articles/A1101–2004Sep6.html; Associated Press, "U.S. Government Seeks $70M from African Official," October 26, 2011.

61. See Pogge's "Achieving Democracy," *Ethics and International Affairs* 15:1 (2001): 3–23, and, for a more recent restatement that goes into other important issues as well, Thomas Pogge, *World Poverty and Human Rights*, 2d ed., Polity Press, Cambridge, 2008, chapter 6. For Academics Stand Against Poverty, see www.academicsstand.org.

62. Leif Wenar, *Blood Oil*, Oxford University Press, New York, 2015. For the organization Clean Trade, see www.cleantrade.org.

63. Wenar, "Property Rights and the Resource Curse," *Philosophy and Public Affairs* 36 (2008): 2–32.

64. See Pogge, *World Poverty and Human Rights*, chapter 6.

65. http://www.cleantrade.org/policy_brief.pdf.

66. For a full discussion, see Wenar, *Blood Oil*, part III.

67. Lorand Bartels, "WTO Law Aspects of Clean Trade," *Social Sciences Research Network*, July 22, 2015, http://papers.ssrn.com/sol3/papers.cfm ?abstract_id=2634567.

68. Brad Roth, *Governmental Illegitimacy in International Law*, Clarendon Press, Oxford, 1999, 162–63.

69. Thomas Jefferson to Gouverneur Morris, November 7, 1792, *Works*, 4th ed. vol. 3, 489, cited in Roth, *Governmental Illegitimacy in International Law*, 321.

70. See Fair Vote, "Problems with the Electoral College," http://www .fairvote.org/reforms/national-popular-vote/the-electoral-college/ problems-with-the-electoral-college/ viewed August 3, 2015.

71. *The Warsaw Declaration*, June 27, 2000, https://www.community -democracies.org/Visioning-Democracy/To-be-a-Democracy-.

72. Community of Democracies, https://www.community-democracies.org/ The-Community-of-Democracies/Our-countries.

4 one law

1. Numbers 31:1–18 (King James Version).

2. See, for example, Deuteronomy 3:1–7, 7:1–26, 20:13–17; I Samuel 15:3; Joshua 8:26–28; Ezekiel 9:5.

3. Lawrence Keeley, *War Before Civilization*, Oxford University Press, New York, 1996. See especially chapter 6.

4. Steven Pinker, *The Better Angels of Our Nature*, Viking, New York, 2011.

5. Richard Wrangham and Dale Peterson, *Demonic Males: Apes and the Origins of Human Violence*, Houghton Mifflin, Boston, 1996, 5–21; see also Jane Goodall, *The Chimpanzees of Gombe*, Harvard University Press, Cambridge, 1986, 530–34.

6. The classic article on this topic is R. L. Trivers, "The Evolution of Reciprocal Altruism," *Quarterly Review of Biology* 46 (1971): 35–57; see also Robert Axelrod, *The Evolution of Cooperation*, Basic Books, New York, 1984.

7. See Tony Ashworth, *Trench Warfare 1914–1918: The Live and Let Live System*, Macmillan, London, 1980.

8. Timothy Garton Ash, *History of the Present*, Allen Lane, London, 1999, 368.

9. Pinker, *The Better Angels of Our Nature*, 47–58.

10. *Charter of the International Military Tribunal*, Article 6; http://www.yale.edu/lawweb/avalon/imt/proc/imtconst.htm.

11. *R. v Bow Street Stipendiary Magistrate and others, ex Pinochet Ugarte (No. 3)* [2000] 1 A.C. 147, [1999] 2 All E R 97; available at http://www.parliament.the-stationery-office.co.uk/pa/ld199899/ldjudgmt/jd990324/pino2.htm.

12. Amnesty International, *The Pinochet Case—Universal Jurisdiction and the Absence of Immunity for Crimes Against Humanity*—Report—EUR 45/01/99 January 1999, United Kingdom, http://www.amnesty.org/ailib/aipub/1999/EUR/44500199.htm.

13. *Attorney-General of Israel v. Eichmann* (1962) 36 Intl.L.R. 5, and, for a summary, see http://www.gwu.edu/~jaysmith/Eichmann.html.

14. See the discussion by Lord Millett in *R. v Bow Street Stipendiary Magistrate and others, ex Pinochet Ugarte (No. 3)* http://www.parliament.the-stationery-office.co.uk/pa/ld199899/ldjudgmt/jd990324/pino7.htm. Though the Supreme Court of Israel did assert universal jurisdiction, Israel also invoked a statute that was more specifically limited to Nazi crimes against Jews. See Gary Bass, "The Adolf Eichmann Case: Universal and National Jurisdictions," in Stephen Macedo, ed., *Universal Jurisdiction: National Courts and the Prosecution of Serious Crimes under International Law*, University of Pennsylvania Press, Philadelphia, 2004.

15. Dionne Searcey, "Hissène Habré, ex-President of Chad, Is Convicted of War Crimes," *New York Times*, May 30, 2016.

16. *R. v Bow Street Stipendiary Magistrate and others, ex Pinochet Ugarte (No. 3)* http://www.parliament.the-stationery-office.co.uk/pa/ld199899/ldjudgmt/jd990324/pino9.htm.

17. Princeton Project on Universal Jurisdiction, *The Princeton Principles on Universal Jurisdiction,* Program in Law and Public Affairs, Princeton University, Princeton, 2001.

18. Ibid., 49, n. 20.

19. Clyde Haberman, "Israel is wary of rights cases across borders," *New York Times,* July 28, 2001.

20. Ben Quinn, "Former Israeli minister Tzipi Livni to visit UK after change in arrest law," *The Guardian,* October 4, 2011.

21. "Bush Urged to Support World Court," *New York Times,* July 17, 2001.

22. Human Rights Watch, "U.S. 'Hague Invasion Act' Becomes Law," August 4, 2002, http://www.hrw.org/news/2002/08/03/us-hague -invasion-act-becomes-law.

23. Mark Mazzetti, "U.S. Cuts in Aid Said to Hurt War on Terror," *New York Times,* July 23, 2006.

24. "Bush Says Terrorists Will Get Better Treatment Than Those Killed Sept. 11," *New York Times,* December 28, 2001.

25. U.S. Department of State, "U.S. Engagement with the ICC and the Outcome of the Recently Concluded Review Conference," Special Briefing, June 15, 2010, http://web.archive.org/web/20120112210935/ http://www.state.gov/j/gcj/us_releases/remarks/143178.htm.

26. BBC News, "ICC finds Congo warlord Thomas Lubanga guilty," March 14, 2012, http://m.bbc.com/news/world-africa-17364988.

27. BBC News, "ICC gives Congo warlord Germain Katanga 12-year jail term," May 23, 2014, http://www.bbc.com/news/world-africa -27531534.

28. Immanuel Kant, *Perpetual Peace: A Philosophic Sketch,* Second Supplement. Available at http://www.mtholyoke.edu/acad/intrel/kant/kantı .htm.

29. John Stuart Mill, "A Few Words on Non-Intervention," in John Stuart Mill, *Essays on Politics and Culture,* ed. Gertrude Himmelfarb, Anchor Books, New York, 1963, 377 (first published in *Fraser's Magazine,* December 1859). For further discussion, see Michael Doyle, "The New Interventionism," *Metaphilosophy* 32/1–2 (January 2001).

30. L. Oppenheim, *International Law,* vol. 1, Longman, 1948 (first published 1905), 279.

31. Michael Walzer, *Just and Unjust Wars*, Penguin, Harmondsworth, 1980, 107.

32. Michael Walzer, "The Argument about Humanitarian Intervention," *Dissent* (Winter 2002): 29–37.

33. Michael Walzer, "The Politics of Rescue," *Dissent* 42 (Winter 1995): 36; Walzer, "The Argument about Humanitarian Intervention," 29.

34. Walzer, *Just and Unjust Wars*, 53–54, 86, 89.

35. Walzer, "The Politics of Rescue," 36.

36. James D. Steakley, *The Homosexual Emancipation Movement in Germany*, Arno Press, New York, 1975, p 110.

37. Kofi Annan, "Two Concepts of Sovereignty," *The Economist*, 18 September 1999, http://www.economist.com/node/324795.

38. Convention on the Prevention and Punishment of the Crime of Genocide, UN General Assembly 260A(III), 9 December 1948; http://www.unhchr.ch/html/menu3/b/p_genoci.htm.

39. Rome Statute of the International Criminal Court, Article 7, http://www.un.org/law/icc/statute/romefra.htm.

40. International Commission on Intervention and State Sovereignty, *The Responsibility to Protect*, International Development Research Centre, Ottawa, 2001, available at http://responsibilitytoprotect.org/ICISS%20Report.pdf.

41. Ibid., paragraph 2.29.

42. United Nations, *Report of the Secretary-General: Implementing the Responsibility to Protect*, paragraph 4, available at http://www.unrol.org/doc.aspx?d=2982.

43. United Nations General Assembly, Resolution adopted by the General Assembly, 60/1 2005 World Summit Outcome, October 24, 2005, A/res/60/1, paragraphs 138–9, available at http://www.un.org/Docs/journal/asp/ws.asp?m=A/RES/60/1.

44. United Nations, *Report of the Secretary-General: Implementing the Responsibility to Protect*, paragraph 11.

45. International Coalition for the Responsibility to Protect, "RtoP at the United Nations: Key Developments on the Responsibility to Protect at the United Nations from 2005–2014," September 2014, http://responsibilitytoprotect.org/index.php/about-rtop/the-un-and-rtop.

46. United Nations Security Council Resolution 1975 (2011) adopted March 30, 2011, http://www.un.org/en/ga/search/view_doc.asp?symbol=S/RES/1975%282011%29.

47. Maria Golovnina and Patrick Worsnip, "U.S. okays military action on Libya," *Reuters*, March 17, 2011, http://www.reuters.com/article/2011/03/17/us-libya-idUSTRE7270JP20110317.

48. United Nations Security Council Resolution 1973 (March 17, 2011) http://www.un.org/en/ga/search/view_doc.asp?symbol=S/RES/1973%282011%29.

49. Gareth Evans, "UN targets Libya with pinpoint accuracy," *Sydney Morning Herald*, March 24, 2011.

50. Chris Keeler, "The End of the Responsibility to Protect?," *Foreign Policy Journal*, October 12, 2011, http://www.foreignpolicyjournal.com/2011/10/12/the-end-of-the-responsibility-to-protect/.

51. Ibid.; David Rieff, "R2P, R.I.P.," *New York Times*, November 7, 2011.

52. Gareth Evans, "R2P: The Next Ten Years," in Alex Bellamy and Tim Dunne, eds., *Oxford Handbook of the Responsibility to Protect*, Oxford University Press, Oxford, 2016. The 2014 Security Council resolutions referred to are United Nations Security Council Resolution 2150, April 16, 2014, http://www.un.org/en/ga/search/view_doc.asp?symbol=S/RES/2150(2014), and Security Council Resolution 2171 (August 21, 2014), http://www.un.org/en/ga/search/view_doc.asp?symbol=S/RES/2171%20%282014%29. I owe these references to the International Coalition for the Responsibility to Protect, "References to Responsibility to Protect in Security Council Resolutions," http://www.responsibilitytoprotect.org/index.php/component/content/article/136-latest-news/5221—references-to-the-responsibility-to-protect-in-security-council-resolutions.

53. SG/SM/7136 GA/9596: Secretary-General presents his annual report to General Assembly; http://www.un.org/press/en/1999/19990920.sgsm7136.html.

54. Martin Gilbert, "The Terrible Twentieth Century," *Globe and Mail* (Canada) January 31, 2007. I owe the reference to Gareth Evans, who modestly concedes that this "may be too big a call." See Gareth Evans, "R2P: The Next Ten Years." For a fuller description of the intellectual foundations on which the responsibility to protect was built, see Gareth Evans, "The Evolution of the Responsibility to Protect: from concept and principle to actionable norm" in *Theorising the Responsibility to Protect*, Ramesh Thakur and William Maley, eds., Cambridge University Press, Cambridge, 2015.

55. Roth, *Governmental Illegitimacy in International Law*, 324.

56. General Assembly Resolution 2625 (XXV), Annex, 25 UN GAOR, Supp. (no. 28), UN Dec A/5217 (1970), at 121, cited in Roth, *Governmental Illegitimacy in International Law*, 161–62.

57. Security Council Resolution 688 (5 April 1991), http://fas.org/news/un/iraq/sres/sres0688.htm. I owe this and the following two examples to Gregory Fox, "The Right to Political Participation in International Law," in Cecelia Lynch and Michael Loriaux, eds., *Law and Moral Action in World Politics*, University of Minnesota Press, Minneapolis, 1999, 91.

58. Security Council Resolution 794 (3 December 1992), http://srcho.un.org:80/documents/sc/res/1992/s92r794e.pdf.

59. Security Council Resolution 841 (16 June 1993), http://srcho.un.org:80/Docs/scres/1993/841e.pdf.

60. United Nations Security Council Resolution 1973 (March 17, 2011), http://www.un.org/en/ga/search/view_doc.asp?symbol=S/RES/1973%282011%29.

61. The thesis goes back to Kant's *Perpetual Peace*, section II, and was also advanced by Joseph Schumpeter in "The Sociology of Imperialism," in *Imperialism and Social Classes*, World Publishing, Cleveland, 1955. See Michael Doyle, "Liberal Institutions and International Ethics," in Kenneth Kipnis and Diana Meyers, eds., *Political Realism and International Morality*, Westview, Boulder, CO, 1987, 185–211; first published as "Liberalism and World Politics," *American Political Science Review* 80:4 (1986): 1152–69. There are many discussions of the "no wars between democracies" thesis on the web; see, for example, http://users.erols.com/mwhite28/demowar.htm.

62. *The Responsibility to Protect*, xi, 12–13, paras 2.7–2.15, 16, para 2.27, and 47–50, paras 6.1–6.18.

63. This objection was pressed by John Broome when I gave an earlier version of this chapter as an Amnesty Lecture at the University of Oxford. My response partially reflects comments made by Nir Eyal, who was also present on that occasion.

64. The preceding paragraph owes much to Leif Wenar's thoughtful comments.

65. Speech to SS Leaders in Posen, October 4, 1943, cited in Karl Dietrich Bracher, *The German Dictatorship*, Praeger, New York, 1971, 423.

66. Doyle, "Liberal Institutions and International Ethics," 220. See this paper generally for a discussion, with many contemporary illustrations, of some of the consequentialist aspects of humanitarian intervention.

67. Thomas Hobbes, *Leviathan,* first published 1651, chapter 13.

68. Tzvetan Todorov, "Right to Intervene or Duty to Assist?," in Nicholas Owen, ed., *Human Rights, Human Wrongs—Oxford Amnesty Lectures, 2001,* Oxford University Press, Oxford, 2002.

69. "Statement by President George W. Bush," United Nations General Assembly, New York, September 12, 2002, http://www.un.org/webcast/ga/57/statements/020912usaE.htm.

70. Center for Refugee and Disaster Response, Bloomberg School of Public Health, Johns Hopkins University, "Updated Iraq Study Confirms Earlier Mortality Estimates," http://www.jhsph.edu/research/centers-and-institutes/center-for-refugee-and-disaster-response/publications_tools/iraq/index.html.

71. David Kirkpatrick, "Ties to Islamic State Cited by Group in Libya Attacks," *New York Times,* February 20, 2015, and David Kirkpatrick, "Wider Chaos Threatens as Fighters Seize Branch of Libya's Central Bank," *New York Times,* January 22, 2015.

72. See, for example, David Pugliese, "Canadian military predicted Libya would descend into civil war if foreign countries helped overthrow Gaddafi," *National Post,* March 1, 2015.

73. Michael Shear and Julie Hirschfeld Davis, "While Offering Support, Obama warns that U.S. Won't be 'Iraqi Air Force,'" *New York Times,* August 8, 2014.

74. Sir William Napier, *History of General Sir Charles Napier's Administration of Scinde, and Campaign in the Cutchee Hills,* Chapman and Hall, London, 1851, 35.

75. For further discussion of the basis of ethics, see my *Practical Ethics,* 3d ed., Cambridge University Press, Cambridge, 2011, chap. 1, and Katarzyna de Lazari-Radek and Peter Singer, *The Point of View of the Universe,* Oxford University Press, Oxford, 2014.

76. See Alvin Gouldner, "The Norm of Reciprocity," *American Sociological Review* 25:2 (1960): 171.

77. For references, see Leonard Swidler, ed., *For All Life: Toward a Universal Declaration of a Global Ethic,* White Cloud Press, Ashland, OR, 1999, 19–21; see also Q. C. Terry, *Golden Rules and Silver Rules of Humanity,* Infinity Publishing, West Conshohocken, PA, rev. ed., 2015.

78. Graeme Wood, "What ISIS Really Wants," *The Atlantic,* March 2015.

79. These figures were calculated from data available in August 2015 (with thanks to Dawn Disette for gathering the data and adding the figures).

80. Quoted from Erskine Childers, "Empowering the people in their United Nations," *Cross Currents* 45 (1995–96): 437–50. For a contemporary defense of the same idea, see George Monbiot, "Let the People Rule the World," *The Guardian,* July 17, 2001.

81. Gareth Evans, "R2P: The Next Ten Years," in Alex Bellamy and Tim Dunne, eds., *Oxford Handbook of the Responsibility to Protect,* Oxford University Press, Oxford, 2016.

5 one community

1. David Barstow and Diana B. Henriques, "Gifts for Rescuers Divide Terror Victims' Families," *New York Times,* December 2, 2001.

2. Joyce Purnick, "Take the Cash. You're Making Us Look Bad," *New York Times,* February 11, 2002, B1; Nick Paumgarten, "Free Money: Trumpery Below Canal," *New Yorker,* February 18, 25, 2002, 58; Joyce Purnick, "For Red Cross, a New Round of Complaints," *New York Times,* February 21, 2002, B1.

3. For a summary, see http://www.unicef.org/media/sowco2presskit/. The full report is also accessible from this page.

4. Purnick, "Take the Cash," B1.

5. Henry Sidgwick, *The Methods of Ethics,* 7th ed., Macmillan, London, 1907, 246.

6. Heinrich Himmler, Speech to SS leaders in Poznan, Poland, October 4, 1943; cited from http://www.historyplace.com/worldwar2/timeline/posen.htm.

7. R. M. Hare, *Freedom and Reason,* Clarendon Press, Oxford, 1963; R. M. Hare, *Moral Thinking,* Clarendon Press, Oxford, 1981.

8. "Famine, Affluence and Morality," *Philosophy and Public Affairs* 1 (1972): 231–32; and reprinted with other essays in Peter Singer, *Famine, Affluence and Morality,* Oxford University Press, New York, 2015.

9. Raymond D. Gastil, "Beyond a Theory of Justice," *Ethics* 85:3 (1975): 185; cf. Samuel Scheffler, "Relationships and Responsibilities," *Philosophy and Public Affairs* 26 (1997): 189–209; David Miller, "Reasonable Partiality Towards Compatriots," *Ethical Theory and Moral Practice* 8 (2005): 63–81.

10. William Godwin, *An Enquiry Concerning Political Justice and its Influence on General Virtue and Happiness,* 1st ed., published 1793, edited and abridged by Raymond Preston, Knopf, New York, 1926, 41–42.

11. Samuel Parr, *A Spital Sermon preached at Christ Church upon Easter Tuesday, April 15, 1800, to which are added notes,* J. Mawman, London, 1801. Henceforth cited as *A Spital Sermon.*

12. Galatians vi:10.

13. *A Spital Sermon,* 4.

14. Nel Noddings, *Caring: A Feminine Approach to Ethics and Moral Education,* University of California Press, Berkeley and Los Angeles, 1986, 86; for a related passage, see also 112.

15. William Godwin, *Memoirs of the Author of a Vindication of the Rights of Woman,* chap. vi, 90, 2d ed., quoted in William Godwin, *Thoughts Occasioned by the Perusal of Dr Parr's Spital Sermon,* Taylor and Wilks, London, 1801; reprinted in J. Marken and B. Pollin, eds., *Uncollected Writings (1785–1822) by William Godwin,* Gainesville, FL, Scholars' Facsimiles and Reprints, 1968, 314–15. As K. Codell Carter notes (op cit., 320, fn), the passage italicised in the original is from Terence (*Heautontimorumenos,* I. 77) and is usually translated as "nothing human is alien to me." Godwin's argument for the importance of "individual attachments" is reminiscent of Aristotle's discussion of the need for friendship in his *Nicomachean Ethics,* bk. IX, sec. 9.

16. R. M. Hare, *Moral Thinking: Its Levels, Method and Point,* Clarendon Press, Oxford, 1981, pt. I.

17. See Yonina Talmon, *Family and Community in the Kibbutz,* Harvard University Press, Cambridge, 1972, 3–34.

18. See Martin Daly and Margo Wilson, *The Truth About Cinderella: A Darwinian View of Parental Love,* Yale University Press, New Haven, 1999.

19. Bernard Williams, "Persons, Character and Morality," in Bernard Williams, *Moral Luck,* Cambridge, Cambridge University Press, 1981, 18.

20. See, for example, W. D. Ross, *The Right and the Good,* Clarendon Press, Oxford, 1930, 21.

21. M. Rosenzweig, "Risk, implicit contracts and the family in rural areas of low-income countries," *Economic Journal* 98 (1988): 1148–70; M. Rosenzweig and O. Stark, "Consumption smoothing, migration and marriage:

Evidence from rural India," *Journal of Political Economy* 97:4 (1989): 905–26. I am grateful to Thomas Pogge for this information.

22. Michael Walzer, *Spheres of Justice*, Basic Books, New York, 1983, 12.

23. Michael Sandel, *Justice: What's the Right Thing to Do?*, Farrar, Straus and Giroux, New York, 2010, 237.

24. Eamonn Callan, *Creating Citizens: Political Education and Liberal Democracy*, Clarendon Press, Oxford, 1997, 96. This and the following quotation are cited from Melissa Williams, "Citizenship as Identity, Citizenship as Shared Fate, and the Functions of Multicultural Education," in Walter Feinberg and Kevin McDonough, eds., *Collective Identities and Cosmopolitan Values*, Oxford University Press, Oxford, 2002.

25. Walter Feinberg, *Common Schools/Uncommon Identities: National Unity and Cultural Difference*, Yale University Press, New Haven, 1998, 119.

26. Benedict Anderson, *Imagined Communities: Reflections on the Origin and Spread of Nationalism*, Verso, London, rev. ed., 1991, 6.

27. Robert Goodin, "What is so special about our fellow countrymen?" *Ethics* 98 (1988): 685; reprinted in Robert Goodin, *Utilitarianism as a Public Philosophy*, Cambridge University Press, Cambridge, 1995, 286. I was reminded of this quotation by Christopher Wellman, "Relational Facts in Liberal Political Theory: Is There Magic in the Pronoun 'My'?," *Ethics* 110 (2000): 537–62.

28. Goodin, *Utilitarianism as a Public Philosophy*, 286.

29. Wellman, "Relational Facts in Liberal Political Theory: Is There Magic in the Pronoun 'My'?", *Ethics*, April 2000. [ms 10–12]; the third point is also made by David Miller, *Principles of Social Justice*, Harvard University Press, Cambridge, 1999, 18.

30. Karl Marx, *Wage Labour and Capital*, in David McLellan, ed., *Karl Marx: Selected Writings*, Oxford University Press, Oxford, 1977, 259.

31. John Rawls, *The Law of Peoples*, Harvard University Press, Cambridge, 1999, 120.

32. John Rawls, *A Theory of Justice*, Oxford University Press, London, 1971, 12; see also 100.

33. John Rawls, *The Law of Peoples*, 40.

34. Ibid., 117.

35. Ibid., 106.

36. For further details, see *A Theory of Justice*, 4f., 453f.

37. Ibid., 108.

38. Ibid., 116; for Beitz's criticisms, see Charles Beitz, *Political Theory and International Relations,* Princeton University Press, Princeton, 1979, and "Social and cosmopolitan liberalism," *International Affairs* 75:3 (1999): 515–29; for Pogge's, see Thomas Pogge, *Realizing Rawls,* Cornell University Press, Ithaca, NY, 1990, and "An Egalitarian Law of Peoples," *Philosophy and Public Affairs* 23:3 (1994).

39. Leif Wenar, "The Legitimacy of Peoples," in C. Cronin and de Greiff, eds., *Global Politics and Transnational Justice,* MIT Press, Cambridge, 2002, 53.

40. See the Organization for Economic Co-operation and Development, "Detailed final 2014 aid figures released by OECD/DAC," http://www.oecd.org/dac/stats/final2014da.htm, and "Aid at a glance charts, Interactive summary charts for all DAC members and total DAC," http://www.oecd.org/dac/stats/aid-at-a-glance.htm.

41. Sarah Hénon, *Measuring Private Development Assistance,* Development Initiatives, Bristol, 2014, 10, figure 5; available at http://devinit.org/staging/wp/wp-content/uploads/2014/08/Measuring-private-development-assistance1.pdf. I am grateful to Anthony Pipa for this reference.

42. See the surveys cited by Bruce Bartlett, "Voter Ignorance Threatens Deficit Reduction," *Fiscal Times,* February 4, 2011, http://www.the fiscaltimes.com/Columns/2011/02/04/Voter-Ignorance-Threatens-Deficit-Reduction.

43. Program on International Policy Attitudes, *Americans on Foreign Aid and World Hunger: A Survey of U.S. Public Attitudes,* February 2, 2001, http://www.pipa.org/OnlineReports/ForeignAid/ForeignAid_Feb01/ForeignAid_Feb01_rpt.pdf.

44. World Opinion Poll, "American Public Opinion on Foreign Aid," November 30, 2010, http://www.worldpublicopinion.org/pipa/pdf/nov10/ForeignAid_Nov10_quaire.pdf.

45. Kaiser Family Foundation, *2013 Survey of Americans on the U.S. Role in Global Health,* November 7, 2013, http://kff.org/global-health-policy/poll-finding/2013-survey-of-americans-on-the-u-s-role-in-global-health/.

46. Ibid.

47. Thomas Aquinas, *Summa Theologica,* II–II, Q66 A 7.

48. Pope Paul VI, *Populorum Progressio* (1967), paragraph 23.

49. Pope Francis, *Fraternity, the Foundation and Pathway to Peace,* available at http://www.vatican.va/holy_father/francesco/messages/

peace/documents/papa-francesco_20131208_messaggio-xlvii-giornata
-mondiale-pace–2014_en.html.

50. Peter Unger, *Living High and Letting Die,* New York: Oxford University
Press, 1996, 136–39.

51. http://www.givewell.org/International/top-charities/amf. GiveWell
considers anything under $5,000 per life saved to be good value, though
the organization also cautions against taking such estimates too literally.
For further discussion, see http://www.givewell.org/international/
technical/criteria/cost-effectiveness. For a list of effective aid organizations partly based on GiveWell's evaluations but using broader criteria
in some cases, see www.thelifeyoucansave.org.

52. Henry Sidgwick, *The Methods of Ethics,* 489–90; for discussion of the
idea of esoteric morality, see Katarzyna de Lazari-Radek and Peter
Singer, *The Point of View of the Universe,* Oxford University Press,
Oxford, 2014, chapter 10.

53. For details of the suggested levels, and for the calculation of how much
this would raise, see Peter Singer, *The Life You Can Save,* Random
House, New York, 2009, chapter 10.

54. Organization for Economic Cooperation and Development, "Aid
at a Glance Charts, Interactive Summary for all DAC members and
Total DAC," https://public.tableau.com/views/AidAtAGlance/DAC
members?:embed=y&:display_count=no?&:showVizHome=no#1,

55. William Easterly, *The White Man's Burden: Why the West's Efforts to Aid
the Rest Have Done So Much Ill and So Little Good,* Penguin, New York,
2006; Dambisa Moyo, *Dead Aid: Why Aid Is Not Working and How
There Is a Better Way for Africa,* Farrar, Straus and Giroux, New York,
2009.

56. Angus Deaton, *The Great Escape: Health, Wealth, and the Origins of
Inequality,* Princeton University Press, Princeton, 2013, chapter 7.

57. Jonathan Muraskas and Kayhan Parsi, "The Cost of Saving the Tiniest
Lives: NICUs versus Prevention," *AMA Journal of Ethics* 10 (2008):
655–58.

58. William MacAskill, *Doing Good Better,* Gotham, New York, 2015, 46.

59. Ibid., 45–46.

60. Garrett Hardin, "Living on a Lifeboat," *Bioscience,* October 1974;
reprinted, with some changes, in William Aiken and Hugh LaFollette,
eds., *World Hunger and Moral Obligation,* Prentice-Hall, Englewood
Cliffs, NJ, 1977.

61. On the relation between fertility and education in India, see Jean Drèze and Mamta Murthi, "Fertility, Education and Development," Discussion paper DEDPS 20 (January 2000), Suntory Centre, London School of Economics and Political Science, available at: http://eprints.lse.ac.uk/6663/1/Fertility,_Education_and_Development.pdf.

6 a better world?

1. Cited from W.-T. Chan, *A Source Book in Chinese Philosophy*, Princeton University Press, Princeeton, 1963, 213. I owe this reference to Hyun Höchsmann.

2. Attributed to Diogenes by Diogenes Laertius, *Life of Diogenes of Sinope, the Cynic*. The same remark is attributed to Socrates by Plutarch, in *Of Banishment*.

3. John Lennon, *Imagine,* copyright © 1971 Lenono Music.

4. Branko Milanovic, "World Income Inequality in the Second Half of the 20th Century," a paper that was available in draft form at www.worldbank.org in June 2001. The draft later became Branko Milanovic, *Worlds Apart,* Princeton University Press, Princeton, 2011, where the sentence may be found on 156.

5. Sewell Chan, "How a Record Number of Migrants Made Their Way to Europe," *New York Times,* December 22, 2015.

6. On this and other ideas about the nature of global institutions, see Daniel Weinstock, "Prospects for Transnational Citizenship and Democracy," *Ethics and International Affairs* 15 (2001): 53–66. Weinstock argues persuasively against some common objections to the idea of global citizenship.

index

The Dwight Harrington Terry Foundation Lectures on Religion in the Light of Science and Philosophy

The deed of gift declares that "the object of this foundation is not the promotion of scientific investigation and discovery, but rather the assimilation and interpretation of that which has been or shall be hereafter discovered, and its application to human welfare, especially by the building of the truths of science and philosophy into the structure of a broadened and purified religion. The founder believes that such a religion will greatly stimulate intelligent effort for the improvement of human conditions and the advancement of the race in strength and excellence of character. To this end it is desired that a series of lectures be given by men eminent in their respective departments, on ethics, the history of civilization and religion, biblical research, all sciences and branches of knowledge which have an important bearing on the subject, all the great laws of nature, especially of evolution . . . also such interpretations of literature and sociology as are in accord with the spirit of this foundation, to the end that the Christian spirit may be nurtured in the fullest light of the world's knowledge and that mankind may be helped to attain its highest possible welfare and happiness upon this earth." The present work constitutes the latest volume published on this foundation.

Other Volumes in the Terry Lectures Series Available from Yale University Press

The Courage to Be Paul Tillich
Psychoanalysis and Religion Erich Fromm
Becoming Gordon W. Allport
A Common Faith John Dewey
Education at the Crossroads Jacques Maritain
Psychology and Religion Carl G. Jung
Freud and Philosophy Paul Ricoeur
Freud and the Problem of God Hans Küng
Master Control Genes in Development and Evolution Walter J. Gehring
Belief in God in an Age of Science John Polkinghorne
Israelis and the Jewish Tradition David Hartman
The Empirical Stance Bas C. van Fraassen
Exorcism and Enlightenment H. C. Erik Midelfort
Reason, Faith, and Revolution: Reflections on the God Debate Terry Eagleton
Thinking in Circles: An Essay on Ring Composition Mary Douglas
The Religion and Science Debate: Why Does It Continue? Edited by Harold W. Attridge
Natural Reflections: Human Cognition at the Nexus of Science and Religion Barbara Herrnstein Smith
Absence of Mind: The Dispelling of Inwardness from the Modern Myth of the Self Marilynne Robinson
Islam, Science, and the Challenge of History Ahmad Dallal
The New Universe and the Human Future: How a Shared Cosmology Could Transform the World Nancy Ellen Abrams and Joel R. Primack
The Scientific Buddha: His Short and Happy Life Donald S. Lopez, Jr.
Life After Faith: The Case for Secular Humanism Philip Kitcher
Private Doubt, Public Dilemma: Religion and Science since Jefferson and Darwin Keith Thomson